Fighting with the German Longsword

oß dem fryen how geuallen
ju dus geuuapper ost

Fighting with the German Longsword

Revised and Expanded Edition

oß dem fryen how gevallen
in die gevangner ort

Christian Henry Tobler

Freelance Academy Press

Freelance Academy Press, Inc., Wheaton, IL 60189
www.freelanceacademypress.com

© 2015 Christian Henry Tobler

Photography by Christopher Valli and Janusz Michael Saba
Cover and Book Design by Robert N. Charrette

Printed in the United States of America
by Publishers' Graphics

22 21 20 19 18 17 16 15 14 13 12 11 10   1 2 3 4 5 6 7 8 9

ISBN 978-1-937439-23-1

Library of Congress Control Number: 2015944835

Dedication

This book is dedicated to my wife Maureen, during whose many patient hours as an "author widow" this book was written, and to the many practitioners of the *Kunst des Fechten*, who make all of this worthwhile.

Acknowledgements

This book would have been impossible without the unflagging dedication and support of my students in the Selohaar Fechtschule, in particular those directly studying with me in Connecticut. To this end, I'd like to thank Rob Kelly, Christopher Valli, Janusz Michael Saba, Mark Keller, Michael DePaola, Joe Grzelak, Ed Borkoski, and Wayne Brosler, my local "research and development" team. The farther-flung members of our school, those studying with our chapters and study groups, have also been most supportive, not only in their enthusiasm for this art, but through their questions and comments. I thank David Teague, Matthew Cacy, Dr. Bill Ernoehazy, Michael Ahrens, Christopher Torres, Todd Sullivan, Eric Slyter, Wayne Osbourne, Aine Connelly, and Sara Matthias for their continued support of our school.

Special thanks are due to Rob Kelly, Janusz Saba and Chris Valli for taking part in the photography sessions and in particular to Chris and Janusz for taking turns behind the camera.

I must, in particular, single out my senior student, Jessica Finley, now an author in her own right. It's an incredible honor to both thank her for being my right hand and to include her work in this book's bibliography. She also crafted the training jackets worn in this book.

I'd be remiss in not once again thanking my friends and colleagues throughout the Western Martial Arts community: Nicole Allen, Jörg Bellinghausen, Devon Boorman, Bob Charrette, Michael Chidester, Claus Drexler, David Farrell, Jeffrey Forgeng, S. Matthew Galas, Bill Grandy, Dierk Hagedorn, Stephen Hand, Maestro Sean Hayes, Hans Heim, my mentor Stephen Hick, Keith Jennings, Craig Johnson, Christoph Kaindel, Peter Kautz, Alex Kiermayer, Jens Peter Kleinau, Jesse Kulla, Tom Leoni, Anders Linnard, Cecil Longino, Roger Norling, Allen Reed, Steven Reich, David Rowe, Roger Siggs, Claus Sørensen, Thomas Stoeppler, Larry Tom, Jeff Tsay, Douglas Wagner, Paul Wagner, Bart Walczak, Roland Warzecha, Theresa Wendland, William Wilson, Guy Windsor, and Grzegorz Zabinski. If I've forgotten some of you, please know you may have momentarily slipped out of my thoughts, but not my heart.

Jessica Finley, Aine Connelly, Sean Hayes, and Pamela Muir did me the very great service of being readers for this book, and I am in their debt for this. Scott Baltic did an exemplary job of proofreading the final text. Bob Charrette's glorious layout design is an integral part of this revised work, not only framing, but informing it.

Lastly, I'd like to thank my partner at Freelance Academy Press, Greg Mele, my boon companion on this journey through the chivalric arts.

Table of Contents

Foreword

What is in a name?

As a subset of Historical European Martial Arts (HEMA), the martial tradition established by Johannes Liechtenauer in the late 14th century is called today by a variety of monikers. The most popular, *Kunst des Fechtens*, is somewhat erroneous, as it simply means "Art of Fencing" in German, and is applicable to all fencing styles; indeed, the term has been applied to the saber and epee far longer, and by far more people, than it has been by modern students of the two-handed sword, messer, or spear. More precise is "the Liechtenauer Tradition," but it is still problematic, as not all of the material in the corpus of 15th and 16th century German sources is clearly attributable to Liechtenauer and his adherents. "German Medieval Martial Arts" is probably the most accurate, but is a rather lack-luster term, and ignores the evolution of the tradition over the course of the 16th century, as it attempted to integrate the new martial realities of a wealthy, armed, mercantile class, the social phenomenon of private dueling, and the dueling weapon par excellence, the rapier, only to be increasingly supplanted throughout the Empire in the 17th c by first the Italian, and then the French, fencing traditions.

Modern man loves his acronyms, and as you can see, modern students of ancient fighting traditions are no different. For the newcomer, Western Martial Arts (WMA) refers to any martial tradition produced by Western culture and civilization, from a reconstruction of Roman Gladiatorial combat to Bare-Knuckle Boxing, German longsword fencing to WWII military combatives. Historical European Martial Arts (HEMA) is a more recent, and more popular term,[1] that refers to pre-20th century fighting traditions, which have specifically needed to be reconstructed and recreated (such as the subject of this book) as opposed to Traditional European Martial Arts (TEMA), which are arts that maintain a living tradition, such as saber fencing, boxing, savate, multiple traditions of European wrestling, and knife and stick-fighting. Further distinction can be made by period, such as Renaissance Martial Arts, or the culture for which it was intended, such as Chivalric Martial Arts, to refer to an art developed by and for the knightly class. For example, Liechtenauer's art is obviously Western, Historical, Medieval, and Chivalric. Or rather, it was in the late 14th century, at the time of its creation. By 1600, the art was Western, Historical, *Renaissance*, and Chivalric – in name; for the better part of a century its most devoted adherents

---

[1] HEMA is a useful catch-term, but its popularity has its own problems. While the term is useful to broadly explain the family of martial arts to outsiders—in much the same way as, say Japanese Martial Arts, or Filipino Martial Arts—it creates an impression of universal homogeneity that takes away from the beauty and uniqueness of each of the various disciplines lumped under the HEMA banner. Very few students of judo, Muay Thai, or Tai Chi feel a need to generalize and genericize the name of the arts they practice, and one hopes that in time French smallsword, Italian rapier, Destreza, Armizare, and so forth will be recognizable in the martial arts community by their own merits.

had been from the wealthy guildsman class. Social history often defies orderly classification, and when a martial art survives its original culture, it becomes increasingly difficult to pigeon-hole.

Have I lost you in the sea of letters yet?

Here is a simpler truth: Whatever we call it, there is a special allure to wielding a 600-year old weapon that is sublime in its deadly efficiency, even though irrelevant in the modern world. Whether because of a love of history, a way to connect to one's cultural heritage, a new athletic challenge, or just that indefinable "romance of the sword," something about this bygone weapon from a lost era speaks to our psyche in a way that is hard to define, yet fills the student of arms with an artist's precision, a sportsman's determination and a child's delight. Here is how Johannes Liechtenauer himself defined his art:

> *Young knight, learn to love God and revere women, so that your honor grows. Practice knighthood, and learn the Art that dignifies you, and brings you honor in wars.*

If you read those words for the first time and don't feel a shudder of momentary transcendence … well, you probably haven't bought this book in the first place.

✛✛✛✛✛✛

It is odd to be in one's 40s, yet an "old-timer" in the recreation of European combat arts. Eleven years ago, I had the privilege to be the editor of the first edition of *Fighting with the German Longsword*, which was the first of its kind: a step-by-step training guide to introduce would-be students into the lost world of German medieval martial arts. At the time of its publication, the term "HEMA" did not even exist, and the Western Martial Arts (WMA) community existed as isolated enthusiasts, mostly in the United States, Australia, the UK, France and Sweden, and as a minority interest amongst modern fencers, Asian martial artists or members of medieval reenactment societies.

Today, the situation is very different. Throughout the Americas, Australasia and every nation of Europe, there is a rapidly expanding network of formal schools, informal clubs and athletic associations where one can learn to wield a sword. An entire industry of specially-designed HEMA training equipment has developed, and there are expansive research websites, discussion forums and social media, even a dedicated, academic journal. Throughout the world, students can attend weekend workshops to refine their skills and share state of the art research, or attend tournaments featuring a modern sport derived from a subset of historical techniques. In short, anything that one can experience in the world of Asian martial arts can be found in the world of HEMA, as well.

All of this flows from the written, often illustrated, works of masters centuries dead. But those works were not written for the novice. Rather, they are a combination of theory and technique, much like a repertoire book for musicians. But what if you can't read music and have never held an instrument?

That is where Christian Tobler steps in as your guide. Having spent years traveling throughout North America teaching workshops on German martial arts, the first edition of this book grew from those experiences, and represented a concise methodology and curriculum synthesizing the teachings of the Liechtenauer tradition. Having helped launch a number of study-groups (many now full-blown schools in their own right), it has been long out of print, and still commands exorbitant prices online. In preparing this foreword I took time to reread my own, battered copy, and was impressed at how well the core of the work has stood against the test of time. But with this new edition, the first goes back onto my shelf for the last time, for in every way, it has been exceeded. Eleven years of research, teaching, pressure-testing, and I suspect some long-hours of false-leads, doubling back, and reevaluation, has produced a meticulous and lovingly crafted training guide that will take a newcomer by the hand and set their feet upon the long and arduous road of mastering the sword.

Although the work is entitled *Fighting with the German Longsword*, and the longsword is undeniably the center-piece of the tradition, Liechtenauer wrote: *A good grappler in wrestling, lance, spear, sword and messer manfully handle, and foil them in other's hands.* Faithful to his master's words, Christian provides you with guidance to begin your exploration of wrestling and spear fencing as well.

Finally, practicing a martial art and teaching it to others are two very different skills. Those already training in the Liechtenauer tradition, but who have struggled with developing a methodology to train others, will find not only a ready-made course, but an easily followed blueprint for developing one of their own.

Christian Tobler has clearly put his heart and soul into this project, and his love of teaching is palpable. For those of you, like me, who once stared at a sword quietly hanging in its case and dreamily thought, "I wonder how they used that," this book will tell you how, and my youthful self envies you its existence!

Gregory D. Mele
Chicago Swordplay Guild
14 July 2015

About the Author

Christian Henry Tobler has been a longtime student of swordsmanship, especially as it applies to the pursuit of the chivalric ideals. He has been focused on the study of medieval *Fechtbücher* ("Fight books") since the late 1990s. He is a passionate advocate of the medieval Liechtenauer School, and his work in translating and interpreting the *Ringeck Fechtbuch* firmly established him as an important contributor to the growing community of Western martial artists. This work was published in the 2001 title *Secrets of German Medieval Swordsmanship: Sigmund Ringeck's Commentaries on Johannes Liechtenauer's Verse*.

A training guide for modern practitioners, revised in this volume, *Fighting with the German Longsword*, followed in 2004. *In Service of the Duke: The 15th Century Fighting Treatise of Paulus Kal*, a facsimile, translation, and analysis of a lavishly illustrated *Fechtbuch* was published in 2006. His most recent releases were *In Saint George's Name: An Anthology of Medieval German Fighting Arts*, in 2010, and *Captain of the Guild: Master Peter Falkner's Art of Knightly Defense*, in 2011. He has also produced two instructional DVDs of the growing German Medieval Martial Arts series—*Volume 1: The Poleaxe* and *Volume 2: Sword, Buckler, and Messer*—along with various articles and downloadable media treating German historic combat.

Mr. Tobler was born in 1963 in Paterson, New Jersey. A graduate of the University of Bridgeport's computer engineering program, he has worked as a software developer, product manager, and marketing specialist in the analytical instrumentation and publishing fields. He is the current Grand Master of the Order of Selohaar, an eclectic order of chivalry that he co-founded in 1979, and serves as Principal Instructor for its associated school of swordsmanship, the Selohaar Fechtschule. A veteran of 25 years of armoured tournament fighting, he is also an avid collector of reproduction arms and armour.

He has taught classes at numerous historic martial arts symposia, and has traveled the United States, Canada, and Europe teaching numerous weekend-long seminars. He has lectured at the 38th International Congress on Medieval Studies in Kalamazoo, Michigan. In 2011, he founded the Chivalric Fighting Arts Association (CFAA), a confraternity of like-minded historic martial arts practitioners and schools.

Mr. Tobler lives in the United States, in rural Oxford, Connecticut, with his wife, Maureen Chalmers, teaching weekly classes on medieval combat, surrounded by far too many books and pieces of arms and armour for the size house that they live in.

The Selohaar Fechtschule

The Selohaar Fechtschule[2] is a historical fencing study group within the Order of Selohaar, an eclectic and mystic chivalric order. The group meets to research, study, and practice the martial arts of medieval and early Renaissance Europe under the guidance of its Principal Instructor, Christian Henry Tobler, an internationally known researcher, instructor, and combatant who has instructed at seminars and symposia around the United States since 2000. Headquartered at its school in Connecticut, the Selohaar Fechtschule also has chapters and study groups in Alaska, Florida, Georgia, New York, Virginia, and Washington.

The Fechtschule focuses on the *Fechtbücher* ("Fight Books") of the masters of the tradition arising from the teachings of the 14th century grandmaster Johannes Liechtenauer. It uses the treatises ascribed to Sigmund Ringeck, Peter von Danzig, Paulus Kal, Hans Talhoffer, Peter Falkner, and others, whose commentaries on Liechtenauer's secret verses constitute the medieval German *Kunst des Fechtens* (Art of Fighting). In addition to encouraging diligent training and scholarship, the Fechtschule and its parent organization stress the importance of good character through study of chivalric ideals and their original cultural context.

Website: www.selohaar.org/fechten.htm
E-mail: orderofselohaar@aol.com

The Chivalric Fighting Arts Association

Founded in 2011, the Chivalric Fighting Arts Association (CFAA) is an international organization of schools and clubs devoted to the study of historical European martial arts, particularly those practiced in a chivalric context, used in war, the tournament, and the duel.

Our member schools share a dedication to the revival of the fighting arts from the past, as well as a belief that the study and practice of these arts is a tool for building character and personal discipline – qualities that we believe can be of benefit to the modern world as much as they were for the ancient one.

CFAA members study diverse martial arts – from lands ranging from Iberia to Britain, from the late Middle Ages to the early modern era, and including weapons ranging from the sword and buckler to the rapier. Ours is a fraternal organization, without a governing body, bound together only by our shared values, mutual support of our endeavors, and passion for ancient martial arts and their cultural milieu.

Website: www.chivalricfighting.org
E-mail: secretary@chivalricfighting.org

---

[2] A *Fechtschule* is a "fencing school" or "fight school." The term also applies historically to public fencing contests.

Preface

From many centuries, the sword was regarded as the "Queen of Weapons." No weapon has ever been so imbued with legend, mystique, and symbolism as the sword. Capable in offense and defense, in spite of its obsolescence on the battlefield for more than a century, the sword remains a potent symbol of war, justice, honor and chivalry. There is something about a sword, whether an antique original or a cunningly crafted replica, that speaks to the hand, heart, and soul. When the sword is taken up, something deep within us whispers of ancestry, noble deeds, and adventure.

Many people are surprised to hear that medieval warriors practiced sophisticated martial arts. Movies, television, and books have created the impression that medieval combat was crude and wholly dependent on strength. Many members of the public believe that medieval swords were ponderous and heavy. They are shocked to hear that the average sword of the time weighed between two and a half and four pounds. Viewing such a weapon in a museum, one is struck by the nobility of its simplicity. The late, revered scholar of the sword, R. Ewart Oakeshott, who created a widely recognized typology for these weapons, writes of the magnificence of the medieval sword:

> *"These swords are beautiful, with an austere perfection of line and proportion – surely the very essence of beauty – comparable with splendid and majestic pottery. A good sword has affinities with, let us say, the work of Chinese potters of the Sung dynasty – affinities whose impact is sharpened by the disparity in their raison d'être."* [3]

Our medieval ancestors must have felt that too. For the warriors of the Middle Ages – the Age of Chivalry – the sword was already an ancient symbol steeped in legend. Vikings and the earliest of the medieval swordsmen named their blades in chronicle, saga, and chanson. The names of the swords wielded by some of these heroes, both historical and fictional (and those populating the grey lands that lie between), have come down to us through these tales: Hrolf Kraki's *Sköfnung*, Roland's *Durendal*, Charlemagne's *Joyeuse*, and, most storied of all, Arthur's *Excalibur*.

When one handles an actual historic sword, it is impossible to believe that the use of such an elegant weapon could have been crude or brutish. These weapons were crafted with skill and care, and many of the warriors who wielded them likely did so using very deliberate methods. In fact, we know that at least some of them did; dozens of fighting treatises survive from the late Middle Ages. We have record of several great traditions, with works surviving from northern Italy, southern Germany, England, northeastern France (Burgundy), Spain and Portugal.

---

[3] R. Ewart Oakeshott, *The Sword in the Age of Chivalry*, p. 12.

This book is an introduction to one of those fighting traditions, the *Kunst des Fechtens* ("Art of Fighting"), the German school of Johannes Liechtenauer, a master of the 14th century. To those who are only familiar with the Asian martial arts, this study should be a pleasant surprise, for this martial art is one of sophistication, elegant movement and, above all, effectiveness, easily on par with its Eastern counterparts. In what follows, you will learn the basics of this art as seen through the lens of its primary and exemplary weapon, the longsword, and later with some of its cousins among the panoply of medieval weapons. Join me now as we take up the sword as our ancestors once did and feel the past come alive in our hands.

Notes Regarding the 2nd Edition

This revised and expanded 2nd Edition includes a number of interpretation changes. I hope students of the art will find the biomechanics presented here cleaner and a number of actions more intelligible.

In addition, eight more chapters appear here than in the first edition. The techniques *Duplieren* and *Mutieren* now have their own chapter, "Breaking the Four Openings", as do the principles of the *Vier Versetzen*, *Nachreisen*, *Indes*, *Überlaufen*, *Absetzen*, *Durchwechseln* and *Zucken*, plus a chapter on the guard *Nebenhut*. This expanded lineup should help the student better understand concepts only briefly addressed in the previous volume.

The reader will also find some material considerably reworked, such as the chapter on *Durchlaufen* (formerly titled "Wrestling Techniques"), wherein I draw more closely from the wrestling at the sword examples described in the Liechtenauer commentaries.

Introduction:
An Ancient and Secret Art of Fighting

A fencing master, likely Master Johannes Liechtenauer, from the 1452 Fechtbuch, or "fight book," Ms A 44 8. He holds a practice longsword in his right hand as he gestures toward a sword and a messer on the wall.

*Young knight learn
to love God and revere women,
so that your honor grows.
Practice knighthood and learn
The Art that dignifies you
And brings you honor in wars.
Wrestle well and grasp
Lance, spear, sword and messer,
manfully handled,
and in others' hands wasted.
Strike bravely and hasten forth;
Rush to, hit or let it go by.
Those with wisdom loathe
the one forced to defend.
This you should grasp:
All arts have length and measure.*

– The Prologue of Master Liechtenauer

The Knightly Art

The Germany of the late Middle Ages was not a country in the sense that we now understand that word. The German lands made up the better part of the Holy Roman Empire, a collection of duchies, bishoprics, free cities and principalities, more or less under the suzerainty of the German Emperor. The imperial court rarely enjoyed strong centralized power, however, and rival nobles often fought each other or leagues of towns in bitter and continual conflicts. The roads were often dangerous; when travelers were not in peril from armed brigands, they might have to contend with robber knights.

On this violent stage, the fencing master was an important player. Fencing guilds, such as the *Federfechter* and *Marxbrüder*, were formed by burghers and tradesmen, while masters such as Sigmund Ringeck, Paulus Kal, and Hans Talhoffer sought noble patronage. Most of these fencers and masters had at least one thing in common: they had all learned the Knightly Art of Master Johannes Liechtenauer.

The memory of the German grandmaster Johannes Liechtenauer looms large over more than two centuries of the *Kunst des Fechtens* ("Art of Fighting"), the German martial art of the late Middle Ages and Renaissance. We know little about this shadowy figure, save that he likely lived in the 14th century. His name might indicate that he came from Liechtenau, in Franconia, though other towns elsewhere in Germany shared that name.

We would know little of the man's teachings were it not for a long succession of other masters who followed in his footsteps, for Master Liechtenauer encrypted his fighting art into roughly 350 lines of rhyming couplets, "*in hidden and secret words, so that not everyone will grasp and understand it…*"[4] These verses are known generally as *Merkeverse* ("Mark Verse"); his treatise, composed of the verses, is known as the *Zettel* ("Epitome"). The verse seems to serve twin purposes: first, as the manuscripts say, to obscure the art from the uninitiated, and second, to serve as a series of mnemonic devices to those who understood his teachings.[5] Concerning the former, if all that history had left to us was the *Zettel*, we could but guess as to what made up this medieval martial art.

Fortunately, the works of Liechtenauer's disciples and successors provide us with a window into the great master's art. In over two dozen manuscripts, these *Fechtmeisters* ("Fencing Masters") deconstruct Liechtenauer's art, presenting his verses and then explaining them to their reader, often some noble patron. The earliest of these manuscripts extant, Hs. 3227a, sometimes (erroneously) attributed to a cleric named Hanko Döbringer,[6] has been dated to 1389, though this may be inaccurate.[7] This work, included in a *Hausbuch* ("Housebook"), a type of medieval home encyclopedia, lacks the characteristic memorial "God have mercy on him", often used in the *Fechtbücher* (Fight Books) to indicate a deceased master, so it is possible that Liechtenauer was still alive at this time. The last known treatises of the tradition appear in the 17th century, including the 1612 printed work of Jakob Sutor – itself an abbreviated redaction of the 1570 magnum opus of Joachim Meyer, the last of the great masters of the Liechtenauer School. Given these dates, we can assume that the tradition endured at least 250 years; Master Liechtenauer cast a long shadow indeed.

The martial arts system of Johannes Liechtenauer encompasses personal combat skills for fighting with and without defensive armour. The art includes the use of the longsword (a sword

---

[4] *Von Danzig Fechtbuch*, 1452, Folio 3r.

[5] Given the popularity of the combination of verses and commentaries throughout the late Medieval German scholastic tradition, it is quite possible that the Merkeverse's primary function was to serve as a series of mnemonics.

[6] Döbringer's name is actually only mentioned once in this manuscript, and rather obliquely at that. The author or, more likely, compiler of the whole manuscript is unknown at this time. A better name for this manuscript might the Nuremberg Housebook or, in German, *Nürnberger Hausbuch*. One can never go wrong by simply referring to it by its shelf number – Hs. 3227a.

[7] The date is based on a calendar included in the *Hausbuch*, but this might be a 'standard' calendar of the time, good for 20 or so years.

that can be wielded with one or both hands on the grip), the lance on horseback, the spear, the dagger, the *messer* (a falchion-like short sword) and techniques for grappling with an opponent with or without weapons. The *Langes Schwert* ("Long Sword") figures centrally in his system.

An exposition of the techniques of unarmoured fighting with the longsword, *Bloßfechten* ("Exposed Fighting"), appears first in his verses and provides the fundamental principles and conceptual framework for the other two disciplines he treats, each focused on the fighting of duels: *Roßfechten* ("Horse Fighting"), which is mounted combat, and *Harnischfechten* ("Harness Fighting"), or fighting in armour. The longsword is an important weapon in these last two disciplines as well, but techniques for lance, spear, and dagger are also included.

The techniques for *Roßfechten* and *Harnischfechten* appear to be optimized for the judicial duel or duel of honor, ritualized affairs of last recourse wherein two antagonists or their champions fight in an enclosed space to resolve a legal issue or point of honor, sometimes to the death. This is not to say, however, that some or most of the techniques involved would not transfer well to the venues of self-defense, the maintenance of civil order, the battlefield, or friendlier tournament combat.

In the mid-16th and early 17th centuries, the German masters of the latter part of the tradition would ultimately discard the teachings that detail fighting in the lists in armour,[8] as the use of the longsword declined as a weapon for battle or dueling and found itself more and more confined to sporting contests. In the 14th and 15th centuries, however, the longsword was still a potent weapon, as it had been during Liechtenauer's lifetime, and we will fix our attention primarily on the techniques written down in those days.

Words and Pictures

Some of the 15th century German *Fechtbücher*, notably those by Masters Hans Talhoffer and Paulus Kal, are lavishly illustrated. Others consist primarily of text, with perhaps the incidental illustration. Common sense would seem to dictate that the illustrated manuscripts would be of greater utility than those with only text. Oddly enough, this is not the case. The finely illustrated manuscripts of Kal and Talhoffer generally offer only snapshots of techniques, with short captions accompanying them. They do not lay out the basic principles of the system, nor do they have the breadth of techniques covered in the text-only commentaries of Sigmund Ringeck, Peter von Danzig, or Jud Lew. While the illustrated manuscripts, which were perhaps written more to advertise a master's skills to his potential patrons, are useful in their own right, we must turn to these text manuscripts to learn Master Liechtenauer's art.

The texts often follow a similar formula: Liechtenauer's verse is presented a couplet at a time, paired with a gloss or commentary explaining the couplet's meaning. Sometimes, the manuscript begins with an exposition of the *Zettel* in its entirety. This pattern of verse and gloss appears in manuscripts from the late 14th through the 16th century.

In producing the syllabus for this book, I have drawn primarily on my research into several roughly contemporary manuscripts of the mid-15th century, plus one from the late 14th century and two from the 16th century. These manuscripts are all compendia; they are collections of various sections probably drawn from various authors. Modern scholars have named them after

---

[8] Handfuls of these techniques do survive in some of the later treatises as *Kampfstücke* ("Dueling Techniques").

masters whose names appear in them, although this may not represent the primary author, even where there is one. In addition, I have consulted the illustrated works of Masters Hans Talhoffer, whose surviving treatises span a period from 1443–1467, and Paulus Kal, whose work dates to the 1470's. Here is a list of the works from which this book derives:

Hs. 3227a (1389?): Perhaps the earliest extant[9] manuscript of the Liechtenauer tradition. The manuscript is quite conceptual in its approach and includes many useful observations on basic strategy, tactics, and kinesthetic theory. It contains an incomplete commentary on Liechtenauer's verse, plus other techniques for the longsword, dagger, and notes on *Ringen* ("Wrestling") attributed to Liechtenauer. The manuscript, a late medieval *Hausbuch*, is more than just a fighting treatise, and contains herbal remedies, techniques for hardening iron, magical formulae, and other miscellanea.

The Ringeck Fechtbuch (early 16th century?), Ms. Dresden C 487: A treatise associated with Master Sigmund Ringeck, who is described as the author of the text's longsword commentaries and as the fencing master to Albrecht, Count Palatine of the Rhine and Duke of Bavaria. It also contains sword and buckler[10] combat and wrestling (including a fragment of Ott the Jew's[11] wrestling techniques), plus commentaries on Liechtenauer's armoured combat on foot and on horseback.[12] Current scholarship now dates the Dresden compendium to the early 16th century, but its source material is likely from the first half of the 15th century. This manuscript is the subject of my first book, *Secrets of German Medieval Swordsmanship*.

The Von Danzig Fechtbuch (1452), Codex 44 A 8: Firmly dated to 1452, this manuscript is a large compendium comprising substantial anonymous commentaries on Liechtenauer's *Bloßfechten*, *Roßfechten*, and *Harnischfechten*. It includes armoured combat, wrestling, sword and buckler, and dagger fighting after a Master Andres Lignitzer. Martin Huntfeltz is attributed for armoured combat, on foot and on horse, and dagger combat. A section on Ott's wrestling is included that is twice the size of that appearing in Ringeck. Finally, another commentary is included on Liechtenauer's armoured combat by Master Peter von Danzig of Ingolstadt, for whom the manuscript is named. A complete translation of this manuscript appears in my book *In Saint George's Name*.

---

[9] This is by no means certain; the 1389 date derives from a multi-year calendar included in the manuscript, and such calendars were often stock items meant to cover a block of years.

[10] A buckler is a small round shield held with the left hand. Buckler techniques appear in the manuscripts of Sigmund Ringeck, Peter von Danzig and Hans Talhoffer, among others, as well as the earliest extant European fighting manuscript, Ms. I.33 "Tower Fechtbuch," a south German work dated to the early 14th century.

[11] Ott the Jew was a wrestling master to the Duke of Austria whose influential techniques appear in numerous manuscripts. Some sources describe him as a "baptized Jew."

[12] Regrettably, the mounted combat commentary is a fragment of what appears in other manuscripts.

The Jud Lew Fechtbuch (c. 1450?), Codex I.6.4°.3: Another diverse compendium, this manuscript contains an anonymous commentary on Liechtenauer's longsword verses. This clearly derives from a source common to the commentaries in the von Danzig manuscript. The manuscript also contains some of the same material attributed to Lignitzer and Huntfeltz in the *von Danzig Fechtbuch*, but the author attributions are at variance with those in that work, some of which are credited here to a Jewish master, known to us only as Lew.

Paulus Kal (c. 1470), CGM 1507: Paulus Kal was in the service of Ludwig IX, Count Palatine of the Rhine, Duke of Upper and Lower Bavaria. He is listed as a *Schirmaister* ("Fencing Master"), but this may refer to his qualifications, rather than his role in the Duke's employ. The work may have been produced for the duke's son, Georg. It includes armoured dueling combat on horse with lance and sword, and on foot with spear, sword, dagger, and poleaxe. Kal also includes unarmoured judicial combat with large specialized dueling shields and sword and buckler combat, as well as longsword, messer, dagger and wrestling. A number of his plates for armoured combat and longsword include snippets of Liechtenauer verse, which makes this illustrated work one of the more useful for studying the great master's art. This volume also includes a listing of some of the masters of the "Society of Liechtenauer," those masters who taught the founding master's art.

Hans Talhoffer (1443–1467): The Swabian Hans Talhoffer is today the best known of the late medieval German fencing masters. He produced manuscripts for several nobles: the Swabian squire Leutold von Königsegg, the brothers David and Buppellin vom Stain, and Count Erberhard im Bart [the Bearded] of Württemberg. Talhoffer's first treatise appeared in 1443, with others following in the 1450's and 1460's. Two of these codices, one from 1459 and the other, the best known to modern audiences, from 1467, appear strikingly similar to those of Paulus Kal, with Talhoffer treating the longsword, messer, sword and buckler, dagger, wrestling, and judicial shields, as well as armoured combat on foot and on horse. Some of his manuscripts begin with a recitation of Master Liechtenauer's verse, occasionally embellished with some of Talhoffer's own couplets.

The Speyer Fechtbuch (1491), M I 29: This compendium repeats much of the material in Jud Lew, with the addition of some introductory material by a master Martin Siber, plus the *Messerfechten* ("Messer Fighting") of Master Johannes Lecküchner, a cleric who adapted Liechtenauer's methods to this weapon sometime in the third quarter of the 15th century.

Joachim Meyer (1570): Meyer's *Thorough Description of the Free, Knightly and Noble Art of Fencing*[13] is significant not only for its sheer size and scope, but because he is the last of the great masters of the Liechtenauer tradition. Although his techniques for the longsword

---

[13] *Gründtliche Beschreibung / der freyen Ritterlichen und Adelichen kunst des Fechtens / in allerley gebreuchlichen Wehren / mit schönen und nützlichen Figuren gezieret unnd fürgestellet* ("A Thorough Description of the Free Knightly and Noble Art of Fencing with All Customary Weapons, Adorned and Presented with Many Fine and Useful Illustrations").

show evidence of its transition into a weapon at least in part intended for sport, rather than earnest combat, the clarity of his instruction makes him an invaluable source. The work also includes techniques for the rapier, *dussack* (here a kind of practice weapon, related to the messer, but often a weapon in its own right), dagger, staff, pike, and halberd.

This list is not exhaustive, as I have read all of the surviving 15th century treatises, but is rather intended a tool for cross-reference for those students eager to dig into the manuscripts themselves.

A Course of Study for Modern Students

In preparing this book, I have drawn on my experience in teaching Liechtenauer's art over the last two decades, both to my own students and to many others at seminars, symposia, and re-enactment events. The masters of the Liechtenauer tradition wrote for an audience that lived with the sword. It was a vital tool and weapon then, whereas today it is a relic and a symbol of a bygone time. The audience of the 15th century grew up knowing the basics of swordplay: how to cut, parry and move appropriately, while we must learn all from scratch.

With this in mind, I have presented the material in this book in an order that is sometimes at odds with the way it is presented in the historic treatises. I have also taken care to assume that the student may be a novice and have included many basics not discussed by Liechtenauer's disciples, such as how to bear your weight when on guard, how to move through the various stances, etc. I have evolved a set of drills, which show general cases for dealing with various types of attacks that you might encounter when facing an opponent. These basics will provide the groundwork for your study and occupy chapters 1–7. Although this material is organized differently than the often less detailed basics in the historic treatises, I draw heavily on the words of the masters to establish its validity.

Chapters 8 through 25 feature specific techniques culled directly from the medieval manuscripts, mostly from the Ringeck, Danzig, and Lew manuscripts. Chapter 26 summarizes these chapters and reviews them in the context of the basics of the earlier part of the book.

Chapters 27, 28, and 29 examine Liechtenauer's art of fighting in armour on foot, *Harnischfechten*. After an initial discussion on the nature of armoured dueling, we will move to the spear, which is an excellent tool for learning the principles of fighting in armour as well as one of the fundamental knightly weapons, before concluding our study with the use of the longsword in armour.

The chapters have been organized in a way that reflects how I teach the system to my students. Please study each chapter in order and work through its techniques and accompanying drills. I begin by teaching basic concepts of movement and tactics and then progress to more complex actions as the chapters unfold; following my curriculum consistently will yield the best results.

All of the techniques are shown with right-handed fighters. This is not to say that left-handers cannot use the system; the masters specifically say they can. However, they too present the system from a right-hander's point of view, and I have presented the material consistent with this. As we are all still learning these ancient methods, I advise the student to work through them right-handed and understand the concepts before attempting to fight left-handed, mirroring the techniques. Since both hands are on the weapon anyway, this should not present too much difficulty. I can say this from experience: I originally fought with the longsword for more than fifteen years left-handed. When I began studying this historic art, I switched to fighting right-handed so that I would not introduce any artifacts into my interpretation of the system.

Historic Works and Their Interpretation

The reader should be aware that this book, and any instructional work on historic fighting arts, is but an *interpretation*, my interpretation, of the fighting system of Johannes Liechtenauer, based on my research and translation of, and working through, the period manuscripts. Although I believe the core concepts of this interpretation will stand the test of time, and overlap greatly with the conclusions of other respected practitioners, some of the interpretations of specific techniques will not survive as our research continues to advance. Readers of my earlier title *Secrets of German Medieval Swordsmanship*, or the first edition of *this* volume for that matter, will note that I now interpret some techniques contained within those works differently.

Sometimes these differences are small, other times they are substantial. This has happened for several reasons. First, I simply know more about the system now, not only from further work with the *Ringeck Fechtbuch* (upon which *Secrets* is based), but through translating and working with its contemporary works. I have also learned a tremendous amount from the many students, scholars, and critics whom I have encountered since, whose questions have helped me to refine my understanding of the art.

The student is therefore advised to be deeply suspicious of any teacher claiming to teach a historic martial art "just as the historic masters would have." Our understanding of these works is growing rapidly, but is imperfect and, given that there are no living masters to correct our errors, likely to remain that way. The process of learning is ongoing in this field, for student and researcher alike. For the true enthusiast of historic combat, this should be no burden but rather a great reassurance that there are many exciting revelations yet to come.

Motivation

Many who do not understand the passion that drives people to study the sword may pose the question: Why study an extinct martial art? The reasons are, to borrow a phrase from the *Von Danzig Fechtbuch* "diverse and manifold."[14] Some practice this art for exercise or the thrill of sporting competition, some to touch a piece of the past that intrigues them, some as a part of academic research, some to flesh out their activities in historical re-enactment, and still others in the hope of resurrecting a martial art that may have some use even today. You can learn a lot about the culture and customs of the late medieval period by researching the *Fechtbücher*, and vigorous practice of this art is certainly a workout. There are modern applications for some of the fighting techniques of the system; the dagger and wrestling plays found throughout the corpus of German or Italian medieval works can be easily adapted for modern self-defense.

My own reasons for studying this art partake of all of the above, but also stem from a desire to use it as a tool for the development of character. This is a *chivalric* art, and my life's path has been

---

[14] Peter Von Danzig, *Fechtbuch*, folio 31r.

one of drawing elements from chivalry's past so that they might find a place in our present-day world, so very much in need of the values of honor, nobility, and service. Our fight school, the Selohaar Fechtschule, operates under the umbrella of the Order of Selohaar, an eclectic chivalric tradition. I strongly believe that, in practicing the fighting arts of our ancestors, we can touch something vital about their lives and better understand the meaning of some of those values through that experience.

These are all valid reasons for studying historic martial arts, and if you do come to find Master Liechtenauer's art even half as enthralling as I have, I hope that you will always find tolerance for those students whose motivations may be different from your own. Regardless of our respective backgrounds, opinions, and reasons for doing this, all students of the sword, and all martial artists in general, have something to teach each other.

The Qualities of a Good Fencer

Paulus Kal, a master in the service of Duke Ludwig IX ("the Rich") of Bavaria in the 2nd half of the 15th century, created an allegorical figure depicting three virtues of fighting. The figure has a falcon's head, the image of a lion over its heart, and legs terminating in deer hooves. *Banderoles*, or speech scrolls, issue from these three elements of the figure, reading, from top to bottom: "I have eyes like a falcon so I will not be fooled," "I have a heart like a lion so I strive forth," and "I have feet like a hind so I spring towards and away." These encapsulate the virtues of judgment, courage, and nimbleness, all necessary qualities for a good swordsman or swordswoman.

All the technical training in the world means nothing without these qualities. Without courage, you cannot face your opponent or prosecute the fight. Without nimbleness, your footwork and carriage will be unequal to the demands of the techniques you wish to employ. Without judgment, you can measure neither the flow of the fight nor the opponent before you.

Take careful note of what this figure—strange though it might seem to us modern folk—and the important message it has for the fighter.

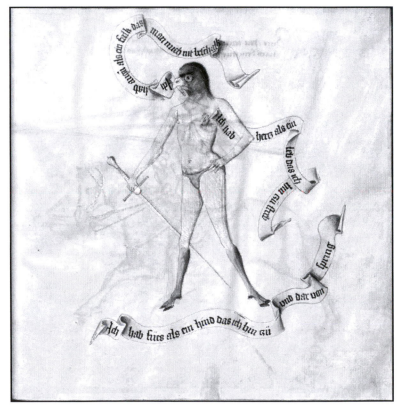

Chapter 1:
Beginning Your Training

*In Saint George's name, here begins
the art of fighting …*
– Master Sigmund Ringeck

The Longsword

The longsword, or *Langes Schwert* in German, is a medieval and early Renaissance weapon designed to be held with both hands, but light enough to be wielded with one if need be. [Fig. 1] Otherwise known as a "bastard sword" or "hand-and-a-half sword," the longsword of the late 14th, 15th, and 16th centuries often tapered to an acute point suitable for thrusting into the narrow gaps between elements of plate armour and into the rings of mail defenses. Earlier 13th-century swords intended for two-handed use usually had more parallel edges ending in a point much less optimized for thrusting. These swords were better suited for the delivering of shearing blows with the edge. A number of longswords are preserved in museums, and they appear often in the iconographic evidence that survives from the late Middle Ages.

An average sized longsword has a roughly 36-inch blade and an overall length of 46–48 inches. The sword has a guard or cross, called the *Gehiltze*, which protects the hands from an opponent's blade sliding down along one's own. The cross can also be used to catch and parry an oncoming blow. Behind the cross is the *Hanthab* (the grip) and after that

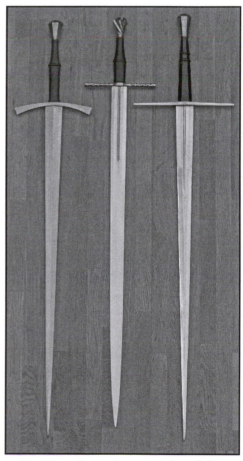

Fig. 1 Reproduction longswords from (left to right) Albion Armorers, Arms & Armor, and Del Tin Armi Antiche.

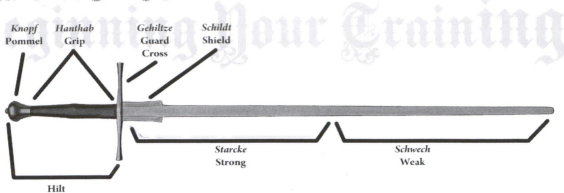

Beginning Your Training

Fig. 2 The parts of a longsword.

the *Knopf* (the pommel). The pommel can be used to strike an opponent and along with the grip can hook an opponent to take them off balance. Together with the cross, these parts make up the hilt of the sword.

The longsword, like most straight-bladed swords of the Age of Chivalry, has two edges. As the sword is grasped in both hands, the edge facing forward and aligned with the knuckles was known as the *Langen Schneide* (long edge), while the trailing edge was called the *Kurzen Schneide* (short edge). [Fig. 2] Perhaps the edges are so named because blows delivered with the long edge have greater reach than those executed with the short. Other fencing traditions often refer to the long edge as the "true edge" and to the short edge as the "false edge." Both edges are employed in German longsword combat in striking and parrying blows or for slicing with the sword, the choice usually being dictated by the desire to hold the sword in a way that keeps the wrists straight at all times.

For fighting on foot without armour, the longsword is usually held with both hands on the grip. However, there are techniques where one hand will let go of the weapon, freeing it to grapple bodily with an opponent or seize their weapon. When fighting on horseback, the sword is generally wielded with one hand, as the left hand is often busied in holding the reins.[15] For armoured dueling on foot, the sword is held at the "half-sword," or *Halb-schwert*, where the right hand holds the grip and the left grasps the middle of the blade, effectively turning the longsword into a short and powerful spear optimized for thrusting into the armour.

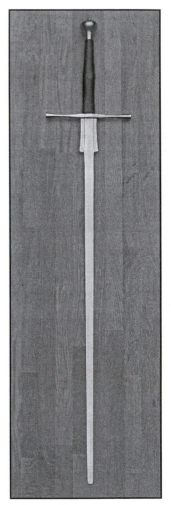

Fig. 3 A blunt training long-sword, produced by Arms & Armor of Minneapolis.

[15] Various German *Fechtbücher* include techniques where one strikes to the opponent's bridle hand, as well as those where one must let go of the reins with the left hand to grapple with an opponent or deflect his weapon.

Sometimes, the sword is even held with both hands on the blade and swung as a bludgeoning weapon, much like another knightly weapon, the late medieval poleaxe.

The blade of the longsword is divided into two halves. The *Starcke* ("Strong") of the sword extends from the cross to the middle of the blade. If you cross swords with someone and this half of your blade is in contact with their blade, you have the benefit of considerable leverage. If however your opponent binds against the upper half of your blade, the *Schwech* ("Weak") of the sword, you have very little leverage.

This is not to say that it is better to bind with one part of the sword or the other. What is important to know is that different responses are called for depending on which part of your sword you have bound with and which part of your opponent's sword is in contact with your sword.

Illustrations in 15th through 17th century *Fechtbücher* often illustrate specialized training longswords with blunted edges, rounded and sometimes spatulate points, and a protective flaring at the base of the blade known as the *Schildt* (shield). We will be using this style of practice sword to depict the partnered techniques in this book. [Fig. 3]

Offense and Defense

A longsword is usually used on foot with both hands on the grip. [Fig. 4] Various grip configurations are employed, depending on the technique one means to execute. At times, the thumb of the right hand braces the underside of the blade, adding stability and enhancing control of the alignment of the edges. The hands may be widely spaced, the left hand holding the pommel, or held close together on the grip. Some manuscript illustrations even show grips where one hand (usually the left) or even both are reversed.

Above all though, your grasp of the sword must be easy, with the fingers relaxed, never tense or overly tight, for tension is the enemy of fluidity and grace in one's movement. You must be able to readily change

Fig. 4 Various grips with the longsword: a simple grip (a), one with the thumb on the base of the blade (b), one with the left hand cupping the pommel (c), and a grip with the left hand fully inverted at the pommel (d).

your grip on the sword, and this is impossible when you carry tension in the hands. As a master from the other side of the Alps, Fillipo Vadi, maintains, one must wield the sword *"with a serene and agile hand."*[16]

A two-handed grip obviously does not leave a hand free to hold a shield, so the longsword must act as both an offensive and a defensive weapon. This requirement determines the form of the guards or stances, as well the footwork and timing needed in longsword fighting. We will see that in all attacks and defensive responses, one must move the sword and the body such that the motion of the sword precedes the movement of the body. Put another way, the sword must create a path of safety for the body to move through.

The sword must provide defensive cover and your body must move in such a way that it follows the movement of the sword. You must not step into range of an opponent's attack or potential attack without your sword clearing a path of safety for you. By moving behind your sword, you benefit from the protection it offers from your opponent's weapon. Further, your sword's movement before you creates a threat that your opponent must address; they can no longer simply attack you with impunity. When approaching the opponent, always create a threat before exposing a target.

Your longsword must at all times threaten your opponent while providing protection for you. Remember: Your sword is your shield.

Training and Safety

Training in historic sword arts entails several activities, all of which are important. Solo work, using either a weapon simulator or sharp replica sword, is valuable for learning how to stand and hold your weapon properly, and learning how to cut and thrust by moving between stances. Learning to strike blows correctly by cutting at practice targets is also valuable. Rolled *tatami* mats, floor coverings made of woven rushes often used by Japanese swordsmanship practitioners, are great test targets, and will provide you with good feedback on how cleanly and effectively you are cutting with your longsword. Our medieval ancestors are also known to have employed a practice target called a *pell*, usually a post of some sort driven into the earth that provided stiff resistance for practicing sword strokes.

Drills may then be done with a partner. You will find them throughout this book, and each technique we explore can itself be practiced as a drill. They should always be done slowly at first so you learn proper form. Much work should be done in this fashion before beginning any kind of competitive freeplay, for if you concentrate on fencing to win too early, you will only reinforce bad form.

As you work through techniques or drill with a partner, always be honest in how you approach the endeavor. If you are the one slated to "fail" in a technique, be a cooperative partner rather than evolving novel counter techniques to your opponent's action during the drill. Remember, it's a drill; there is no winner or loser, only two people learning. Trying to "win" a drill is disrespectful to your training partner, robs you both of the opportunity to learn, and, worst of all, compromises safety.

---

[16] Porzio and Mele, *Arte Gladiatoria Dimicandi*, p. 70.

When you train in any martial art, your own safety, and that of your training partner, is your responsibility. Control, both of your own body's movement and your temper, is the most important aspect of this, for without it no safety equipment is sufficient for preventing injury. Any training sword, no matter what its design, swung in anger or without control, can cause injury to your training partner. I often remind students that wooden swords, or *wasters*, as they were called in the Middle Ages, are really no more than elegantly carved baseball bats, with all the dangers the comparison implies.

The fencers in this book are shown in most of the photographs wielding training swords without protective gear. This has been done to provide the greatest clarity in depicting the unarmoured techniques, but these posed pictures should in no way be construed as depictions of how one should train or bout with such weapons. Quite the contrary, there is no weapon simulator that allows fighters to safely fence with contact without at least some measure of protection. This is not to say, however, that the techniques of this book cannot be worked through with control without a lot of safety gear, provided that safety is held paramount, ahead of "scoring a hit."

The type of safety gear you choose should depend on your training goals and choice of weapon simulators. Blunt steel swords require some combination of protection and control. If you use *more* control, you can use *less* protective gear. The higher the speed you play at, the more likely are failures in control and the higher the consequences of those failures.

For full-speed fencing freeplay, the following should be regarded as the minimum protection: a padded jacket or *gambeson* (a kind of medieval padded fabric body armour); a fencing mask featuring protection for the back of the head or a helmet; a *gorget* (an armoured collar providing protection for the throat); and rigid protection for the hands, elbows, and knees. An athletic cup for men and groin and breast protection for women are also highly recommended. Please note also that any helmet used must have eye slots that do not allow entry of the sword's point.

Ultimately, the choice of gear is personal, and can vary with the situation. Some practitioners prefer modern sporting equipment for freeplay, while others (including me) prefer to use elements of reproduction medieval armour. My choice is informed by both my "purist" sensibilities and by the fact that I train a wide spectrum of the art, including fully armoured combat.

This aside, you will find complete agreement among all reputable teachers and enthusiasts of medieval swordsmanship on the necessity of good control. If you treat your training partner as your sister or brother in arms and are mindful at all times of the inherent dangers of training in the martial arts, then you will train in safety and in good temper always.

Notes on the Clothing, Arms, and Armour in This Book

The Selohaar Fechtschule uniforms worn in this book are meant to evoke the doublets of the 15th century. The shoes and boots are similar to late medieval *turnshoes* (so-called from their having been constructed inside-out and then turned right side out after sewing) and have smooth leather soles without heels, just as the originals did. To the modern mind accustomed to high-grip athletic footwear, it may seem strange to train wearing such slippery shoes, but medieval fighting footwork requires pivoting on the ball of the foot and good sensitivity to the floor or terrain. While wrestling shoes and the like are usable substitutes, bear in mind that most modern footwear doesn't work that way and can introduce distortions in technique. This is not to say that concessions shouldn't be made when training under particularly slippery conditions, such as on a highly polished floor. However, it is imperative that your shoes do not have a built-up heel.

The armour worn in this volume's technique photos is based on examples from the late 14th century, a transitional period in the history of armour, incorporating varying elements of mail, fabric defenses (such as the gambeson), and plate armour. It was the relative accessibility of armour reproductions from this era that led to 14th century armour being so heavily represented in this book. I'd like students to learn how to fight in armour, and it would be discouraging for the two-year waiting list and multi-thousand dollar expense for full 15th century armour to be the limiting factors for beginning such study.

Chapter 2:
Line, Footwork, Measure & Time

To fight with the entire body,
is what you powerfully want to do.
– Johannes Liechtenauer

The basics of any system of fighting are rooted in the proper carriage of the body, a good sense of timing and an understanding of distance. Of these, carriage

and its most important aspect, footwork, comprise the area that vexes students, novices and experienced combatants alike, the most. Students most often fail to execute techniques correctly simply because their footwork was faulty or their bodyweight placed improperly. Footwork is the foundation upon which all movement in the system is built. We will therefore begin by learning how to stand and step correctly, for an appreciation of time and distance is useless without proper carriage.

Line

The "line of engagement" is the imaginary line connecting two fencers as they face each other. You can step away from the line, or across it, depending on the situation.

The idea of line can also be used to describe angles of attack. To make an attack on the "high inside line" is make an attack to the opponent's upper left quarter, while one made on the "low outside line" threatens the lower right quarter.

You can deceive your opponent by threatening to attack on one line but then actually attacking on another.

Finally, your sword can either be in-line, when your point is a direct threat to the opponent (the point is also said then to be "in presence"), or off-line, when it is angled such that it poses no direct threat. [Fig. 1] If you must parry an opponent's attack, it is usually desirable to do so in a manner that keeps your point in presence. Otherwise, you are generally reckoned to have over-committed your parry. There are exceptions to this rule however, as we will see later.

Fig. 1 Christian (foreground) with his sword in-line, or "in presence" (a); and off-line, or "out of presence" (b).

Footwork

The basic stance depicted and described in all medieval combat manuscripts is one where one leg is presented forward, with the leading foot facing one's opponent, while the other is held back, with that foot forming an angle with the leading foot. The toes of the leading foot should be turned a little outward, about 5–10 degrees off the line of engagement, so that the hips are opened and primed for movement. The back and neck must be straight and the body should be held upright, but relaxed. The body's weight must be carried between the legs, on the balls of the feet, with the knees supple. The weight of the body can be carried slightly forward, with more of the weight focused on the forward foot, or slightly backward, with more weight on the rear foot, depending on the guard assumed and other tactical considerations. [Fig. 2]

Changing from a forward-weighted to a backward weighted stance can have an important tactical benefit. If your opponent attacks you, you may be able to slip just out of range of their attack by shifting your weight backward, which moves your hips, and thus your upper body, back. Conversely, you might lie in wait with your weight carried backward, your opponent seemingly out of your range, and then shift forward to initiate an attack.

The position of the basic stance affords various benefits. First, because the body is held upright as opposed to being held forward, one's opponent is provided with a more limited target. Secondly, a longer weapon such as a longsword may be held in such a way when in this stance that it both protects a side of the body and still presents a threat to the opponent. Lastly, a change of which foot leads, by stepping, can deny one target area, while bringing the other side of one's body into an attack.

Fig. 2 Stances: Evenly weighted (a), forward weighted (b), and backward weighted (c).

In all, your stance should be well-balanced, but ready for action. Remember Paulus Kal's words: I have feet like a hind so that I spring towards and away.

One must employ several steps in fighting with Master Liechtenauer's system. These are passing, compass, advancing, and gathering steps.[17]

The Passing Step

A passing step is any step in which one foot passes the other, thereby changing which foot leads. Passing steps can be used to approach or retreat from the opponent, as needed. Each time you pass, you move only one foot at a time. In passing forward, you pivot on the forward foot while stepping forward with the rear. In a backward pass, you pivot on the rear foot while stepping backward with the leading foot.

The importance of placing your weight on the balls of your feet is paramount: If you are not on the ball of the foot, the pivot is awkward. You must also be sure that your body's weight glides smoothly forward or backward; do not "throw" your weight as you step. Think of this almost like pouring water from one glass into another: an easy, graceful transition of weight.

Passes can vary in their direction of movement. At times, you may step straight toward the opponent, simply by stepping forward with the rear leg [Fig. 3]. More commonly, a strong outward component is involved, which allows you to flank your opponent by stepping away from the line of engagement. In this pass, which we can term an "oblique pass," the trailing foot not only passes the forward foot, it moves out to the side as well. The most common way to do this is to step away from the line of engagement. [Fig. 4] This allows you to step around your opponent and to their side. As the commentary in Hs. 3227a says:

> *Also, he [i.e., Liechtenauer] means here that one should neither strike nor go and step directly but instead a little to the side and crookedly around, so that one comes to his side where one can have all manner of things to reach him with than from the front.[18]*

---

[17] Note that I am applying modern terminology here. While the German masters describe footwork in detail, they usually do not name their steps.

[18] *Nürnberger Hausbuch* (Hs. 3227a), folio 19v.

This is the most important step for fighting with the longsword, as it allows you to sidestep your opponent's attack to a degree and at the same time, still attack them while covering yourself with your sword. Unless otherwise noted, any passes described in this book will be oblique,

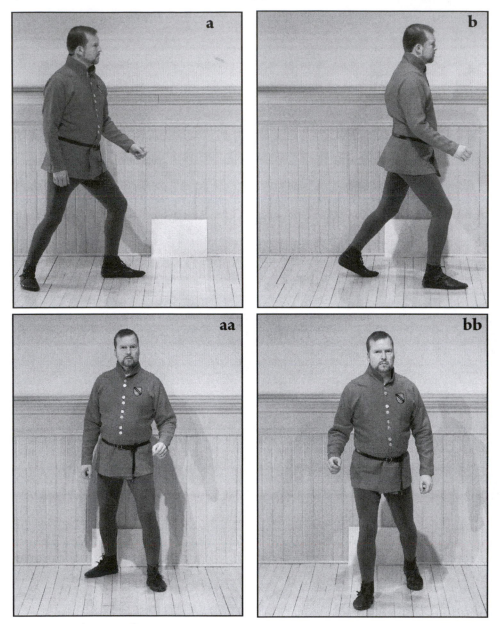

Fig. 3 A straight pass with the right foot (a/aa-b/bb).

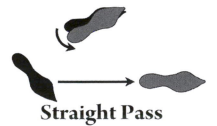

Straight Pass

that is, incorporating a flanking component. As with a straight pass, you may use this step for retreating as well as advancing.

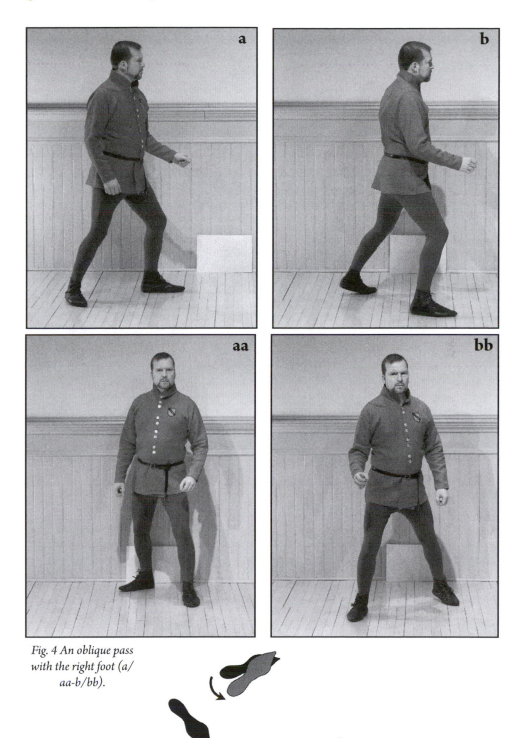

Fig. 4 An oblique pass with the right foot (a/aa-b/bb).

Oblique Pass

Oblique passes are sometimes described by the masters as "springing out away from the blow," indicating a step with an explosive, or leaping, quality, though this must be done in a way that preserves one's balance. Further, they often stress the importance of moving significantly away from the line of engagement, with specific instructions like "step well to your right side…"

One final form of passing step bears note. In some cases, it is desirable to step across the line of engagement, rather than away from it. Performing this cross-line pass[19] allows you to deeply flank an opponent's outside, especially when combined with other footwork, as we shall see below. [Fig. 5]

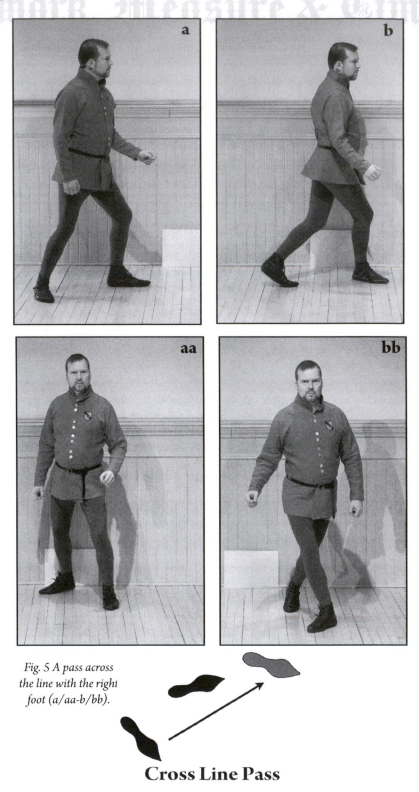

Fig. 5 A pass across the line with the right foot (a/aa-b/bb).

Cross Line Pass

---

[19] I am indebted to my friend and colleague Tom Leoni for this term, and the term "oblique pass," used earlier. These are elegant modern equivalents for steps described in paragraph form in the period sources. Mr. Leoni presents these terms in his book, *The Complete Renaissance Swordsman* (Freelance Academy Press, 2010).

Advancing and Gathering Steps

Advancing and gathering steps are used for gaining or giving ground without changing which leg leads. An advance is simply a step taken forward with the already leading foot, thereby widening the distance between the feet. [Fig. 6]

A gathering step is one where one foot moves closer to the other; that is, one foot is gathered up to meet the other. The other foot then moves to re-establish a balanced stance. This step is very useful when you want to alter your distance to the opponent without changing from a left to a right side guard or vice-versa. This is an especially important concern in armoured fighting, as we shall see very much later in this book.

To execute an advancing gathering step, move your rear foot forward, toward your front foot, and then step forward the same distance with the front foot. [Fig 7] To perform a retreating gathering step, move the front foot backward, toward the rear foot, and then move the rear foot backward the same distance. [Fig. 8] In either case, the movement of each foot should be conservative, so that you remain balanced with your weight between your legs at all times.

Note that an advancing or gathering step need not be performed straight forward or back; the foot may move either away from or across the line, as needed.

Finally, a small gathering step is often used in concert with a passing step. If you perform an aggressive passing step you may find yourself unbalanced unless you gather up the now trailing foot to regain your proper stance.

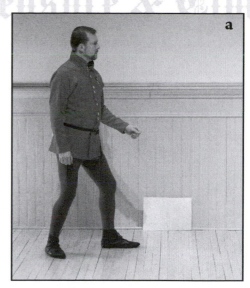

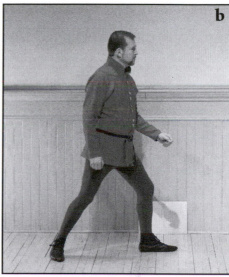

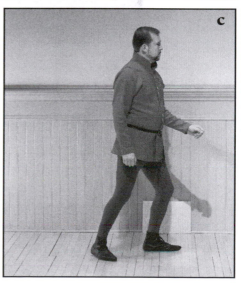

Fig. 6 An advance of the left foot, with the right brought up after to recover (a-c).

Advancing Step

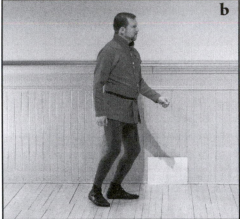

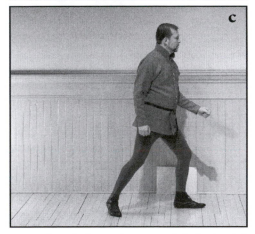

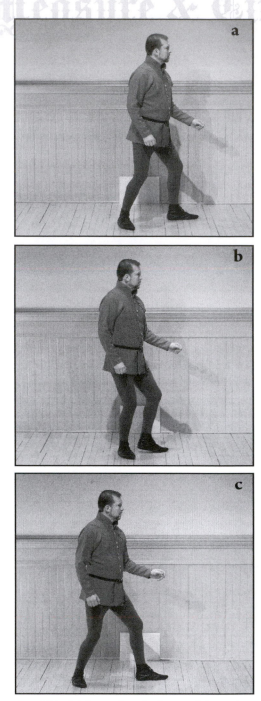

Fig. 7 The right foot gathers toward the leading left foot, which then advances forward (a-c).

Fig. 8 The left foot gathers back toward the trailing right foot, which then retreats (a-c).

Advancing Gathering Step

Retreating Gathering Step

The Compass Step

A compass step is one where you pivot on one foot while swinging the other around it, like a compass' motion about its axis. Compass pacing is useful in voiding an attack while remaining on guard with a weapon on the same side of the body, because the leading foot does not change. It can also be used in positioning against an opponent in grappling techniques, where its pivoting action provides the power for a throw, as we will see later.

To compass step forward, step forward and outward with your rear foot while pivoting on the front foot. However, do not move so far as to pass your front foot with your rear foot; the leading foot should not change. Instead, you change the angle at which you face your opponent while continuing to lead with the same foot. [Fig. 9] To compass step backward, pivot on your leading foot while swinging your trailing foot backward and outward. [Fig. 10] In both cases, your body's weight must move smoothly in an arc. Do not attempt to perform the compass step with just your feet or by throwing your weight forward or backward; the step conforms to the same smooth movements found in the previous steps.

A compass step can immediately follow a passing step, particularly a pass that covers considerable ground, as a means of better recovering one's balance and flanking the opponent.

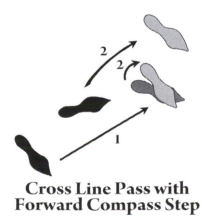

**Cross Line Pass with
Forward Compass Step**

Fig. 9 A forward compass step of the left foot (c), used to realign the body after a cross-line pass (a-b).

Measure

Liechtenauer said in his prologue that "all arts have length and measure." By this he means to tell us just how important control of measure, or distance, is to the arts of combat. One comes into wide measure when it is possible to strike the opponent with a single step. All else is "out of measure." Further, once this step is taken, the opponent is now within close measure. From here, no step is necessary to strike the opponent, or be struck by them.

Fig. 10 A backward compass step of the right foot (a-b).

Backward Compass Step

Control of measure, that is, management of distance, is related to how the German masters describe the phases of an encounter. The first phase, the *Zufechten*, which roughly means the approach to or onset of the fight, includes all actions leading up to the first strike delivered by either opponent. Many techniques are described as beginning here, often using a phrase such as "when you come to him in the *Zufechten*."

You must take care in this phase of the fight. Do not wander in haphazardly toward your opponent without a prepared threat, lest you find yourself at the mercy of an attack from them that requires no step.

A fight can begin and end in the *Zufechten*. A devastating attack to an opponent's head can make for a short fight. However, if the fight continues after you close, then another phase of the fight begins. This is known variously as *Krieg* ("War"), *Handarbeit* ("Handwork"), or *Mittel* ("Middle"). In this middle phase of the fight, it is the motion of the hands, and thereby the swords they wield, that arbitrates the fight. This phase occurs at a range where the swords have crossed or are within range where they can cross. To hit your opponent you need not step; they are already in range of you, and vice-versa. Things can happen quickly here, and only a finely honed sense of the opponent's intent can avail.

Joachim Meyer explicitly describes a third phase of the fight, one implied by the earlier masters of the 15th century, the *Abzug* ("Withdrawal"), the safe removal of one's person from the opponent. This might take place after a successful attack, bearing in mind that even a grievously wounded opponent can still be dangerous, or after an exchange where neither opponent has struck the other, allowing the fencer(s) to regroup for another pass.

One tool in the *Abzug* is a concept briefly touched on in the masters' commentaries on Liechtenauer's verse: the *Zecke* ("Tag Hit"). This is a light blow used as one withdraws safely away from a bind. If the opponent keeps their sword low as they bind, cut down onto their arms as you pivot away. [Fig. 11] Your direction of withdrawal will vary depending on how committed they are in the bind. [Fig. 12] If they instead lift their sword, strike below it to their body as you withdraw. [Fig. 13]

Understanding how to safely close distance in the *Zufechten*, prosecute the fight up close in the *Krieg*, and safely withdraw in the *Abzug*, are critical skills in mastering this art. Shielding oneself with the sword is of paramount importance in all three of these phases.

NOTE: Be mindful when performing any of the partnered drills in this book that they tend to describe discrete actions, not a fight. It is important to practice individual techniques, but once you've done so, you should add an entry and a withdrawal from the action, as described above. Otherwise you will inadvertently train yourself to "freeze" after performing a technique, an undesirable consequence to say the least.

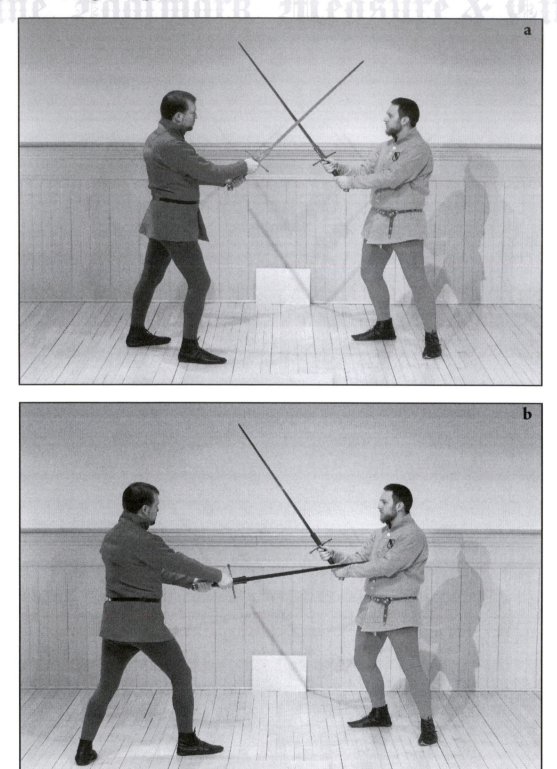

*Fig. 11 Meeting a weak parry by Janusz (a), Christian compass
steps back with the left foot to cut down onto the arms (b).*

*Fig. 12 Meeting a strong parry (a),
Christian frees his sword from the bind
(b) with a pass of the left foot to cut down
onto the arms on the other side of Janusz's
sword, using a backward compass step of
the right foot to gain further safety (c).*

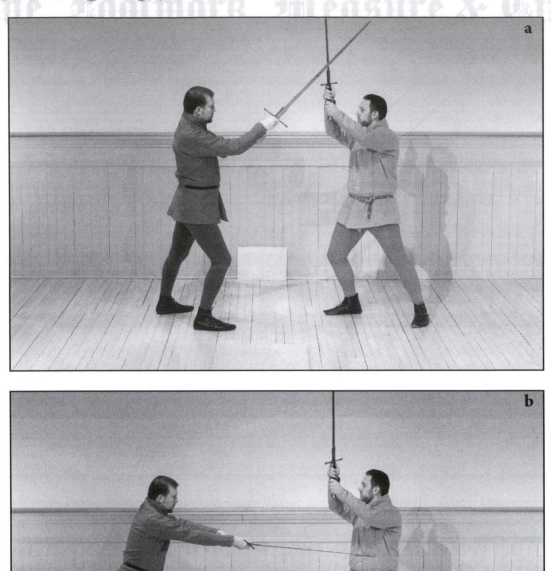

Fig. 13 Janusz lifts his sword high in the bind (a), so Christian drops his point to strike to the body with a backward pass of the right foot (b).

Time and Timing

It is meaningless to discuss measure in fencing without discussing time: the two are intertwined and one cannot learn one without the other.

While the German masters do not give a specific interval of time in fencing a name, their brethren across the Alps, the Italian masters, describe the idea of *tempo* (which simply means "time"). Drawing on the teachings of Aristotle, which were in wide currency in the late Middle Ages, a tempo is the interval of time between two moments of stillness. Thus, if you take a guard, make a cutting stroke with the sword, and then recover in another guard, this occupies a single *tempo*, or fencing time.

Drawing further on the teachings of the Philosopher (a common epithet for Aristotle in many a medieval treatise), we can describe a fencing time as either "perfect" or "imperfect." The simple example of the stroke described above describes a perfect time; no opposing force alters its course. If, however, an opponent were to parry that blow, and you were to allow your stroke to flow into a thrust in response to the parry, this would constitute a single imperfect time. There is no stillness between the two actions of the cut and its follow-on thrust, but your original trajectory has been transformed through the opponent's parry. Some fencing authorities call this imperfect time tempo indivisible, for the two actions may not be separated; they are one. In short, even a single fencing time can contain more than one action, so long as one flows seamlessly into the other.

Some techniques in Master Liechtenauer's art can be performed within a single fencing time, while others require more. The most sophisticated techniques are single-time actions where in one movement you defend against an opponent's attack and hit them at the same time. Other techniques require one time to defend against an attack and then another time to then give offense to the opponent: if you parry an opponent's attack, and then strike at them as a distinct, second action, this takes two fencing times (or *tempi*). Sometimes these two actions can flow together so seamlessly that there is no break between the two movements and hence no beat separating the two times. This is the single imperfect time, described above. The single-time action is the one most favored by Master Liechtenauer and, interestingly, if one of these fails to hit an opponent, it usually sets up a follow-on action requiring another fencing time. It is one of the beauties of this art that when one technique doesn't quite work, it lays the groundwork for another.

Note that a fencing time occupies no fixed interval of time. Some single-time actions require longer times than others. Further, you should understand that actions requiring longer times could be defeated by actions requiring shorter times. If you can respond within the time of an opponent's attack, you can answer it successfully.

Fencing times are how intervals of time in the fight are described. What of proper timing? How does one know the right moment to begin a defense or initiate an attack? These matters are tightly woven together with Master Liechtenauer's concepts of the flow of initiative in the fight. To seize the initiative, particularly when the opponent has elected to act first, we must know how to time our own actions – how to respond within the time of their action. We will study initiative in a later chapter and will then understand how one can properly time both attack and defense.

✛✛✛✛✛

Line, footwork, measure, and time are fundamentals that you must learn and practice if you want to fight well. You cannot keep your balance and bring the strength of your body to bear against your opponent if your footwork is poor, cannot reach them with your attacks, or prevent them from attacking you with impunity, if you've no sense of distance, and cannot exploit opportunities as they arise if you've not developed your timing. These aspects of swordplay are fundamental, yet they require years of practice to achieve true excellence. So, as you learn the techniques of the longsword that follow, be ever mindful of them so that you may continue to hone these basic skills as well. Remember, even a master of the sword is continually re-learning the basics.

Chapter 3: Vier Leger

*Four guards alone hold
and disdain the common
Ochs, Pflug, Alber,
vom Tag should not be unknown to you.*

— Johannes Liechtenauer

Master Liechtenauer advocated the use of four primary fighting stances or guards, the *Vier Leger* ("Four Positions"). These are *Ochs* ("Ox"), *Pflug* ("Plow"), *Alber* ("Fool"), and *vom Tag* ("From the Roof"). The guards are at once positions from which to begin a fight and places to transition through or pause briefly in during the fight. In addition to these four guards, there are several secondary guards in the system that are described by subsequent masters interpreting Liechtenauer's art, or which have been grafted from other traditions paralleling or deriving from his teachings. As all major actions within the system start and finish in these four positions (or subtle variations of them), it is essential to become acquainted with them and their function before exploring any techniques.

We will begin by learning of the *Vier Leger* and their applications and follow with the secondary guards and their relationship to these four primary ones.

The Vier Leger *("Four Positions"), from left to right,* Pflug, Ochs, vom Tag, *and* Alber, *from the 1452* Von Danzig Fechtbuch, *folios 1v–2r.*

Ochs – The Ox

The first of the four guards, *Ochs* ("Ox") is held with the hilt beside the head and the point slightly dipping to threaten the opponent's face. This position can be assumed on either side of the body. The right *Ochs* is performed with the left leg leading and the sword held at the right side of the head [Fig. 1]. The left *Ochs* is performed with the right leg leading and the sword held beside the left side of the head [Fig. 2]. Its name stems from its appearance. The blade's position beside the head mimics the horn of an ox. While Master Ringeck is silent on the orientation of the sword's edge in this guard, the Von Danzig manuscript indicates that the right *Ochs* should have the long edge

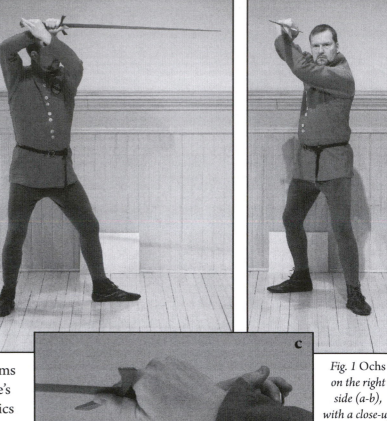

Fig. 1 Ochs on the right side (a-b), with a close-up showing the crossed hand position, the thumb bracing the base of the blade (c).

oriented outward and that the left *Ochs* should have the short edge oriented outward. The blade need not be held perfectly horizontal, but the edge should be presented outward. When you are in either *Ochs*, you should stabilize your blade by keeping your right thumb on the underside of the base of the blade. Do not attempt, however, to force your whole thumb onto the blade, only just enough to have a comfortable degree of control of the sword's orientation. The fingers of both hands should be supple and relaxed.

Your weight should be distributed such that there is more weight placed on the rear foot as you stand on guard. Be careful not to overdo this; 40% of the weight should be on the leading foot, and 60% should be on the trailing foot. As the *Ochs* is held high and somewhat back, this is important for keeping yourself balanced. It is the only one of the four primary guards held with the weight so placed. Be sure that your weight is placed on the balls of the feet in this and every other guard. Another consequence of keeping the weight on the rear foot is that it prevents you from extending your point too far as you approach into the fight. However, when you step forward into *Ochs* from another guard, your weight will naturally be more focused on the lead

Fig. 2 Ochs on the left side (a-b) with the thumb on the base of the blade (c).

foot. The weight is back when standing on guard, forward as you press forward to attack or defend in *Ochs*.

The orientation of the point implies this guard's primary function: It is used as a starting point for thrusts originating from above. From the *Ochs* on either side of the body you can thrust downward to hit the face, breast, or lower body. If such a thrust is executed in close proximity to an opponent, you will remain in a slightly forward version of the guard as you thrust, your body shifting forward from the backward weighted stance into the forward weighted one. If, however, you are thrusting from a greater distance, you must thrust from the *Ochs* into a position with the hands extended in front of your body. This fully extended position is one of the secondary guards that we will explore later in this chapter, *Langenort* ("Long-point"), and this is the final position of all thrusts made at long range, that is, from the *Zufechten*.

A slightly extended version of *Ochs* is also one of the two positions that you should be in when you cross swords with your opponent. In this capacity, it is also known as the "Upper Hanging" with the sword, for the point hangs down from the hands. When you are in this position, you are protected from sword blows that come from above on that side. Thus, the right *Ochs* protects you from a high strike from your opponent's left side, while the left *Ochs* protects you from high strikes coming from their right side. It is no accident that this defensive capability also has offensive potential; the point remains a threat to your attacker even as you defend yourself. This act of deflecting an attack while threatening with the point is called *Absetzen* ("Setting Aside"). By assuming the ox guard, a defender can set aside their opponent's attack while making one of their own with the extended point, with the horn of the Ox.

Pflug – The Plow

The second guard, *Pflug* ("Plow"), takes its name from the orientation of an old-fashioned push plow's blade as it furrows the earth. It is held with the sword hilt beside the hip, the point angled up towards the opponent's face. As with the *Ochs*, *Pflug* can be held symmetrically, that is, on either side of the body. To stand in the right *Pflug*, lead with your left foot and hold the hilt beside the right hip [Fig. 3]. The left *Pflug* is held at the left hip with your right foot leading [Fig. 4]. The von Danzig manuscript offers some advice on how to orient the edges of the blade. The right *Pflug* should have the short edge held upward, while the left *Pflug* has the long edge turned upward. In contrast to the *Ochs*, your weight should be more evenly balanced between your feet.

Pflug is very much the lower counterpart to *Ochs*. Both guards are thrusting positions. As *Ochs* is the starting point for thrusts originating from above, so *Pflug* is the point of origin for thrusts from below. As with *Ochs*, thrusts initiated from long range from *Pflug* also terminate in the guard *Langenort* ("Longpoint").

Pflug is another position appropriate for crossing swords with your opponent. In this capacity, it is the "Lower Hanging," that is, now it is the pommel which hangs down. When you assume the guard of the plow, you protect your side from strikes or thrusts. Again, as with *Ochs*, this defensive position contains a potent offense: the point remains a threat to your opponent at all times. You can employ *Absetzen* from *Pflug* too. Set aside a stroke or thrust and at the same time deliver a counter-thrust by assuming the guard of the Plow.

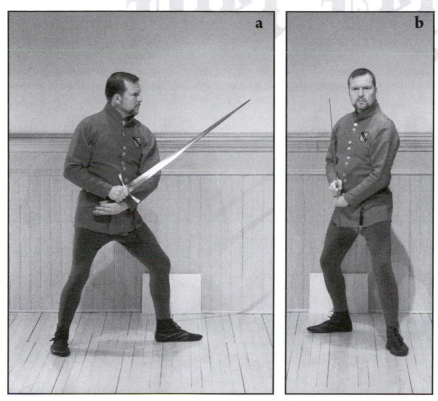

Fig. 3 Pflug *on the right side (a-b).*

Fig. 4 Pflug *on the left side (a-b).*

Alber – The Fool

The third of Master Liechtenauer's four guards is called *Alber* ("Fool"). Its name would seem to be in reference to its function: it lures fools into attacking what appears to be a very vulnerable position. *Alber* is held with the hilt lowered and the point facing the earth at a forty-five degree angle [Fig. 5]. In the manuscripts associated with the 15th century masters Sigmund Ringeck and Peter von Danzig, the right leg is the one leading. Interestingly, the manuscript associated with the Jewish Master Lew[20] (mid-15th century) describes the guard with the left leg leading [Fig. 6]. *Alber* should be held with more weight on the leading foot than the rear foot.

Alber is a guard of provocation: It invites attack, as the head and body appear to be unprotected by the lowered sword. However, once attacked, the swordsman can quickly lift the sword from *Alber* into *Ochs* or *Pflug* to intercept an incoming blow. Alternatively, the sword can be lifted straight up to interrupt a vertical attack. This parrying position, with the sword blade facing upward, is called *Kron* (the Crown). Once the attack is caught or deflected on the strong of the blade or the cross, the swordsman can then follow up with a thrust or rush in toward their foe to grapple with or disarm them.

Attacks can also be initiated from the Fool's Guard. A strike with the "short" or false edge can be executed by pulling the sword hard upward from *Alber*. A strong upward thrust can also be performed from it. It is important to know how to attack from this position, as it is a likely place for you to recover to when striking downward blows.

The guard *Alber* was also called the *Eisenpforte* ("Iron Gate") in some manuscripts,[21] notably in Hans Talhoffer's 1467 codex and in Hs. 3227a, where it is listed among the techniques "of other masters." Sometimes the name *Eisenpforte* seems to represent a guard distinct from *Alber*, perhaps held off to the side, much like the *Nebenhut* or *Wechselhut* that will discuss shortly. Interestingly, the northern Italian traditions refer to a series of low guards as *Porta di Ferro* ("Iron Gate"), perhaps showing some relationship between these two traditions separated by the Alps.

---

[20] The commentaries in the Lew manuscript closely follow those in the von Danzig manuscript, but with some interesting exceptions, such as this variant on *Alber*.

[21] Perhaps this alternative name derives from a fighting tradition that parallels Liechtenauer's.

Fig. 5 Alber *on the left side (a-b).*

Fig. 6 Alber *on the right side (a-b).*

Vom Tag – From the Roof

Vom Tag ("From the Roof") is a powerful striking guard whose name indicates that the strikes come from above. Alternative translations hold it to mean "from the day" or "clear as day". It is variously spelled in period manuscripts as *vom Dach*, *vom Tach*, and *vom Tage*. Both the Ringeck and von Danzig manuscripts describe it as being held in one of two ways. The first has the sword held on the right shoulder with the blade angled slightly backward [Fig. 7].

A left side version of this guard may be inferred: this is assumed on the left shoulder

Fig. 7 Vom Tag on the right shoulder (a-b), with a variant showing the flat laid upon the shoulder (c).

with the right leg leading [Fig. 8], although this is not the strongest position for a right-handed swordsman to strike from, as the hands cross when striking from the left side. Blows struck from the left are also shortened. The leading hand's shoulder (the right) stays behind in this case, limiting one's range. These are likely the reasons why the left side version isn't called out explicitly in the manuscript – its existence is implied in some of the techniques however, which refer to one's opponent striking "from his left shoulder."[22] On either side of the body, the long edge should always be presented toward your opponent, although the edge may need to face somewhat outward on the left side to avoid breaking the wrists.

A variant of the guard, attested in the Lew and Speyer codices, optimizes a particular stroke by laying the flat of the sword against the right shoulder. This will be explored in the chapter to come about the *Zwerchhau* ("Thwart Stroke").

The other basic form of *vom Tag* is held with the sword directly above the head with the blade angled slightly backward or pointing straight up. [Fig. 9] The latter version appears in the illustrated

---

[22] Peter von Danzig, *Fechtbuch*, folio 16r – 16v.

Fig. 8 Vom Tag *on the left shoulder (a-b).*

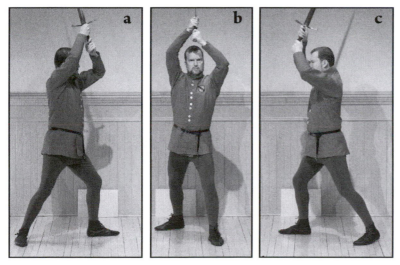

Fig. 9 High vom Tag *with the left leg leading (a-b) and with the right leg leading (c).*

manuscripts of the Bavarian *Fechtmeister*, Paulus Kal. The Jud Lew manuscript commentaries explicitly describe only this version of *vom Tag*, although the "on the shoulder" variant is described in many of the technique descriptions.

The shouldered version and the one over the head each have advantages and disadvantages. From the shoulder, it is easier to strike angled blows, while vertical strokes are easier to deliver from above the head. If you wish to switch between the two, however, be sure you make the transition before coming into range in the *Zufechten*, as moving between them causes your arm to momentarily occlude your vision, providing your opponent with an opportunity to act against you. *Vom Tag* should be held with the body's weight carried equally by both feet.

You can strike a blow vertically down, diagonally down, horizontally, or in a line sweeping up from below (by lifting the hilt and dropping the point as your strike) from *vom Tag*. As we shall see later, all of Master Liechtenauer's "five secret strikes," the Meisterhaue,[23] originate from this guard. A simple transition from *vom Tag* into either *Pflug* or *Ochs* (on either side) can also be made to set aside incoming attacks.

---

[23] *Haue* is the plural of *Hau*.

Moving Between the Four Guards

Most actions within Liechtenauer's fighting system comprise transitions from one guard to another, sometimes passing through yet another guard. As the guards constitute the basic building blocks of the art, it is essential to be able to move from one guard to another efficiently.

In the following drills, wherever footwork is necessary to make a transition from one guard to another, I've specified it with a pass forward. The student should be advised that each transition can also be performed in reverse, that is, with a pass backward instead. It's important to become fluid in one's movement through each transition with both forward and backward motion, because at times you may need to create distance rather than close it.

Hints for Practicing the Above Drills:

- Be sure that when you pass, whether forward or backward, that there is an outward component to your movement and the step is oblique (i.e. you never step directly toward your opponent, unless closing to grapple).

- It is critical as you transition between the *Ochs* and *Pflug* on each side so that your point remains facing your opponent at all times. The threat of the point must be maintained always when moving between those guards.

- Always begin moving your sword before you begin moving your foot. Remember: Your sword is also your defense, so it must begin moving into position to protect your person before you put yourself in harm's way.

- At this stage of your training, avoid the temptation to strike from *vom Tag* into *Alber* or vice-versa. Instead, do this slowly to first learn the proper footwork and positioning of the body. You will be rewarded with good form as you progress toward learning how to strike and thrust. Once you know how to do that, you will be able to perform these drills with greater speed and power.

Drill 1: Transitioning Between *Pflug* and *Ochs* on Both Sides

Part A – With passing steps

- Stand in the right *Pflug*, in the left leg lead stance with the hilt at your right hip.

- Move from the right *Pflug* into the left *Pflug* with a pass forward so that your right leg now leads.

- Move from the left *Pflug* into the right *Ochs* with a pass forward so that your left leg leads again.

- Move from the right *Ochs* into the left *Ochs* with a pass forward so that your right leg leads.

- Move from the left *Ochs* into the right *Pflug* with a pass forward foots that your left leg leads.

- Repeat steps 1 – 5, this time with backward passing steps, rather than forward ones.

Part B – Without steps

- With a right leg lead, move repeatedly between left Pflug and left Ochs.

- With a left leg lead, move repeatedly between right *Pflug* and right *Ochs*.

Drill 2: Transitioning Between *vom Tag* and *Alber*

- Stand in the guard *vom Tag*, with your sword on your right shoulder and your left leg leading.

- Bring your sword down into left *Alber* with a pass of the right foot.

- Lift your sword up into the variant of *vom Tag* where the sword is over the head with a pass of the left foot.

- Bring your sword down into left *Alber* as in Step 2, once again with a pass of the right foot.

- Compass step 180° around on the right foot to form *vom Tag* on your left shoulder with your right leg leading.

- Bring your sword down into right *Alber* with a pass of the left foot.

- Lift your sword up into the over-the-head variant of *vom Tag* with a pass of the right foot.

- Bring your sword down once more into right *Alber* with a pass of the left foot.

- Compass step 180° around on the left foot and form right *vom Tag* to re-start the cycle at step 1.

- Repeat steps 1–9, this time with backward passing steps, rather than forward ones.

Drill 3: Using All Four Primary Guards

- Stand in *vom Tag*, with your sword on your right shoulder and your left leg leading.

- Move forward into the left *Ochs* with a pass of the right foot.

- Move forward into the right *Pflug* with a pass of the left foot.

- Move forward into the left *Alber* with a pass of the right foot.

- Lift your sword to your left shoulder to form left *vom Tag*.

- Move forward into right *Alber* with a pass of the left foot.

- Lift your sword up into the right *Ochs*.

- Move forward into the left *Pflug* with a pass of the right foot.

- Move forward to return to right *vom Tag* with a pass of the left foot.

- Next, you can mix and match the above steps, varying which side you assume the *Ochs* and *Pflug* and by practicing your transitions with backward (i.e., retreating) passing footwork.

The Secondary Guards

Several secondary guards appeared throughout the manuscripts of the Liechtenauer tradition during the 14th and 15th centuries. At least one, *Langenort* ("Longpoint"), is actually terminology surviving from a time pre-dating the extant manuscripts, and perhaps the tradition itself. This guard appears in the Royal Armouries Manuscript I.33 sword and buckler manuscript from the late 13th or early 14th century. The other secondary positions that we will cover are the *Schranckhut* ("Barrier Guard"), *Nebenhut* ("Side Guard"), and a parrying position called *Kron* ("Crown").

Liechtenauer's verse strongly admonishes us to hold only four guards. Why then do these other positions figure throughout the system? My own feeling is that the four primary guards represent the best places to begin an encounter because each is optimized for either threatening with the point or edge or, in the case of *Alber*, luring an opponent. The function of each of these guards is fundamental. The other positions either offer a compromise between those two functions or represent places you might momentarily find yourself in while executing techniques. There is the tendency, found in many martial systems, for subsequent masters of a given tradition to add their own innovations as time goes by. By the 16th century, still more positions were added to the Liechtenauer tradition's system of guards. Master Joachim Meyer describes a number of these additional guards in his 1570 work, but even he, at this late date, takes pains to distinguish the importance of Liechtenauer's original four.

Understanding the secondary guards accords us a better grasp of the movement between the primary guards during the course of techniques, and provide for some tactical variations when used carefully. Let us look at each and preview their functions.

Langenort – The Longpoint

The *Langenort* ("Longpoint") is a position held with the blade extended outward toward your opponent's face. It is the natural termination of thrusts delivered from *Ochs* or *Pflug* and in fact looks very much like the guard *Pflug*, but with the arms held farther away from the body.

Langenort is the point of focus for all blows struck with the sword from above. As this position is where one is likely to make contact with one's opponent, the energy and intent of the attack should be concentrated here.

Lastly, this guard is also a position you can assume to keep an opponent at bay at a distance. This can even be used to provoke an opponent, for an aggressive enemy will want to try to beat aside the sword to reach their opponent. As the Long Point's extension means that one cannot beat the sword away and hit its wielder in one movement, this creates an opening for a counterattack from this guard.

Langenort can be assumed with either the left [Fig. 10] or right [Fig. 11] leg leading. The blade should be held with the short edge facing up, the arms extended away from the body, the point menacing the opponent's face. However, you should resist the temptation to lock the elbows out straight to maximize your reach. This is both unnecessary and dangerous because locking your elbows makes you much more vulnerable to grappling techniques. As with *Pflug*, you should have slightly more weight upon your forward foot as you stand in this guard.

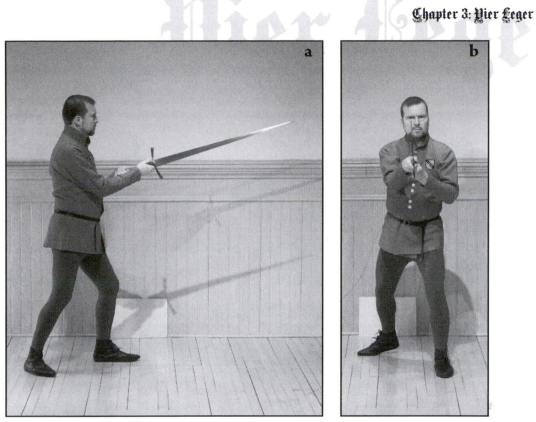

Fig. 10 Langenort *with the left leg leading (a-b).*

Fig. 11 Langenort *with the right leg leading (a-b).*

Schranckhut – The Barrier Guard

The *Schranckhut* ("Barrier Guard") is a low guard. Unlike *Alber*, however, it is not held with the point forward, but with it slanting toward the ground at a right angle to the line of engagement with the opponent, thus forming a barrier. Because of this orientation, it is primed for the launching of powerful blows, much like a low version of *vom Tag*. However, it also partakes of one of the qualities of the guard *Alber*, in that it leaves the wielder completely exposed, inviting an attack to either the upper or the lower openings. The Von Danzig text speaks of standing in this guard and so provoking your opponent:

> When you come to him in the Zufechten (the approach), then stand with your left foot forward and hold your sword with the point beside your right side toward the ground with the long edge up, and provide an opening with your left side.[24]

The *Schranckhut* is held on the right [Fig. 12] with the left foot forward and with the hilt held above the waist with the point sloping downward at a roughly forty-five degree angle toward the earth. The long edge should face upward. On the left side of the body [Fig. 13], the right leg leads and the short edge faces upward, with the arms crossed at the wrists. In each case, I find it works best to have the leading foot carry slightly more of the body's weight than the trailing foot.

Schranckhut can be used for setting off incoming blows by quickly moving into the guards *Ochs* or *Pflug* on the opposite side or for delivering powerful blows. It is particularly well suited as a starting, and ending, point for blows that sweep across your body to hit your opponent as you pass safely away from one of their blows, as we shall see in a later chapter.

---

[24] Peter von Danzig, *Fechtbuch*, folio 17r.

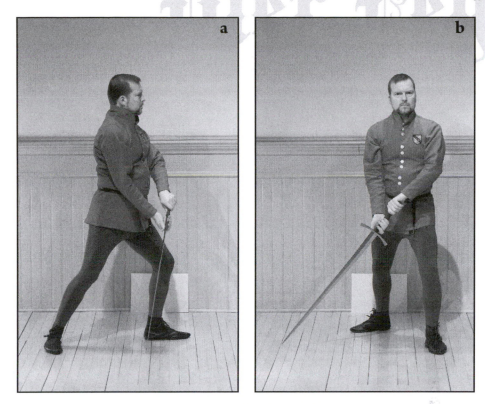

Fig. 12 Right Schranckhut *(a-b)*.

Fig. 13 Left Schranckhut *(a-b)*.

Nebenhut – The Side Guard

*N*ebenhut ("Side Guard") is held at the side of the body and near the trailing leg. It is similar to the Tail Guard that appears in contemporary Italian treatises, but my interpretation of it is that it is not carried as far back as that guard is. *Nebenhut* is framed similarly to *Schranckhut*, but with the blade along the side of the body and roughly parallel to the line of engagement, rather than perpendicular to it.

While similar looking, though unnamed, postures appear in some illustrated manuscripts such as the *Codex Wallerstein* or Talhoffer's *Fechtbücher*, the only place the guard is directly called out in the earlier treatises is a series of techniques appearing after the main commentaries on Liechtenauer's teachings in the Ringeck manuscript (and some copies thereof). Here, a series of methods are described for slashing upward with the short edge from the left *Nebenhut*, which the author lauds as being better than performing them from the right. Because of this, I have elected to depict the left *Nebenhut* as presenting either edge forward. To stand in the left *Nebenhut*, stand in the right-leg-leading stance, with your hilt at waist height and the point low at your left side with your short edge facing forward, or with the point trailing and the long edge facing forward. [Fig. 14] Other sources, such as the later work of Joachim Meyer, and the early 16th century anonymous treatise on the messer, refer to the short edge forward position as the *Wechselhut* ("Change Guard"), perhaps because, once you've struck a full stroke from above, this is a position wherein the blow finds its completion and you must now change directions.

Other than what seems to be illustrated in some manuscripts, we have little information on the right side *Nebenhut* from either the 14th or the 15th century treatises. However, Meyer's 1570 treatise discusses it, and as the Ringeck material infers its existence, I present it here as well, with the long edge presented forward. To form the right *Nebenhut*, stand with your left leg leading, your hilt at waist height and the point low at your right side, the long edge facing forward.[25] [Fig. 15]

There are unnamed positions that appear in various manuscripts that look like *Nebenhut*. Sometimes they are shown with the weight distribution favoring the forward foot, but sometimes it is the trailing foot. My advice is that if you are attempting to lure your opponent into attacking you, keep your weight back, but if you intend to initiate an attack, shift it forward.

Nebenhut is a good launching place for powerful blows from below, or with an arcing motion, those that sweep upward and descend from above. Like the *Schranckhut*, it is a guard of provocation. It must be used prudently, for if one is not particular mindful of the opponent's timing, it is often hard to bring your own sword to your defense when it is held so far back from your opponent. More succinctly, any action proceeding from here requires a long tempo.

---

[25] Following Meyer, a case can be made for a version on the right side of the body where the short edge faces forward, just as both orientations can be inferred on the left. Such a position is good place from which to deliver an upward slash as an entering action.

Fig. 14 *Left* Nebenhut *(a-b) with the short edge forward, and with the long edge forward (c).*

Fig. 15 *Right* Nebenhut *(a-b).*

Kron – The Crown

Kron ("Crown") is not really so much a guard as it is a position through which to pass. This is not a position to lie in on guard, but is useful as a transition point. If you are attacked while you stand in the guard *Alber*, you can rise up out of that guard and briefly into *Kron* to intercept the attack. From this position, you must quickly move to another by either turning your sword into *Ochs* to thrust or by rushing in to come to grips with your opponent. This is because the *Kron* is not a stable position to bind in, as it offers no threat with the point.

This guard is held much like *Langenort*, except that the point is angled upward more and the sword's cross is presented somewhat flat towards the opponent so that it can catch incoming blows.[26] The name *Kron* likely derives from its appearance. When you form *Kron*, your hilt will be at approximately the height where a crown would adorn your brow.

When you move from *Alber* to *Kron*, you can do so without stepping and then step in to grapple. From a right-leg-leading *Alber*, you'd therefore lift up into a right-leg-leading *Kron* [Fig. 16]. However, there may be times where you might find yourself in the left-leg-leading version of *Alber* specified by the commentaries in the Lew manuscript, and this would in turn give rise to a version of *Kron* where the left leg leads. [Fig. 17] As with *Alber*, the likely starting point for moving into *Kron*, this guard should be formed with your weight focused more on your leading foot.

---

[26] Later versions of this position have the sword angled down, with the left hand holding the middle of the blade, as it does in the armoured half-sword combat.

Fig. 16 Kron *with the right foot forward.*

Fig. 17 Kron *with the left foot forward (a-b).*

Drill 4: Moving through All the Guards

This drill for exercising all of the guard positions was created by my friend and fellow fencer Jeffrey Tsay and his students. You'll likely need to perform this drill outdoors, as it requires a bit of room. In many cases, the transitions represent techniques that we will explore later: cutting strokes, thrusts, parries. All of the transitions, save for those from Alber to Kron and the two turnarounds, require passing footwork.

- Begin in right *vom Tag*

- Move into left *Nebenhut*

- Move into right *Nebenhut*

- Move into left *Ochs*

- Move into right *Langenort*

- Move into left *Pflug*

- Move into right *Schranckhut*

- Move into left *vom Tag*

- Move into right *Alber*

- Move into right *Kron*

- Compass step around 180° on the left foot while assuming left *vom Tag*

- Move into right *Nebenhut*

- Move into left *Nebenhut*

- Move into right *Ochs*

- Move into left *Langenort*

- Move into right *Pflug*

- Move into left *Schranckhut*

- Move into high *vom Tag*

- Move into left *Alber*

- Move into left *Kron*

- Compass step around 180° on the right foot to assume right *vom Tag*, from which you can repeat the above steps.

Chapter 4: Three Wounders

Also you should
Test stroke, thrust, or slice,
in all hits,
if you want to fool the masters.
— Johannes Liechtenauer

Master Liechtenauer's verse speaks of *Drei Wunder*, or "Three Wounders," three different ways to wound an opponent with the longsword. Each of these attacks must be used only as appropriate. An important part of developing good tactical skills with this system involves knowing when you should employ one or the other.

The first type of attack is a stroke of the sword, which the German masters called *Hauen*, or "hewing." These are powerful cutting strokes with the sword and are capable of cutting deeply into the body, rending limbs, and severing heads.

The second attack is called Stechen, or "thrusting." With its tapering blade, the longsword is an admirable weapon for delivering attacks with the point. Even the most casual experimentation reveals that it requires frighteningly little force to push the point of a longsword through clothing and flesh. We will see that, because of this advantage, it is highly desirable to perform many of the techniques in a way that allows us to readily bring the point to bear against a foe.

The third and last attack is called *Abschneiden*, or "slicing off." These are cuts made by forcefully placing the blade against an exposed part of the body—a wrist, the neck, or the face—and either pushing or pulling the blade along it, cutting into it. These attacks can be harassing in nature or, if directed against a wrist or throat, can impede an opponent's ability to fight. When applied to the hands or arms, these are always executed while simultaneously pushing the opponent away from you.

One of the great advantages of this fighting system is how the three attacks play off each other. For instance, if you strike at someone with your sword and they recoil just enough for you to miss, the odds are that your point will come on line and set up a thrust as your follow-on technique. If instead, in your stroke you fail to develop sufficient power, your edge may still come into play against your foe so that you can slice into them by pulling or pushing your edge against them. In a similar vein, if you thrust past your opponent, you can slice them as you pull your point back.

Hauen - Striking with the Sword

> Listen to what is wrong,
> do not fight above on the left if you are right handed;
> and if you are left-handed,
> on the right you limp as well.

— Johannes Liechtenauer

Liechtenauer advised that one should favor the striking of blows with the sword from one's strong side. A right-hander should favor striking from their right side and a left-hander from their left side. This is for a couple of reasons. First, you have the best reach when striking from the side where your hand is leading. If you're right-handed, your right hand will be topmost on the grip of the sword and you will have the best extension with your right shoulder put forward as you strike. Secondly, striking from your strong side avoids having your wrists or arms cross during the blow. When your arms cross, you can become "tangled up" and can be more easily disarmed by a skilled combatant.

This is not to say that a right-hander should never strike blows from their left, or vice-versa. Do be aware that your surest attacks will come from your strong side.

The two most important and primary strokes of the sword are the *Oberhau* and the *Unterhau*, the stroke from above and the stroke from below. All other strokes are but permutations of these. As the passage in Hs. 3227a says:

> *Also know that there are only two strokes from which derive all other strokes, namely, the* Oberhau *and the* Unterhau *from both sides. These are the main strokes and the foundation of all other strokes, which in their cause and fundamentals come from the point of the sword, which is the kernel and center of all techniques.*[27]

He means here that these strokes each culminate with a threat from the point, an extremely important feature of Liechtenauer's system. Whether you fence with the stroke above or the stroke below, if you are parried, your point has nonetheless been brought in line for a thrust against your opponent. Mark this well, for the quote cited above is no exaggeration.

Later in this book, we will explore specialized sword strokes – the Five Secret Strokes, later known as the *Meisterhaue* or "Master Strokes," which are signature techniques of the *Kunst des Fechtens*. For now, let us begin by turning our attention to the basic strokes of the sword in Master Liechtenauer's art, for all other strokes are but variations on these basics.

The *Oberhau* – A Stroke from Above

An *Oberhau* is any blow struck from above. It can descend toward the opponent along either a vertical or a diagonal line. These blows are often delivered from the guard *vom Tag*, though they can originate from the guards *Schranckhut* or *Nebenhut* when struck through a wide arc that comes from below and then up and over. Strokes from above are the most powerful, but to realize their full offensive and defensive potential, they should be delivered with the entire body

---

[27] Hs. 3227a, folios 23v – 24r.

working in harmony. We have discussed before how the sword's movement must precede the body's movement. This also holds true for striking blows with the sword.

Master Liechtenauer's verse contains an extremely useful reminder of this concept, appropriate to all striking with the sword, wherein he says, "*If you want to behold the art, see that you go with the left and strike with the right. And left to right, is how you strongly want to fight.*"[28] In his commentary on this part of the verse, Master Ringeck says:

> *If you strike an Oberhau from the right side then, follow the blow with your right foot. If you do not the blow is wrong and ineffective, because your right side stays behind. Because of this, the blow will fall short and cannot travel in its proper arc towards the left side. If you strike from the left side and you do not follow the blow, it too is wrong. That is why no matter from which side you are striking follow the blow with the same foot. So you will succeed in all techniques. This is how you shall strike all blows.*[29]

To strike an *Oberhau* from the right, place yourself in the guard *vom Tag*, with your left foot leading and your sword held on your right shoulder. Envision now that you are to strike to an imaginary opponent's head or collarbone. Start moving your sword by pushing out with the top hand as you pull in with the bottom hand, utilizing the lever nature of a two-handed hilt. Now move your sword in a downward and extending arc towards your opponent and in one smooth movement let your shoulders, then your hips follow this movement. To maximize your reach in an attack, keep your hands high, and keep the angle of the attack steep (no less than 70 degrees for a diagonal attack). Finally, let your right foot follow your sword with a pass forward. Strike with your sword's long edge[30] and with your arms outstretched, but not so much that your elbows lock straight. If your footwork feels stiff or awkward, try again and be sure you are putting your weight down on the balls of your feet.

Your weight must smoothly transition from being more focused on your left foot to being more focused on your right as you pass forward. By doing this, you will impart your body's momentum to the stroke and in such a way that you are never off-balance. When the blow is finished, your weight should be forward on the right foot, but not so that you are over-balanced. Rather, it should feel identical to the passing steps you practiced before ever taking up the weapon. Be sure that your hips, back, and shoulders follow the motion of the sword, coiling and charging your left hip so that it is poised to provide energy for any stroke from the left that may follow. At the end of a blow from the right your right foot, hip and shoulder will be forward; at the end of a blow from the left this will be reversed. Be sure that you can feel your entire body bringing the stroke to bear, not just your arms. This is what Master Sigmund Ringeck means when he says:

> "*Always, if you wish to fence, this do with all the strength of your body.*"[31]

---

[28] Sigmund Ringeck, *Fechtbuch*, folio 11v.

[29] Ibid., folio 12r.

[30] Later in this book, we will examine a type of *Oberhau* performed with the short edge.

[31] Sigmund Ringeck, *Fechtbuch*, folio 13v.

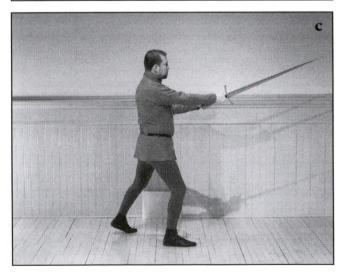

Fig. 1 An Oberhau *from right* vom Tag *seen from the side, terminating in* Langenort *(a-c).*

Fig. 1 An Oberhau *from right* vom Tag *seen from the front, terminating in* Langenort *(aa-cc).*

Now, here is an important note about timing and focus in your sword strokes. When you strike the *Oberhau*, you should focus the power of your stroke at the point in space corresponding to the guard *Langenort*. As it steps, your right foot should land on the ground, just as your sword passes through this point. If you were striking an opponent, this would be the point of contact and hence where you want the most power.

Langenort is the point of focus for all strokes from above, but not always where the stroke will terminate. If you are striking vertically and you don't make contact, or strike a powerful "full" blow, you may follow through to the guard *Alber*. If you are striking down diagonally, however, you may finish in an extended version of the left *Pflug* should your opponent bind against your sword, or in the guard *Nebenhut*, if your stroke misses or cuts strongly through the target.

You should be able to stop your sword in *Langenort*. This last option is, in fact, a very safe way to enter into the fight. This cannot be overstated. It is of profound importance when entering the fight, should your blow fall short, that you continue to threaten the opponent with your point.

Lead with your left leg and practice the *Oberhau* by striking diagonally from right *vom Tag*. Vary your level of commitment by completing the blow just as it passes through *Langenort*, [Fig. 1] and by striking a full blow through to *Nebenhut*. [Fig. 2]

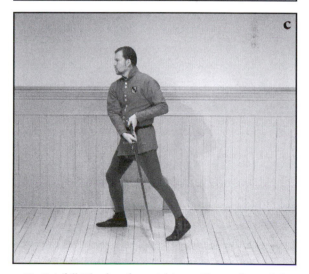

Fig. 2 A full Oberhau *from right* vom Tag, *ending in left* Nebenhut *(a-c).*

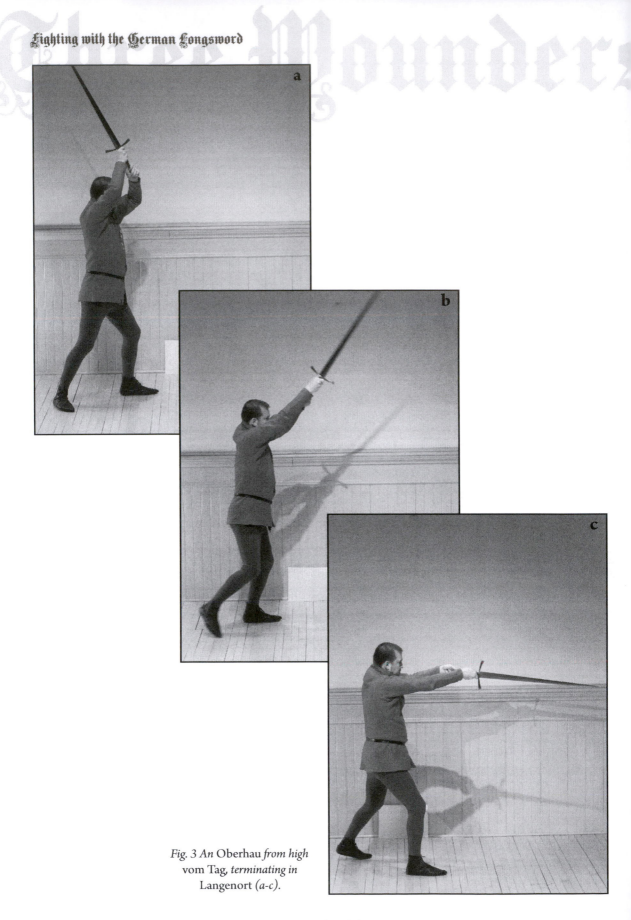

Fig. 3 An Oberhau *from high* vom Tag, *terminating in* Langenort *(a-c)*.

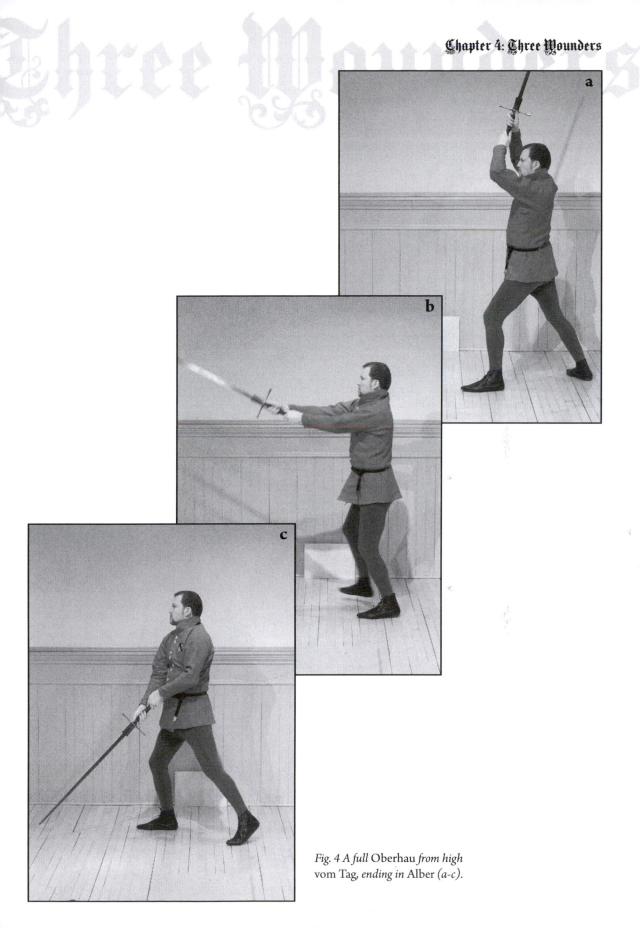

Fig. 4 A full Oberhau *from high* vom Tag, *ending in* Alber *(a-c).*

Also practice striking vertically from high *vom Tag*, varying between strokes that finish in *Langenort* [Fig. 3] and full blows that follow through to *Alber*. [Fig. 4]

Also, practice the *Oberhau* from the other side. To do this, begin by standing in *vom Tag* on the left side, with your right leg leading. As you strike, pass forward with your left foot. [Fig. 5] Once again, you must focus your power and intent in the *Langenort*. As before, your body's weight must smoothly move forward as you strike, your hips, shoulders and back following the movement of the blade and in turn charging the hips.

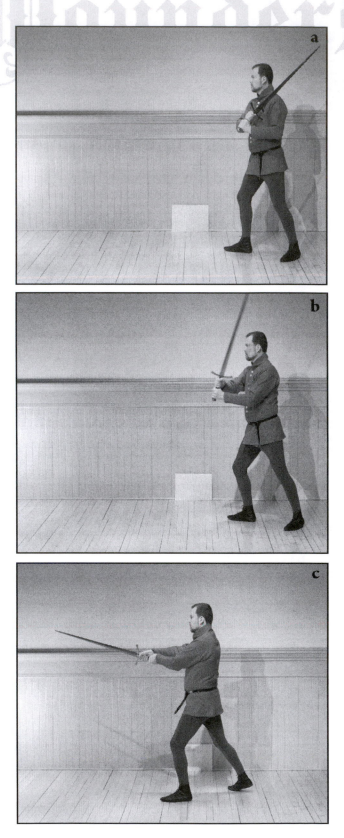

Fig. 5 An Oberhau *from left* vom Tag *(a-c).*

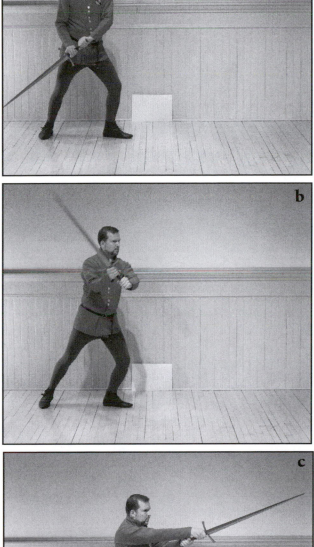

Once you have learned these strokes, try them from the *Nebenhut* [Fig. 6] and from the *Schranckhut* [Fig. 7]. Do this from the right and from the left and remember that, although you are creating a longer arc of travel for your sword as it comes up around and down, you must always focus your strength in *Langenort*.

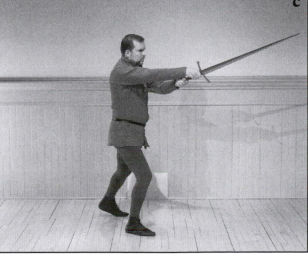

Fig. 6 An Oberhau *from right* Nebenhut *(a-c).*

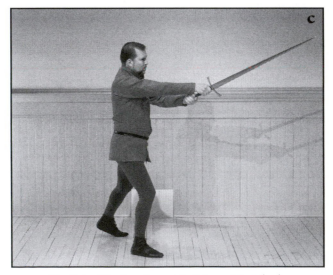

Fig. 7 An Oberhau *from right* Schranckhut *(a-c).*

The *Unterhau* – A Stroke from Below

As an *Oberhau* is any stroke from above, an *Unterhau* is any stroke from below. These can originate from any of the low guards on either side; this includes the *Alber*, *Schranckhut*, and *Nebenhut*. They can also originate from *vom Tag* on either side. Although *vom Tag* is a high guard, you can still sweep up from below by pulling your hilt upward while letting your point drop – this can be put to good use in deceiving your opponent, who may expect an *Oberhau*, but end up on the receiving end of an *Unterhau* instead.

Both the long and short edges of the sword may be used when striking an *Unterhau*.[32] From *Alber* and left *Nebenhut* it is often easier to simply strike a slashing blow upward with the short edge, particular after striking an *Oberhau* from your right side. This "one-two" combination of *Oberhau* and *Unterhau* is very powerful and very fast.

When you strike an *Unterhau* with the long edge, your stroke will terminate in the *Ochs* on either side, whether you hit, miss, or bind with your opponent. If, however, you strike up from below by slashing upward with your sword's short edge, you will find it important, as with the *Oberhau*, to focus your strength in *Langenort*. If you miss your opponent, you will recover in high *vom Tag*, but if you bind against your opponent's sword, this will most likely occur at a position corresponding to the Kron.

An *Unterhau* delivered with the long edge can be very deceptive and hard to parry, but be aware that because it is likely to connect with the opponent while passing through the *Ochs* (a guard with a short reach) their limited range can be outreached by a skilled swordsman, who will slip out of its range and strike an *Oberhau* in return. The advantage of reach that an *Oberhau* has over the *Unterhau* is ensconced in one of Liechtenauer's primary techniques, *Überlaufen* ("Overrunning"), of which the von Danzig commentaries say:

> Note, when you come to him in the Zufechten *and he strikes from below to your lower openings, then do not parry this, but strike strongly above to his head. Or if he strikes with the* Unterhau, *then note before he comes up with the* Unterhau, *and shoot the point in above long to his face or chest, and plant it on him above so that he cannot reach you below, since all thrusts above break and defeat those below.*[33]

Owing to this disadvantage it is best to either strike the *Unterhau* with the long edge from *vom Tag* on either side of the body, as you can feint an *Oberhau* and turn it sneakily into an *Unterhau* to catch your opponent unaware, or immediately thrust when your *Unterhau* comes in line against your opponent.

To strike an *Unterhau* with the long edge, position yourself in *vom Tag* on the right, with your left foot leading. As with the *Oberhau*, begin moving your sword first (remember, your sword is your shield and must precede you). Do this by pulling your hilt up a bit and letting your point

---

[32] Generally, the masters describe the *Unterhau* proper as being struck with the long edge. However they imply that all blows which strike upward from below are *Unterhau*, so I have included the upward slashing blows with the short edge under this umbrella term.

[33] Peter von Danzig, *Fechtbuch*, folio 30r.

drop down, allowing your sword to almost move through the *Nebenhut*. Your shoulders should follow your blade, your hips twisting with the motion, and finally your right foot, which should pass forward. Your foot should land as your sword sweeps up toward its target. As with the *Oberhau*, your weight must smoothly transition forward, imparting power to the blow, but without disturbing your balance. You will find the same natural orientation of arm, shoulder, hip, and leg, and the same commitment of bodyweight as discussed under the *Oberhau*, above.

Practice this from right *vom Tag* [Fig. 8] as described above. When this begins to feel comfortable and natural to you, practice it from *vom Tag* on the left [Fig. 9]. From a right leg lead, pass forward with your left foot as you strike the blow.

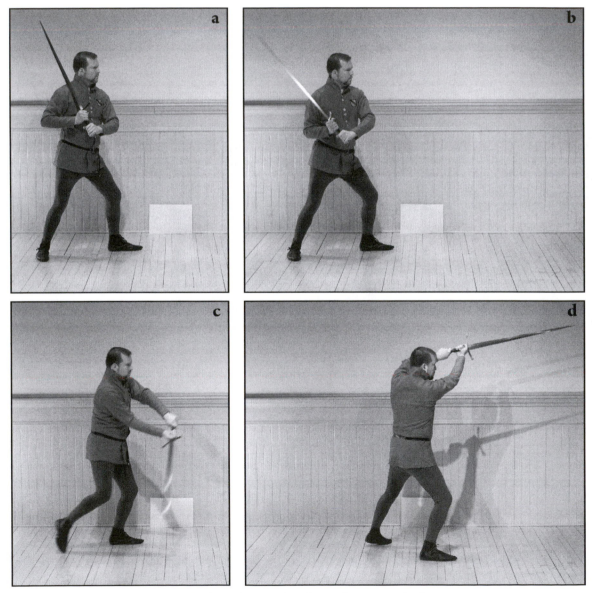

Fig. 8 A long edge Unterhau *from right* vom Tag *(a-c).*

Practice the long-edge *Unterhau* from both the right [Fig. 10] and left [Fig. 11] *Nebenhut*. Use this version judiciously as it can be predictable and, without the element of surprise, the *Unterhau* is at disadvantage due to its diminished reach. With a slight adjustment, you can perform this same action from the right and left *Schranckhut* as well, though this will not be as powerful a blow as when it is struck from the *Nebenhut*.

The upward slashing strokes[34] with the short edge are fast and have a greater range as they pass through the guard *Langenort*, the guard with the greatest forward extension. These are excellent techniques to have in your repertoire because they can flow naturally from a completed *Oberhau*.

To strike an *Unterhau* with the short edge, begin in either left *Nebenhut* [Fig. 12] or in *Alber* [Fig. 13]. Pass forward with the left foot as you snap your blade upward. This should be done with a levering action. Your right hand should pull up and toward you while your left hand pushes slightly down and away. Remember to do this with the whole body contributing to the stroke. The hips, shoulders, and back should all be involved, so that the cut is not simply a "flick" with the false edge made by your hands. Recover the blow in high *vom Tag*.

---

[34] In the Ringeck manuscript, these are called *Streichen* ("Slashing"). In some 15th century sources, notably the 1467 Talhoffer *Fechtbuch*, it seems to be called a *Wechselhau* ("Change Stroke"), as it comes out of the *Wechselhut* ("Change Guard"), the position similar to the Nebenhut in which the short edge faces forward.

Fig. 9 A long edge Unterhau from left vom Tag (a-c).

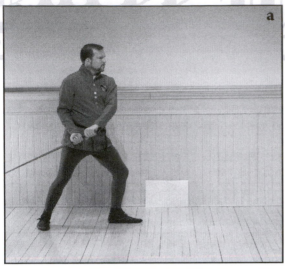

a

a

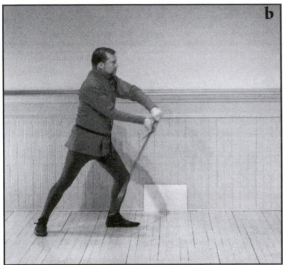

b

b

c

c

Fig. 10 A long edge Unterhau *from right* Nebenhut *(a-c).*

Fig. 11 A long edge Unterhau *from left* Nebenhut *(a-c).*

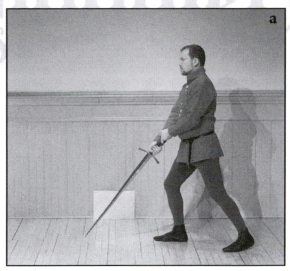

Fig. 12 Slashing up with the short edge from left Nebenhut *(a-c).*

Fig. 13 Slashing up with the short edge from Alber *(a-c).*

The *Mittelhau* – The Middle Stroke

A Mittelhau is a horizontal stroke with the sword, and can be thought of as either an *Oberhau* or *Unterhau* whose trajectory flattens out. This stroke does not figure prominently in the earlier works of the Liechtenauer tradition, where it is mentioned only obliquely or as the starting point for techniques with the messer or the sword and buckler. By the time of Joachim Meyer's magnum opus of 1570, however, it was considered one of the fundamental blows. It can be struck from *vom Tag* on either side of the body or from either *Nebenhut* with the long edge of the sword.

In addition, while they are powerful blows, you should be aware that *Mittelhaue* are readily parried by the guard *Pflug*, so expect them to serve only as entrances into the fight when you are fencing with a skilled combatant. If your opponent does parry your *Mittelhau*, you in turn will bind in the guard *Pflug*, but if your strike misses, you will recover in the *Nebenhut* on the opposite side of the body from which you started the blow.

When you strike a *Mittelhau*, your body should move as if you are striking an *Oberhau*. The difference is that your blade should flatten out as you strike so that it moves horizontally. Be sure you drive your weight forward as you step and that you bring the turning of your hips, back, and shoulders to bear in powering the blow.

Practice the *Mittelhau* from the guard *vom Tag* on the right [Fig. 14] and left [Fig. 15], and then from the right [Fig. 16] and left [Fig. 17] *Nebenhut*.

Drill 5: Striking with the Sword

- Begin in right *vom Tag*.
- Strike a diagonal *Oberhau*, passing forward with the right foot, recovering into left *Nebenhut*.
- Cut upward with an *Unterhau* with the short edge from left *Nebenhut*, passing forward with the left foot, recovering into *vom Tag* above the head.
- Strike a vertical *Oberhau*, passing forward with the right foot, recovering in left Alber.
- Lift your sword up into left *vom Tag*.
- Strike a backhanded diagonal *Oberhau*, passing forward with the left foot, recovering into right *Nebenhut*.
- Strike an *Unterhau* with the long edge, passing forward with the right foot, recovering in left *Ochs*.
- Bring your sword back into left *vom Tag*.
- Strike an *Unterhau* with the long edge, passing forward with the left foot, recovering into right *Ochs*.
- Bring your sword back into right *vom Tag*.
- Strike a *Mittelhau*, passing forward with the right foot, recovering into left *Nebenhut*.
- Strike a *Mittelhau*, passing forward with the left foot, recovering into right *Nebenhut*.
- Return to right *vom Tag*, from which you can repeat the above steps.

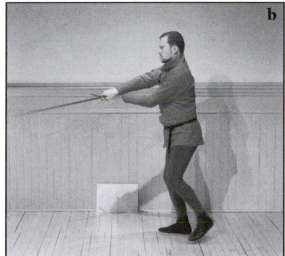

Fig. 14 The Mittelhau *from right* vom Tag *(a-c).*   *Fig. 15 The* Mittelhau *from left* vom Tag *(a-c).*

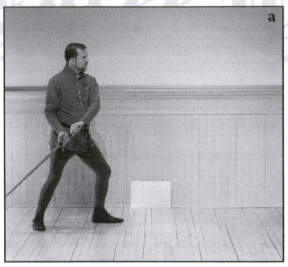

Fig. 16 The Mittelhau *from right* Nebenhut *(a-c).*   *Fig. 17 The* Mittelhau *from left* Nebenhut *(a-c).*

Stechen – Thrusting with the Sword

> *Set upon the four ends.*
> *Stay upon them, learn if you want to bring it to an end.*
> - Johannes Liechtenauer

There are four basic thrusts with the longsword. These originate from the guards *Ochs* and *Pflug* on both sides of the body. Hence, there are two thrusts from above and two from below. Each of these thrusts terminates in *Langenort*. These four thrusts are sometimes called the *Vier Ansetzen*, which can be translated as "Four Settings Upon," "Four Plantings," or, more loosely, "Four Thrusts."

Thrusts can be delivered from wide measure in the approach to the fight (that is, from the *Zufechten*), or they can be made while you are bound against your opponent's sword. From the *Zufechten*, you will need to step, passing forward, in order to close distance as you thrust. Remember to do this by moving your sword first, before you move your body and then your foot.

From the *Zufechten*, you should practice thrusting from *Ochs*, first from the right [Fig. 18] and then from the left [Fig. 19]. You must straighten your blade as you do so, from the more or less horizontal edge orientation of *Ochs* to the vertical orientation of the thrust's termination in *Langenort*. Then, practice thrusting from right *Pflug* [Fig. 20] and left *Pflug* [Fig. 21].

Now, practice thrusting in place, as if you were bound to your opponent's sword. In this case, you should not step, for you are already in range and wish to remain in contact with their sword. Thrust from right *Ochs* and left *Ochs* [Fig. 22] and then right *Pflug* and left *Pflug* [Fig. 23].

A thrust may begin from a non-thrusting guard by first passing through one. Thus, you can start in, say, *vom Tag* on the shoulder and drop through *Pflug* to thrust. You can also thrust upward from *Alber*. This should be practiced with a step forward and a step backward and, in each case, should extend up from *Alber*, through *Pflug*, and into *Langenort*. [Fig. 24]

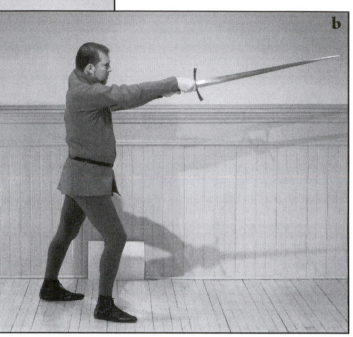

Fig. 18 A thrust from right Ochs performed with a step (a-b).

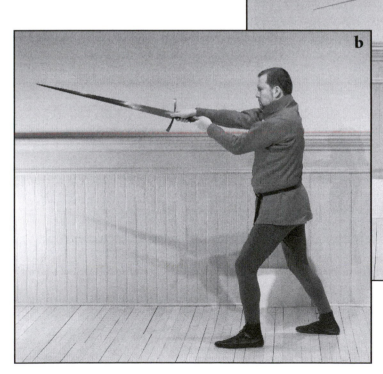

Fig. 19 A thrust from left Ochs performed with a step (a-b).

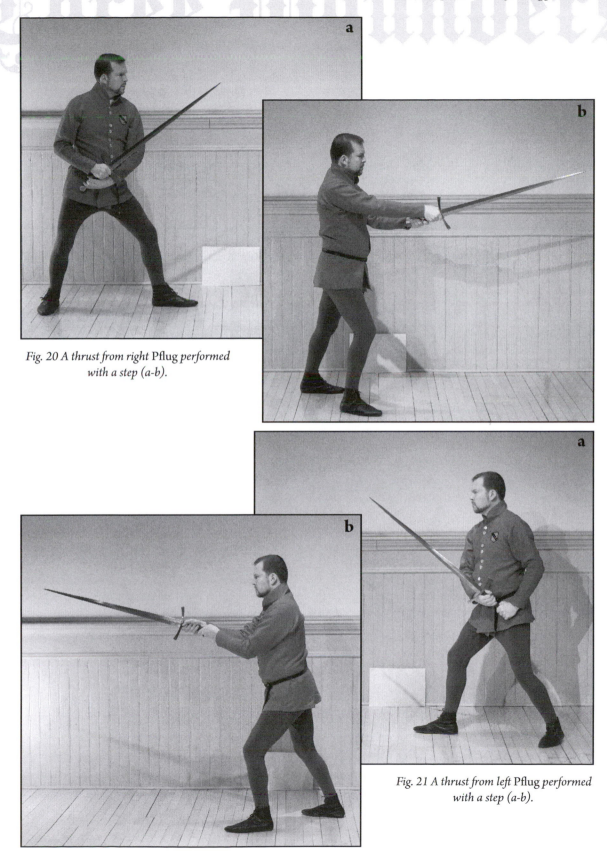

Fig. 20 A thrust from right Pflug performed with a step (a-b).

Fig. 21 A thrust from left Pflug performed with a step (a-b).

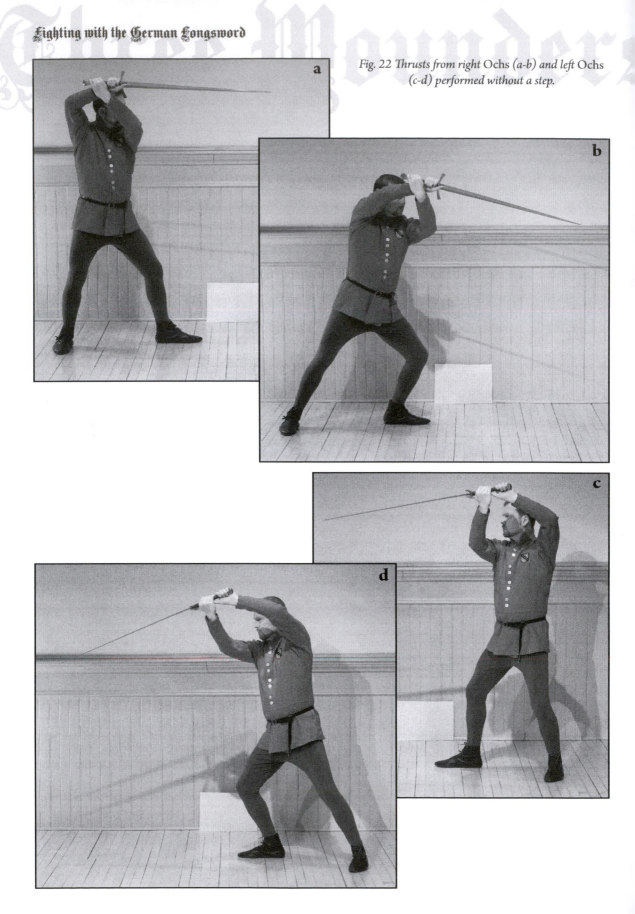

Fig. 22 Thrusts from right Ochs (a-b) and left Ochs (c-d) performed without a step.

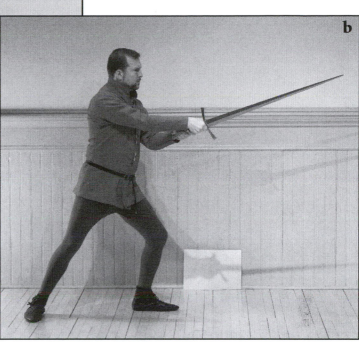

Fig. 23 *Thrusts from right Pflug (a-b) and left Pflug (c-d) performed without a step.*

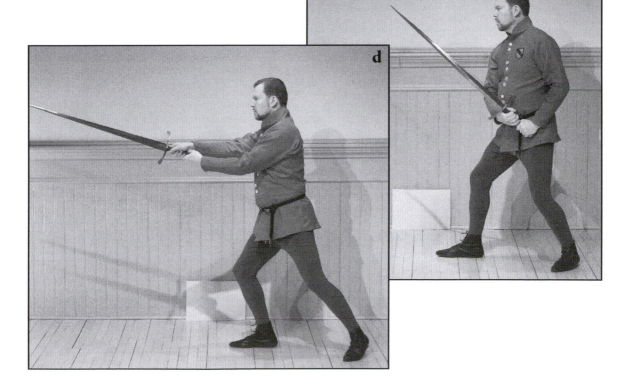

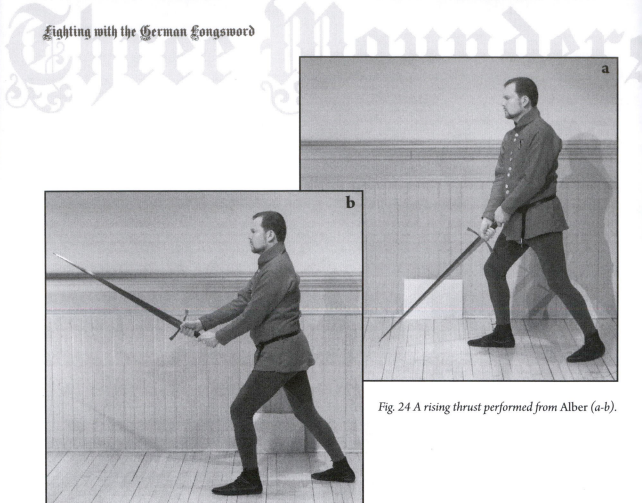

Fig. 24 A rising thrust performed from Alber *(a-b).*

Drill 6: Thrusting with the Sword

- Begin in right Pflug.

- Thrust into *Langenort*, passing forward with the right foot, recovering into left *Pflug*.

- Thrust into *Langenort*, passing forward with the left foot, recovering into right *Ochs*.

- Thrust into *Langenort*, passing forward with the right foot, recovering into left *Ochs*.

- Thrust into *Langenort*, passing forward with the left foot, recovering into right *Pflug*.

- Drop your point to form right *Alber*.

- Thrust up into *Langenort*, passing forward with the right foot, recovering into left *Alber*.

- Thrust up into *Langenort*, passing forward with the left foot, recovering into right *Pflug*.

- Repeat the above steps.

Abschneiden – **Slicing with the Sword**

> *Four are the slices:*
> *two below and two above.*
>
> — Johannes Liechtenauer

Schnitte, or slices, are the last of the "Three Wounders," and their use in forcing an opponent away from you comprises one of Liechtenauer's primary techniques, the *Hauptstücke*: *Abschneiden*, or "Slicing Away." These attacks are made with either edge by placing it forcefully into contact with the opponent's body and then either drawing or pushing the edge along against them. They are usually accompanied by a forceful push outward of the weapon that forces them and their weapon away from you. These attacks are always made at close range, that is, in the *Krieg* (close range) phase of combat. They are excellent responses to an opponent's attempt to rush or crowd you.

There are four slices, two made from *Ochs* and two made from *Pflug*. A slice from below made from the guard *Ochs* on either side of the body is called an *Unterschnitt* ("Under Slice"), while one made from above from either *Pflug* is called an *Oberschnitt* ("Over Slice"). The upward slices from the right *Ochs* are performed with the long edge against your foe. Those from the left *Ochs* slice them with the short edge. From either side *Pflug* it is stronger to slice downward with the long edge.

The slices from above, that is, those from *Pflug*, are best used when an opponent goes to strike around from one side to the other after binding against your sword or if they try to rush in under your sword. Lay your sword atop their arms or wrists in *Pflug* and push down and away from you with your sword. Shift your weight forward and downward as you push and slice so that your entire body contributes to the cut [Fig. 25]. The slices from below from *Ochs* work best against the hands of an opponent who attempts to rush you by bearing down on you from above.

Fig. 25 The Oberschnitt.	*Fig. 26 The* Unterschnitt.

If your opponent tries to overwhelm you from above, move your sword up into *Ochs* to catch their wrists or hands with your edge and force them away from you. Shift your weight forward and upward, driving the edge against them with your whole body. [Fig. 26]

This slice from *Ochs* can be continued and transformed into a slice from above. Once you have stopped their attack with the *Unterschnitt*, you can convert your slice into an *Oberschnitt* by rotating your edge around their wrists and continuing to push and slice them. This rather ghastly technique, a slice all the way around their wrists, is called *Hende Drucken* ("Pressing of the Hands") [Fig. 27] and is ranked in its own right among Master Liechtenauer's 17 primary techniques (the *Hauptstücke*).

When using either form of *Schnitt*, the use of weight shifts to drive the technique cannot be overstated. Without the power of the entire body, these slices are reduced to mere harassing actions instead of the vicious combination of cutting and manipulating the opponent's body that Liechtenauer meant for them to be. In addition to weight shift, it is also the body's turning motion that harnesses its large muscle groups. A simple shift without this turning is in fact merely a "sway," which conveys almost no power.

Drill 7: Slicing with the Sword

- Begin in right *vom Tag*.

- Move forward into left *Ochs* by passing with your right foot. Remember to push your weight and your sword's short edge upward and outward.

- Compass step backward with your left foot, pushing your weight and your sword's long edge down into left *Pflug*.

- Compass step forward with your left foot, driving your weight and your sword's long edge up and outward into right *Ochs*.

- Compass step backward with your right foot, pushing your long edge down into left *Pflug*.

- Bring your sword back to your right shoulder to form *vom Tag* again, from which you can repeat the above steps.

Fig. 27 Hende Drucken ("Pressing of the Hands"): Christian performs the Unterschnitt (a) which flows into the Oberschnitt (b), pushing his opponent away.

✛✛✛✛✛✛

The three wounders each have different ranges associated with them. Both the stroke and the thrust may be used long range from the *Zufechten* (the "Approach" or "Onset" of the fight). The thrust has a bit more range than the stroke, but is easier to parry, so be particularly prepared to work with follow-on techniques when you thrust from this range. Slicing attacks, however, are strictly used in the *Krieg* (the "War" or close combat) and are never used to initiate the fight. Instead, they should be used when you are rushed by your opponent, or from the binding of the swords. The stroke and thrust may also be used in the *Krieg*. Once you have bound swords, you can always strike or thrust to another opening, if and as appropriate.

Chapter 5:
Four Openings

Four openings know,
aim: so you hit certainly,
without any danger
without regard for how he acts.
— Johannes Liechtenauer

In the last chapter, we learned of the three types of attack with the longsword: strokes, thrusts, and slicing cuts. These attacks may be aimed at various targets on the body: the head, torso, and arms. The legs are rarely attacked in Master Liechtenauer's system because of the geometric advantage a high-targeted stroke has over one targeted so low. If you strike to someone's leg, it is easy for them to pull the leg away from your attack, but still hit you with a high stroke.

Master Liechtenauer divided the body into four target areas or "openings." These are the *Vier Blößen* ("Four Openings"). [Fig. 1] There are two openings above the belt, one on the left and one on the right side of the body, and two below the belt, on the left and on the right. The left and right side of the head are included in the left and right upper openings.

High Right
High Left
Low Right
Low Left

Fig. 1 The four openings: high-left,
low-left, high-right and low-right.

Attacks may be aimed at any of the openings, although some openings are easier to hit with some attacks than others. For instance, it is much easier to hit an upper opening with an *Oberhau* (a stroke from above). Conversely, a lower opening is easier to reach with an *Unterhau* (a stroke from below).

Which opening is easiest for you to hit is also dependent on which side you are attacking from. If you are striking from your right side, it is usually easiest to hit your opponent's left side. Hence, an *Oberhau* from the right can most readily be aimed at your opponent's upper left opening, while an *Unterhau* from your left side can best strike their lower right opening.

In general, it is best to target the upper openings first with an *Oberhau* and resort to the lower openings only when you have crossed swords. This is again because of the principle of *Überlaufen* ("Overrunning")—if you strike low, you may be struck above. However, there may be times when your opponent is quite focused on parrying strokes high where they become vulnerable to the stroke below. Be sure, though, to protect your head with your hilt as you strike the *Unterhau*.

Knowing the four openings and the means to attack them is essential when fencing with Master Liechtenauer's art. You must be aware of your opponent's openings as they are exposed, and you must be prepared to continue your onslaught from one opening to another as your opponent commits to their defense. So long as your sword maintains a defensive line as you do so, you may attack your opponent's openings, as Master Liechtenauer has it, without regard for how he acts.

Four Openings

Drill 8: Meyer's Cutting Diagram

One of the diagrams in Joachim Meyer's late 16th century treatise depicts a set of cutting drills targeting the four openings. The blows in the upper two quadrants are *Oberhaue*; those for the lower quadrants are *Unterhaue*. Each "ring" is a set of four cuts. Hence, the outermost ring calls out the following four cuts, to be strung together fluidly:

Part A – 1st (Outermost) Ring

- An *Oberhau* from the right, performed with a pass of the right foot

- An *Unterhau* from the left, performed with a pass of the left foot.

- An *Unterhau* from the right, performed with a pass of the right foot.

- An *Oberhau* from the left, performed with a pass of the left foot.

Part B – 2nd Ring

- An *Unterhau* from the right, performed with a pass of the right foot

- An *Oberhau* from the left, performed with a pass of the left foot.

- An *Oberhau* from the right, performed with a pass of the right foot.

- An *Unterhau* from the left, performed with a pass of the left foot.

This drill, using drill the outermost ring, can continue on, with step 4 flowing back into step 1, completing the cycle.

Working inward, the completion of this ring can also, instead of repeating, dovetail into performing the sequence of the second ring:

Again working inward, the completion of the 2nd ring can flow into performing the sequence of the 3rd ring. Note though that, when you finish the 2nd ring and move into the 3rd ring, you'll have to incorporate a small gathering step, rather than a pass, as you cut, as your left leg will already be leading:

Part C – 3rd Ring

- An *Oberhau* from the left, performed with a pass of the left foot (or without, if transitioning from the 2nd ring).

- An *Unterhau* from the right, performed with a pass of the right foot.

- An *Unterhau* from the left, performed with a pass of the left foot.

- An *Oberhau* from the right, performed with a pass of the right foot.

Part D – 4th (Innermost) Ring

- An *Unterhau* from the left, performed with a pass of the left foot.

- An *Oberhau* from the right, performed with a pass of the right foot.

- An *Oberhau* from the left, performed with a pass of the left foot.

- An *Unterhau* from the right, performed with a pass of the right foot.

Lastly, the completion of the 3rd ring can flow into performing the sequence of the 4th ring.

Practice each of these sequences independently. This will develop flow and grace in your striking, allowing you to attack any opening as it avails itself. Then, string all four together, from outermost to innermost. Note that if you wish to repeat all four together, returning to the first ring, then you will once again need to omit a passing step as you transition between the 4th ring's step 4 and the 1st ring's step 1.

Chapter 6: Initiative

Before and After, these two things,
are to all skill a wellspring.
— Johannes Liechtenauer

The most important tactical concept of Liechtenauer's system of fighting is that of initiative. It is crucial that you maintain control of the fight, and should you lose it you must immediately work to regain it. When you have the initiative, you can stay on the offensive, while your opponent is forced to protect from your attacks. When you control the fight, it is only a matter of time before your opponent is overcome.

It is of great importance that the student understands the importance of initiative in this fighting system, for it informs the means of accomplishing every action and the framing of every stance or guard. The master describes the dynamics of initiative in the fight with three words: *Vor*, *Nach*, and *Indes*.

Initiative

Vor – The Before

The *Vor*, or "Before", is the offensive principle in Liechtenauer's art. When you fight in the *Vor*, you have the initiative, while your opponent must concentrate on countering you. You can be in the *Vor* by simply attacking before your foe has a chance to, or by doing something to wrest the control of the fight from them.

There are various ways of seizing the initiative. This can be done by delivering a stroke of the sword to the nearest exposed opening. [Fig. 1] This should not be an overcommitted attack. Your approach should be conservative. Be sure that your point remains a threat during the blow's travel to the opponent. It is better to cut across the face, rather than risk being struck by attempting to deliver a "decapitating" stroke. You can also employ the thrust in the same way.[35] [Fig. 2]

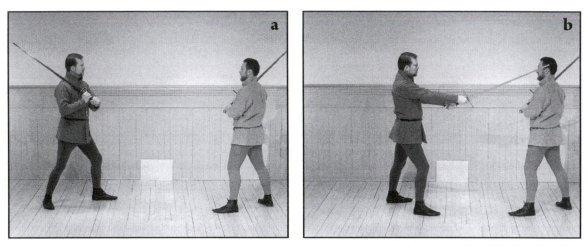

Fig. 1 Seizing the initiative with an Oberhau *(a-b).*

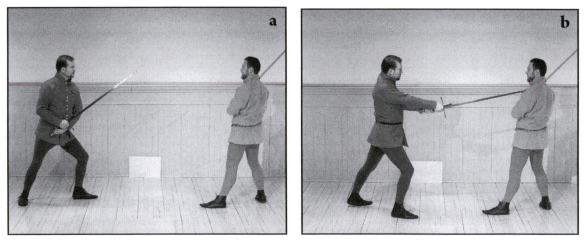

Fig. 2 Seizing the initiative with a thrust (a-b).

---

[35] The concept of *Nachreisen* also applies when bound against another's sword. You can "stick" to his sword as he moves, following his motion, and seeking another opening to attack as it becomes available.

A good time to attack is when your opponent is preparing to attack you by charging a stroke or thrust. [Fig. 3] This method of using your opponents' timing against them is called *Nachreisen* ("Chasing" or "Traveling After"). By *following* their movement, you can anticipate and strike as they prepare to hit you.

While there is no guarantee that you will hit with either a stroke or thrust, you will at least provoke a response to your attack. Therefore, you will still have put your opponent on the defensive, and if they are forced to parry your attack, you can continue to work offensively (*maintaining the initiative*) from the binding of the swords.

We are also advised to keep up the onslaught. *Hs. 3227a*, possibly our earliest Liechtenauer source, advises that once one has struck the *Vorschlag* ("Before Stroke"), a term used in that manuscript for an initiative-seizing first attack, one should immediately strike the *Nachschlag* ("After Stroke"), regardless of whether the *Vorschlag* hit or missed.

Fig. 3 As Janusz pulls back into vom Tag *to charge a blow, Christian follows after him with an* Oberhau *(a-c).*

Another way of seizing the initiative is to provoke your opponent in a manner that entices them to respond without being hit. *Langenort* lets you do just that. If you extend your point against their face, they cannot both move your sword aside and hit you at the same time. The distance you have created forces them to do this in two separate actions, which can work to your advantage. [Fig. 4] Also, you can slash your sword upward from below (repeatedly, even), to "draw their fire" before striking in earnest. This can make your opponent react, thereby making them vulnerable because they are caught during a wasted tempo. [Fig. 5]

One can also fight in the *Vor* by employing an attack that is designed to "break" an opponent's guard. By attacking in a particular way, you can strike while safely closing off any potential line of attack from their guard. Each of the four primary guards has an attack that is designed to counter it, and we will see later in this book how to use them.

Fig. 4 Christian provokes his opponent in Langenort.

Fig. 5 Christian disrupts Janusz's timing by slashing upward, before launching his Oberhau attack (a-d).

Nach – The After

The *Nach*, or "After," is the system's defensive or responsive principle. If your opponent attacks first, or otherwise seizes the initiative, you must respond. The techniques of the *Nach* are designed to give you back the initiative, that is, to get you back into fighting in the *Vor*. This can be done by out-timing your opponent, simultaneously defending and counter-attacking, or using leverage once you have crossed swords.

In all of these cases, your response to an attack must create a threat, rather than merely provide for defense. The words of Master Sigmund Ringeck speak well to this point: "*And beware of all parries used by bad fencers. Note: Strike when he strikes, thrust when he thrusts.*"[36] So be sure that you do not use a "bad parry," one that has a defensive component but no offense. [Fig. 6] There are some actions in the system, such as lifting the sword into *Kron*, that appear to be purely defensive, but which actually set up an immediate threat.

Responding in the *Nach* is often as simple as changing from one fighting stance to another. You can defend yourself against a sword stroke or thrust by moving into the guards *Ochs* or *Pflug* on either side of the body as appropriate. Remember that *Ochs* protects against high attacks, [Fig. 7] while *Pflug* defends against attacks directed against the lower openings of the body. [Fig. 8] As both of these are thrusting guards, you also come into an offensive position while doing so. This action of parrying while placing the point in line with the opponent is called *Absetzen*, or "setting aside."

The concept of *Nachreisen* was described in the previous section as a way of exploiting your opponent's timing in the *Vor*, but it can also be used in the *Nach*. If your opponent strikes first to you, but misjudges the distance and strikes short of you, you can then exploit the interval needed to recover after the missed blow. This mistake occurs when a fencer either has not truly come into the *Zufechten* before an attack or doesn't strike with sufficient extension. As their sword goes past you, regain the initiative by following the movement and striking while they are vulnerable, taking advantage of their errors in both timing and distance.

Fig. 6 A bad parry: Christian defends himself, but strikes so far to his left that he offers no counter-threat to his opponent.

Fig. 7 A good parry: Christian defends a high attack in the guard Ochs so that he offers a threat with the point.

Fig. 8 Another good parry: Christian defends a low attack in the guard Pflug so that he offers a threat with the point.

[36] Sigmund Ringeck, *Fechtbuch*, folio 35r.

Indes – **Instantly**

Indes is the hardest of the three words to translate, though its meaning is clear. It indicates a condition of simultaneity, and represents the kind of response you must use in the *Nach* ("After") to get back to the *Vor* ("Before"). When your opponent seizes the initiative, you must immediately (*Indes*) react to the attack, whether that attack begins with a strike or has bound to your sword. That is to say that you must act *during* or *within the tempo* of their action.

If your opponent begins to deliver a sword stroke toward you, you must *instantly* decide how to respond by striking into the incoming blow, setting the strike aside by deflecting it, or through the application of other techniques. Similarly, if you find yourself in a bind [Fig. 9], you must determine *instantly* what to do depending on how much pressure is applied against your sword and where their blade is positioned in relation to your sword and your person.

This sense of blade pressure is called *Fühlen* ("Feeling"), and it goes hand-in-hand with *Indes*. You cannot determine how to react immediately while in a bind without first sensing the opponent's intentions through their sword. This sense of blade pressure must be developed through practice until you no longer need think about what to do, but simply do it.

Fig. 9 A bind: each fencer must rely on Fühlen *("Feeling") to determine their opponent's intent and decide upon the proper response.*

✛✛✛✛✛✛

The concept of initiative informs every technique and every other principle in Master Liechtenauer's system, so much so that it can be used as a "sanity check" when trying to execute specific techniques. Practitioners should always ask themselves when responding to an opponent's actions, "Will my response facilitate my seizing the initiative?" If the answer is no, the action should always be re-evaluated.

When you have learned to use the inseparable concepts of *Indes* and *Fühlen*, you will be fencing with Master Liechtenauer's system in its highest manifestation. As his 15th century disciple Master Sigmund Ringeck says:

> *Indes is a sharp word that cuts all fencers who don't know anything about it. And* Indes *is the key that unlocks the art of fencing.*[37]

Drill 9: Developing Sensitivity—*Fühlen*

- You and a partner both assume left *Pflug* with your blades crossed on the inside.

- In a steady and controlled manner, each of you try to keep your point in line with the other's face or chest while making sure your opponent's point isn't facing you.

- Using the feedback of pressure against your sword, exert pressure, give way, or re-angle your point to keep it in line.

- Reset with both partners crossing blades in right *Pflug*.

- Repeat steps 2 – 3.

- Reset with both partners crossing blades in left *Ochs*.

- Repeat steps 2 – 3.

- Reset with both partners crossing blades in right *Ochs*.

- Repeat steps 2 – 3.

Further iterations of this drill can be done with one partner in *Pflug* and the other in *Ochs* on the opposite side. Note how this gives the combatant in *Ochs* a considerable advantage because of superior leverage. Remember this; it will be very important later!

---

[37] Ringeck *Fechtbuch*, folio 39r.

Chapter 7: Defending with Attacks

Strike when he strikes; thrust when he thrusts.
— Master Sigmund Ringeck

We will now put together, for the first time, all of the basic principles we have studied thus far. We have learned how to stand, how to step, and how to hold the sword in the guards, and we have learned the importance of maintaining or regaining the initiative. Further, the methods here will serve as templates for understanding those hallmark techniques of Master Liechtenauer's art, the *Meisterhaue* ("Master Strokes"). The *Scheitelhau* ("Scalp Stroke") is a vertically directed *Oberhau* targeting the top of the head or face. It is used to outreach low strokes and to attack the guard *Alber*.

You must maintain proper body carriage and step with the proper footwork at all times, whether you are standing in a guard or moving from one guard to another.

All important actions in this fighting system are composed of transitions from one guard to another, sometimes passing through other guards on the way.

There are three types of attack—the *Drei Wunder* ("Three Wounders")—with the blade of a longsword: strokes, thrusts, and slicing cuts. Each of these actions is simply a vigorous transition from one guard to another. You must use whichever is appropriate at the time.

Often, the failure of one type of attack will nevertheless set up one of the others. If your stroke runs out of energy and hits only lightly, change this attack into a slice instead. If your stroke falls short, thrust when your point comes in line.

There are four targets that may be attacked, the "Four Openings." Any of these openings may be attacked with either stroke, thrust or slice. If your opponent defends one opening strongly, this consequently exposes another opening. Be vigilant and attack whatever becomes exposed.

All tactics are driven by the notion of *Vor* ("Initiative"). When you hold the initiative, you are in the *Vor*. When you must respond to your opponent's initiative, you are in the *Nach*. You should seize the *Vor* if you can, and you must regain the *Vor* if your opponent seizes it. You must at all times fix your mind upon seizing the *Vor* or regaining it when it has momentarily been lost.

Now that our memories have been refreshed, we will engage in work for two students. This will take the form of set plays wherein one partner launches a specified attack, against which the other must defend while still giving offense. There are eight response plays. Four begin with both the attacker and defender starting in *vom Tag* on the right side of the body. The remainder commence with the attacker standing in *vom Tag* on the left side and the defender in *Alber* with the right leg leading.

The plays use four attacks, a nearly vertical downward stroke, a diagonal downward stroke, a stroke from above to the leading leg and, lastly, an *Unterhau*, a stroke from below. The vertical *Oberhau* is defended by passing forward into *Ochs* and either thrusting to your opponent's face or hitting them with your edge at the same time. The diagonal *Oberhau* is defended by passing forward into *Pflug* and thrusting to your opponent. The *Oberhau* down to the leg is defended by passing backward, thereby removing the leg from harm's way, while either striking vertically to your opponent or thrusting into *Langenort* against them. Lastly, the *Unterhau* is defended by deeply passing forward and away from your opponent's stroke while striking across your person to hit their hands with the very end of your sword. This is the safest way to defend the *Unterhau* as its trajectory is likely to run parallel to the positions of our binding guards *Ochs* and *Pflug*, making them unsafe defenses in this case.

Defenses from the Right Side

Response 1 – *Vom Tag* to *Ochs*, against a Vertical *Oberhau*

Attack: From a left-leg-leading stance with the sword held on the right shoulder in *vom Tag*, strike a nearly vertical blow downward to the head or upper body with a pass forward with the right foot.

Response: From a left-leg-leading stance with the sword held on the right shoulder in *vom Tag*, transition into left *Ochs* with a pass forward with the right foot. As this transition is performed, be sure to shift your right hand's grip on the sword to place your thumb on the lower flat of the blade.

Outcome: The defender parries the incoming blow to the upper left while thrusting to the attacker's face, hitting the left side of the head, or slicing the head or neck with the *short edge* of the sword. [Fig. 1] Should the defender's blade fall a little short of the opponent's head, the defender should thrust, completing an *Absetzen*, a setting aside of the attack followed by a thrust in opposition with the opponent's blade.

What to Remember: *Ochs* on either side protects the head and the upper openings of the body and, in doing so, gives offense to one's opponent. As you execute this transition, be sure that you hold your hilt high in front of you with your right thumb under the strong of the blade, providing your head with protective cover.

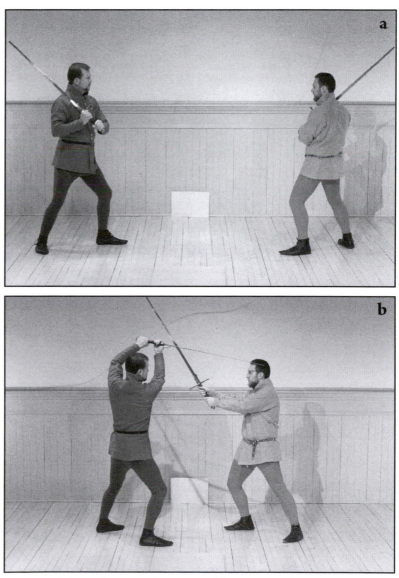

Fig. 1 Both fencers begin in right vom Tag *(a). Janusz attacks with a high* Oberhau, *so Christian passes into left* Ochs *to counterattack with a thrust or stroke (b).*

Response 2 – *Vom Tag* to *Pflug*, against a Diagonal *Oberhau*

Attack: From a left-leg-leading stance with the sword held on the right shoulder in *vom Tag*, strike a diagonal blow downward to the body with a pass forward with the right foot.

Response: From a left-leg-leading stance with the sword held on the right shoulder in *vom Tag*, transition into left *Pflug* with a pass forward with the right foot. This transition should be made by passing through *Langenort*, so that the attacker is menaced by the defender's point at all times.

Outcome: The defender parries the incoming blow to the lower left while thrusting to the attacker's face or chest. [Fig. 2]

What to Remember: *Pflug* on either side protects the lower openings of the body while threatening your opponent with the point.

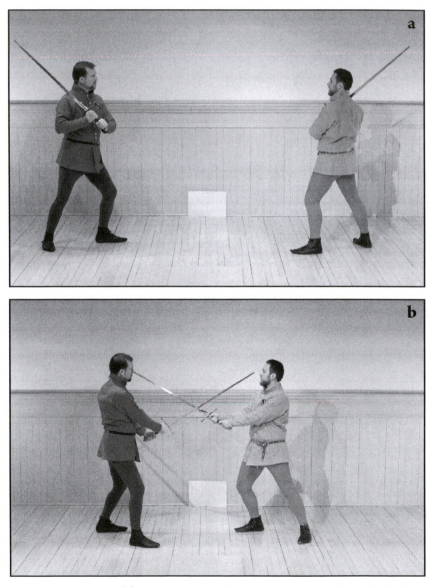

Fig. 2 From vom Tag *(a), Janusz attacks with a lower targeted* Oberhau, *which Christian defends by passing forward into left* Pflug *to counterthrust (b).*

Defending with Attacks

Response 3 – *Vom Tag* to *Langenort*, against an *Oberhau* to the Leg

Attack: From a left-leg-leading stance with the sword held on the right shoulder in *vom Tag*, strike a downward blow aimed at the defender's forward leg with a pass forward with the right foot.

Response: From a left-leg-leading stance with the sword held on the right shoulder in the guard *vom Tag*, extend your sword forward and outward into *Langenort* with a pass backward of the left foot. This should be a conservative step backward; be sure you can still reach your opponent.

Outcome: The defender denies the leg target to the attacker by passing back with the leading leg. At the same time, the defender strikes straight down with their arms extended to hit the attacker's head. [Fig. 3]

What to Remember: A low-angled attack compromises the sword's range, so evade your opponent's low stroke while outreaching their attack with your own.

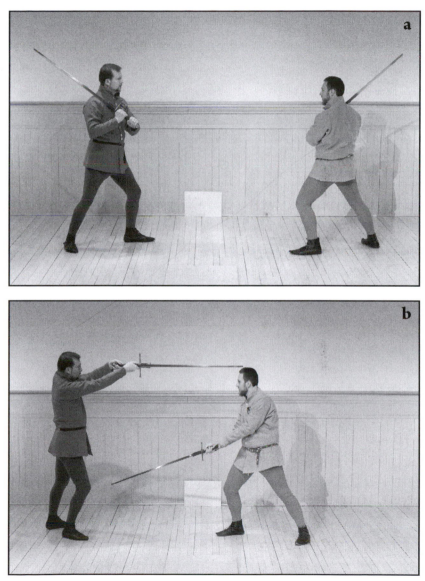

Fig. 3 Both fencers begin in right vom Tag *(a). Janusz attacks Christian's leg, so Christian passes back with the left foot, avoiding the leg strike and counterattacking to Janusz's head (b).*

Response 4 – *Vom Tag* to *Schranckhut*, against an *Unterhau*

Attack: From a left-leg-leading stance with the sword held on the right shoulder in *vom Tag*, strike an *Unterhau*, a stroke that sweeps up from below, toward the head with a pass forward with the right foot.

Response: From a left-leg-leading stance with the sword held on the right shoulder in *vom Tag*, transition into the left *Schranckhut* with a deep pass forward with the right foot. Your blade should pass before you counter-clockwise from right to left, across the line of engagement.

Outcome: The defender strikes the attacker with the tip of the sword on the hands. [Fig. 4]

What to Remember: Be sure to take a good deep step forward and to your right. Keep your hilt high as you strike to your opponent's hands. This way, if you fall short with your strike, your blade will be sloping downward from above, protecting you.

Fig. 4 Both fencers begin again in right vom Tag *(a). Janusz strikes an* Unterhau, *so Christian springs out to his right side, striking Janusz's arms with the long edge, his hands crossed (b).*

Defenses from the Left Side

Response 5 – *Alber* to *Ochs*, against a Vertical *Oberhau*

Attack: From a right-leg-leading stance with the sword held at the left shoulder in *vom Tag*, strike a nearly vertical blow downward to the head or upper body with a pass forward with the left foot.

Response: From a right-leg-leading stance with the sword held in *Alber*, transition into right *Ochs* with a pass forward with the left foot.

Outcome: The defender parries the incoming blow to the upper right while thrusting to the attacker's face. [Fig. 5]

What to Remember: *Ochs* on either side protects the head and the upper openings of the body and, in doing so, gives offense to one's opponent. Be sure that you hold your hilt high in front of you with your right thumb under the strong of the blade, providing your head with protective cover, as you execute this transition.

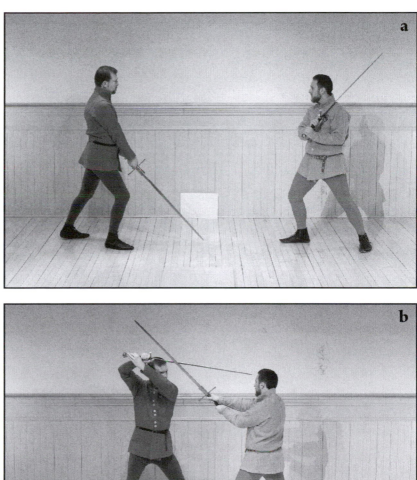

Fig. 5 Christian begins in Alber, with Janusz forming left vom Tag (a). Janusz strikes a high Oberhau, so Christian responds by passing with his left foot as he delivers a counterattack in right Ochs (b).

Response 6 – *Alber* to *Pflug*, against a Diagonal *Oberhau*

Attack: From a right-leg-leading stance with the sword held at the left shoulder in *vom Tag*, strike a diagonal blow downward to the body with a pass forward of the left foot.

Response: From a right-leg-leading stance with the sword held in *Alber*, transition into right *Pflug* with a pass forward with the left foot. This transition should be made by passing through *Langenort*, so that the attacker is menaced by the defender's point at all times.

Outcome: The defender parries the incoming blow to the lower right while thrusting to the attacker's face or chest. [Fig. 6]

What to Remember: *Pflug* on either side protects the lower openings of the body while threatening your opponent with the point.

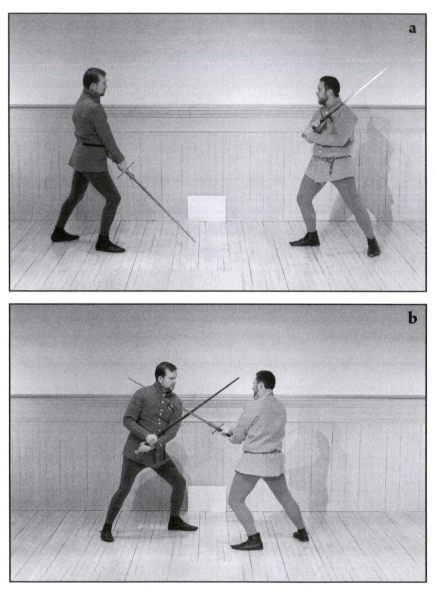

Fig. 6 *Christian resumes* Alber, *with Janusz in left* vom Tag *(a).* Janusz *strikes a low* Oberhau *which Christian defends by passing into right* Pflug *(b).*

Response 7 – *Alber* to *Langenort*, against an *Oberhau* to the Leg

Attack: From a right-leg-leading stance with the sword held at the left shoulder in *vom Tag*, strike a downward blow aimed at the defender's forward leg with a pass forward of the left foot.

Response: From a right-leg-leading stance with the sword held low in *Alber*, extend your sword upward and forward into *Langenort* with a pass backward with the right foot. As with Response 3, this should be a conservative step backward; be sure you can still reach your opponent.

Outcome: The defender denies the leg target to the attacker by passing backward with their lead leg. At the same time, the defender pulls their arms upward quickly to hit the attacker's hands with a stroke or slicing cut with the short edge, or to thrust to the chest. [Fig. 7]

What to Remember: A low-angled attack compromises the sword's range, so evade your opponent's low stroke while outreaching their attack with one that extends out from below.

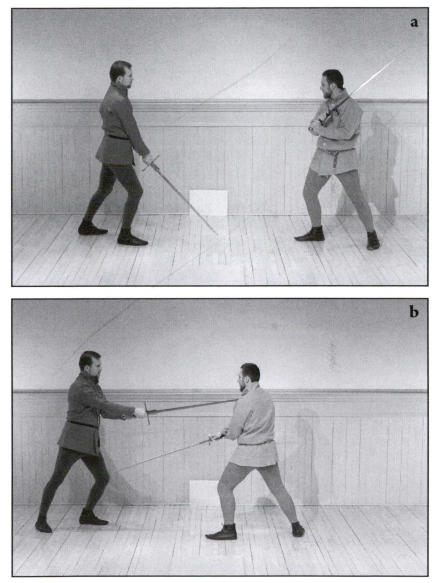

Fig. 7 Christian forms Alber, with Janusz holding left vom Tag (a). Janusz strikes down to Christian's leg, so Christian passes back with the right foot to counterthrust and void the attack (b).

Response 8 – *Alber* to *Schranckhut*, against an *Unterhau*

Attack: From a right-leg-leading stance with the sword held at the left shoulder in *vom Tag*, strike an *Unterhau*, a stroke that sweeps up from below with the long edge, toward the head with a pass forward of the left foot.

Response: From a right-leg-leading stance with the sword held in *Alber*, transition into the right *Schranckhut* with a deep pass forward with the left foot. Your blade should pass before you clockwise from left to right, across the line of engagement, to strike your opponent's hand with the short edge.

Outcome: The defender strikes the attacker with the tip of the sword on the hands. [Fig. 8]

What to Remember: Be sure to take a good deep step forward and to your left. Keep your hilt high as you strike to your opponent's hands. This way, if you fall short with your strike, your blade will be sloping downward from above, protecting you.

✠✠✠✠✠✠

Practice these response exercises diligently, for they are keys to understanding much of what follows in the chapters ahead.

Fig. 8 From Alber *(a), Christian responds to Janusz's* Unterhau *by springing out to his left side to attack Janusz's hands with the short edge (b).*

Drill 10: Defending with Attacks

Part A – Defenses from the Right Side

- Have both partners begin in right *Vom Tag* with the left foot leading. Player A is the attacker; Player B is the defender.

- A attacks with a vertical *Oberhau*. B employs Response 1.

- A attacks with a diagonal *Oberhau*. B employs Response 2.

- A attacks the legs. B employs Response 3.

- A attacks with an *Unterhau*. B employs Response 4.

- A now repeats steps 2 – 5, randomly picking attacks. B must choose the appropriate response.

- Partners A and B switch roles and repeat all the above steps.

Part B – Defenses from the Left Side

- A assumes left *Vom Tag* with the right foot leading. B assumes left *Alber* with the right foot leading.

- A attacks with a vertical *Oberhau*. B employs Response 5.

- A attacks with a diagonal *Oberhau*. B employs Response 6.

- A attacks the legs. B employs Response 7.

- A attacks with an *Unterhau*. B employs Response 8.

- A now repeats steps 2 – 5, randomly picking attacks. B must choose the appropriate response.

- Partners A and B switch roles and repeat all the above steps.

Drill 10: Variations

Many variations on these eight responses are possible. For instance, the first set of four, those starting from the right side of the body, could be performed with the defender standing in *Schranckhut* or *Nebenhut*, while the second set of four responses, those beginning with the defender lying in *Alber*, could be performed with the defender instead standing in *Vom Tag*, *Schranckhut*, or *Nebenhut* on the left side.

You can also begin the response exercises with the defender in *Ochs* or *Pflug*. The trick here lies in responding to the *Unterhau*, as you may not be able to generate sufficient power from either guard to strike into the *Schranckhut* against their hands. Instead, pass forward into the *Schranckhut* from *Ochs* or *Pflug* and catch their stroke with your sword beneath theirs.

Another variation is to have the attacker thrust from either *Ochs* or *Pflug*. If the attacker thrusts from right *Ochs*, you can use the transition from right *Vom Tag* to left *Ochs* to intercept the attack and thrust down to their chest while your blade opposes theirs. If the attacker thrusts from right *Pflug*, transition to left *Pflug* to defend the thrust and counterthrust to their face. From left *Vom Tag* or left *Alber*, you can oppose your opponent's thrust from left *Ochs* or *Pflug* by transitioning to right *Ochs* or *Pflug*, respectively. These actions are all *Absetzen*, which will be more fully explored in a later chapter.

Chapter 8:
The Five Strokes

Learn five strokes
from the right hand against the opposition.
Then we promise
that your arts will be rewarded.

— Johannes Liechtenauer

Master Liechtenauer's "Five Secret Strokes" are specialized blows with the sword designed to provide defense and offense in a single movement. By the 16th century, these were known as the *Meisterhaue* ("Master Strokes"). Of their effectiveness, and the difficulty in countering them, the von Danzig commentaries have this to say:

> *These are the five secret strokes that many masters of the sword know nothing about. You should learn to strike them correctly from the right side. The combatant who can break these strokes with true skill without coming into harm is commended by other masters and shall be praised in his art more than another combatant.*[38]

The techniques for the five strokes are very important for two reasons. The blows themselves are extremely useful, both in answering an opponent's attack and in attacking them while they are on guard. These techniques also provide a framework wherein Liechtenauer posits his principles by example.

Liechtenauer presents the five strokes in his verse before even discussing the system's four primary guards. This might seem a strange choice in the material's organization, but is consistent with medieval thinking, which valued the exposition of ideas through examples of their application. The verse discusses first some very basic principles of swordsmanship, then the five strokes, and finally, the guards and other chief techniques (*Hauptstücke*). However, these chief techniques are first exposed among the techniques associated with the five strokes. Therefore, a study of these five blows will teach the student much of Liechtenauer's art.

---

[38] Peter Von Danzig, *Fechtbuch*, f 12v.

The five strokes, in the order in which Liechtenauer presents them, are:

> The *Zornhau* ("Stroke of Wrath") is a diagonal *Oberhau* that meets an opponent's attack and threatens them with the point. As this is the first and simplest of the five strokes, many concepts of Liechtenauer's art appear in the techniques for its application.

> The *Krumphau* ("Crooked Stroke") is an *Oberhau* that sweeps across the line of engagement. It is also used to attack an opponent standing in the *Ochs* guard.

> The *Zwerchhau* ("Thwart Stroke") is a high horizontal stroke that disrupts an opponent's attack, or potential attack, from above. It is also used to attack the guard *Vom Tag*.

> The *Schielhau* ("Squinting Stroke") is an *Oberhau* performed with the blade turned over so that the short edge strikes the opponent. It is used to attack an adversary who has assumed the guard *Pflug*.

> The *Scheitelhau* ("Scalp Stroke") is a vertically directed *Oberhau* targeting the top of the head or face. It is used to outreach low strokes and to attack the guard *Alber*.

The chapter on the *Zornhau* is very important for learning the various responses you should know once you are bound with your opponent's sword. Like the medieval masters, I've elected to use the *Zornhau* as the platform for teaching these actions.

The remaining four strokes—*Krumphau, Zwerchhau, Schielhau,* and *Scheitelhau*—are important too, but for a different reason. They are designed, among other things, to provide optimal attacks against an opponent standing in one of the four primary guards.

The five strokes, together with the techniques for *Winden* ("Winding"), which we will see later, are the signature techniques of Liechtenauer's art. We will explore each stroke in the next few chapters and they will be easier to learn if you have practiced the drills of Chapter 7 diligently, for those exercises provide the raw material for the master's five secret strokes.

Chapter 9: Zornhau

Who strikes at you above,
the Wrath Stroke threatens him with the point
— Johannes Liechtenauer

The *Zornhau* ("Wrath Stroke") is an *Oberhau* struck diagonally with the long edge. In general, any stroke of the sword performed in this fashion is a *Zornhau,* and its name doubtless derives from the fact that an angry (i.e., wrathful) opponent will instinctively strike in this fashion. In view of this, the von Danzig commentaries include this description, which seems at once both disclaimer and praise:

> Note, the Wrath Stroke breaks with the point all strokes from above and yet is nothing but what a poor peasant strikes.[39]

Anyone can strike a *Zornhau,* but Liechtenauer's application of this blow is sophisticated in a way that the mere ruffian will not perceive. The novice fighter will naturally try to swing a powerful blow at their foe, but this does not necessarily prevent their being struck in the bargain. So, instead, Liechtenauer advises that the *Zornhau* be used to strike into an opponent's stroke and to thrust as soon as contact is made, all the while maintaining opposition with their sword. The line of attack must be effectively closed so that the counter-attack may be made in safety. It is the point of the sword that then threatens the opponent.

We have already explored the proper way to strike a *Zornhau:* In this regard, it is simply the diagonal *Oberhau* we learned in chapter four. Remember to strike with your whole body—arms, shoulders, back, hips and legs—acting in concert. [Fig. 1] If you strike from your right side, be sure that your right hip rotates into the blow, in turn charging the left hip with the potential energy a follow-on stroke from the left will need. Should you strike from your left, the left hip rotates through, storing potential energy in the right hip.

---

[39] Peter von Danzig, *Fechtbuch,* folio 13r.

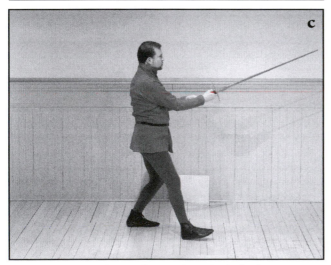

Fig. 1 The Zornhau *performed solo (a-c).*

When you strike a *Zornhau*, you will likely make initial contact with an opponent's sword as you pass through a position somewhere between *Pflug* and *Langenort*. Do not allow your point to drift out of the opponent's presence, but remain a threat to them with this stroke.

The plays associated with the *Zornhau* are exemplars of many of Liechtenauer's chief techniques, the *Hauptstücke*. As we explore each, be mindful that as you bind swords, you must use the sense of *Fühlen* to feel how hard or soft your opponent is at the sword, and what your eyes tell you about the blade's position, to act instantly (*Indes*) and appropriately.[40] You must "*test the bind*"[41] to determine if you should work *Am Schwert* ("at the sword") or *Vom Schwert* ("from the sword"), that is, whether you should remain in the bind or depart from it.

When you test the bind, you learn whether the opponent is applying strong pressure, equal pressure, or weak pressure against your sword. There are, naturally, degrees to either the strong or weak extremes, but this division into three conditions allows us to group the actions we must use for each situation.

If your opponent is "soft at the sword", applying weak pressure in the bind, you should thrust to the face or chest. If your opponent is "hard at the sword" and pushes your blade aside, you should depart from the bind using either the techniques *Zucken* or *Durchwechseln* that follow in this chapter.

---

[40] As stated earlier, *Indes* and *Fühlen* go hand in hand with each other.

[41] Liechtenauer's verse, line 217.

However, if your opponent is hard at the sword, matching your strength, but their point stands before you, you must not leave the bind, because you will be vulnerable to a thrust as you do so. Instead, you must now work on the sword by *winding*, as we will see in the last set of techniques of the chapter. [Fig. 2]

There are other techniques for dealing with binds, both hard and soft; we will explore them in subsequent chapters of this volume. These three options represent basics that apply in every bind and will serve you well with all the weapons in Master Liechtenauer's arsenal.

Drill 11: The *Zornhau*

- From right *Vom Tag*, strike a right *Zornhau* with a pass forward of the right foot.

- Pass back with the right foot, resuming right *Vom Tag*.

- Repeat steps 1 – 2 several times.

- From left *Vom Tag*, strike a left *Zornhau* with a pass forward of the left foot.

- Pass back with the left foot, resuming left *Vom Tag*.

- Repeat steps 4 – 5 several times.

- From right *Vom Tag*, strike a right *Zornhau* with a pass forward of the right foot.

- Recover briefly to left *Vom Tag*.

- Strike a left *Zornhau* with a pass forward of the left foot.

- Repeat steps 7 – 9 several times.

Fig. 2 Three different binds: the opponent is weak, or "soft", at the sword (a); the opponent is strong, or "hard", at the sword (b); and an equal bind, where neither swordsman has the advantage but both points are in presence (c).

Exploiting a Weak Bind – Thrusting from the *Zornhau*

The simplest technique with the *Zornhau* is to strike against their *Oberhau* and thrust to them as you make contact. We have already practiced this in effect in Response 2 from Chapter 7. If

you stand in *Vom Tag* on the right side and your opponent strikes above to you from their right side, strike against their sword with wrath as you pass forward with your right foot. If your opponent is soft at the sword as you bind, then let your sword flow seamlessly from the stroke into a thrust along their sword to their face or chest. [Fig. 3]

It is *imperative* that you create a "cone of defense" as your *Zornhau* meets the opponent's stroke. On contact, your hilt should be angled slightly outward to your left, with your point striking the *right* side of their face, neck, or upper chest. Targeting the right side of the face helps to ensure that you have kept their attacking blade out of the center and to your left, allowing you to hit them while defending yourself.

Do not over-commit your body in executing the *Zornhau*. Rather, you should be able to comfortably extend your point into *Langenort* on the thrust's completion. If you lean too far forward into the stroke, you may not be able to clear your opponent's person and convey your point before their face.

Note that this technique, often known as *Zornhau-Ort* (the thrust from the *Zornhau*), is a prime example of the "single imperfect fencing time" described in the earlier part of this book. It is also arguably the foundational action of the entire system, a way of disrupting an attack by striking into it safely, while still giving counter-offense to the opponent.

Much training time should be given to perfecting this simple, but formidable technique.

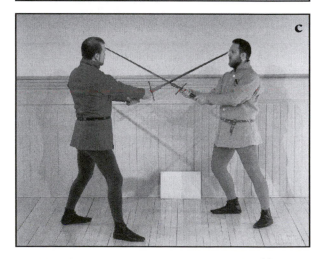

Fig. 3 Zornhau-Ort. Both fencers begin in vom Tag (a). Janusz strikes an Oberhau, so Christian counterstrikes into the attack, binding the opposing sword and allowing his stroke to flow into a thrust to the face or chest (b-c).

Leaving a Strong Bind – *Abnehmen* and *Zucken*

When your opponent is hard at the sword, pushing your stroke aside when you strike a *Zornhau*, you will not be able to put your point in line against their face or chest for the thrust. At first, such a strong parry might appear to be the opponent's safest response, for after all, one should be safer the farther aside they beat an opponent's sword. However, the reverse is true, for the more committed a parry is, the more it exposes the openings opposite those it defends. Over-commitment to the defense of one opening imperils another opening. Rather than opposing their strong parry with strength of your own, you must instead take your sword out of the bind and attack another opening. We will examine three methods for doing this.

The choice of which technique to use is determined by how much strength is brought to bear by your opponent in the bind. It's a matter of degrees of commitment on your opponent's part. This may sound complicated, but it actually isn't. When you allow your opponent's actions to guide your own movements, the appropriate level of effort needed to free yourself from the bind will be apparent. You must "go with the flow" when you bind at the sword.

If your opponent applies moderate strength in the bind, you can use a technique called *Abnehmen* ("Taking Off"). To do this, lift your blade upward from the bind until it clears their point. Once your sword clears your opponent's point, immediately bring the blade back down on the opposite side of their blade, hitting them in the head with your long edge as you continue to keep contact with their sword. From a bind ensuing from a right *Zornhau*, a simple turn of the shoulders and hips is all that is needed to power the stroke on the other side of their sword. [Fig. 4] This technique, which is very quick and requires only a modicum of movement, should be used if your opponent has parried your sword only slightly to the side. Limit the motion of your arms and body. Most of the action is performed by levering the sword between your two hands.

If your opponent pushes your blade farther to your right, however, you will need to forcefully pull your blade from the bind. The pulling action itself is called *Zucken*—"Pulling," "Withdrawing," or "Twitching" and is one of Liechtenauer's primary techniques, appearing not only here, but also in the combat on horse and on foot in armour. If your sword is strongly parried to your right side, pull your sword back out of the bind as you pass forward with your left foot to attack the right side of your opponent's head or body. This follow-on attack can be another stroke of the sword [Fig. 5] or a thrust.

These methods exemplify the German fighting adage "Use strength against weakness, weakness against strength." Rather than engaging in a contest of strength by fighting against your opponent's strong bind, you yield to it and use their attempt at defense as an opportunity to attack another opening. However, you should leave the bind only when your opponent pushes your sword sufficiently to the side so that their point is not directly threatening you. Otherwise, as soon as you leave the bind, they will thrust to your face or chest. In determining your actions, their position is just as important as the amount of pressure they are applying. There are other remedies later in this chapter for the situation where your opponent binds strongly, but keeps their point facing you.

Fig. 5 Responding to Janusz's now more powerful parry (a), Christian leaves the bind, stepping to attack Janusz's now exposed right side (b).

Fig. 4 Janusz responds to Christian's counterattack by parrying (a). Christian then slashes upward to clear Janusz's point (b) and strikes down to the head along the other side of his sword (c), a turn of the hips and shoulders powering the action.

Sliding Out from a Strong Bind – *Durchwechseln*

Durchwechseln ("Changing Through") is a similar technique to *Zucken*, as they are both means of escaping a forceful parry. The difference lies in how you break contact with your opponent's sword. With *Zucken*, this involves a pulling action. With *Durchwechseln*, you disengage by letting your point drop through under the bind in a circular motion. This can be done with little physical effort.

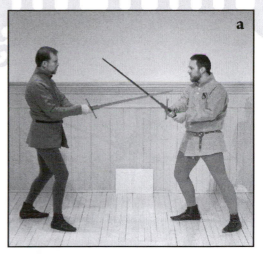

Changing-through works best in those situations where your opponent tries to beat your blade aside by striking too near your point. This does allow them to gain considerable leverage against your sword, but at the cost of taking their own point very much off line from you and gaining little purchase in the bind. The von Danzig commentaries recommend that you should employ *Durchwechseln … against those combatants who are keen to parry, and cut to the sword and not to the openings of the body.*[42]

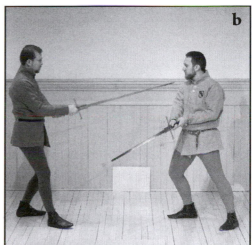

The technique is so named because in letting your point slide free from the bind, you "change through" from one side of their sword to the other. If your opponent parries the end of your blade aside, simply keep your grip supple and let your point slide free beneath the bind and come back in line against their face or chest. [Fig. 6] When you use *Durchwechseln* correctly, it will practically happen by itself.

There is another form of *Durchwechseln*, a "Changing Through with the Pommel." If your opponent strongly binds against your sword, drive your pommel under and through the bind to the other side of their blade and, with a pass forward of the left foot, hit them in the face with the pommel. Your blade should provide cover for you on your right side as you complete the blow with the pommel. You can even use your left hand to check your opponent's right elbow as you step in. [Fig. 7]

Fig. 6 Janusz responds to Christian's counterattacking Zornhau by striking aside the point (a). Christian allows the tip of his sword to drop under and through the bind to thrust on the other side of Janusz's sword (b-c).

---

[42] Peter von Danzig, *Fechtbuch*, folio 31r.

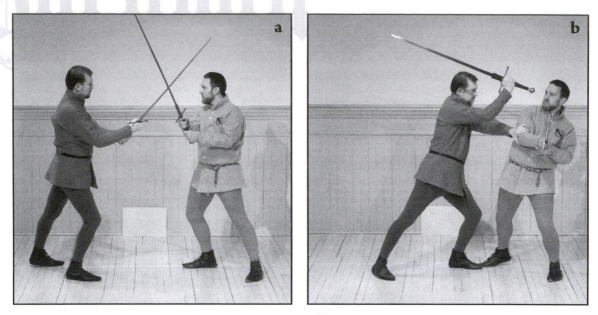

Fig. 7 Janusz again strongly parries Christian's counterattack (a), so Christian passes directly forward with his foot to smash his opponent's face with the pommel, controlling the upper body by grabbing the upper arm with his left hand (b).

Equal Pressure in the Bind – *Winden*

The keen fencer will not meet your sword soft, so that you can thrust to them, nor too hard, so that their own point goes astray, but will instead bind hard with their point threatening your face. In this case, you dare not move to leave the bind as that will provide a momentary opportunity for your opponent to thrust or strike at you with impunity. In this situation, you must work against your opponent while in contact with their blade to maintain a measure of control over their movements in addition to using *Fühlen* to ascertain their intentions. However, if they are strong in the bind, you must mitigate that advantage. This is done by winding or turning your sword against theirs to gain the advantage of superior leverage and is called *Winden Am Schwert* ("Winding at the Sword").

The winding is done in the bind by lifting your hilt up and outward so that your sword moves from the Lower Hanging to the Upper Hanging, that is, from an extended version of *Pflug* to an extended version of *Ochs*, without ever breaking contact with their weapon. If you bind after striking from your right, do this so that your short edge is presented outward and in contact with their sword, with your right thumb on the flat of the underside of your blade. This guard transition – from left *Pflug* to left *Ochs* – brings the strong of your blade against the weak of theirs so that you have a tremendous advantage in leverage and now *command the bind*. As your sword comes into *Ochs*, you thrust to the face or chest. [Fig. 8] In one elegant movement, you deny their point and bring yours against them.

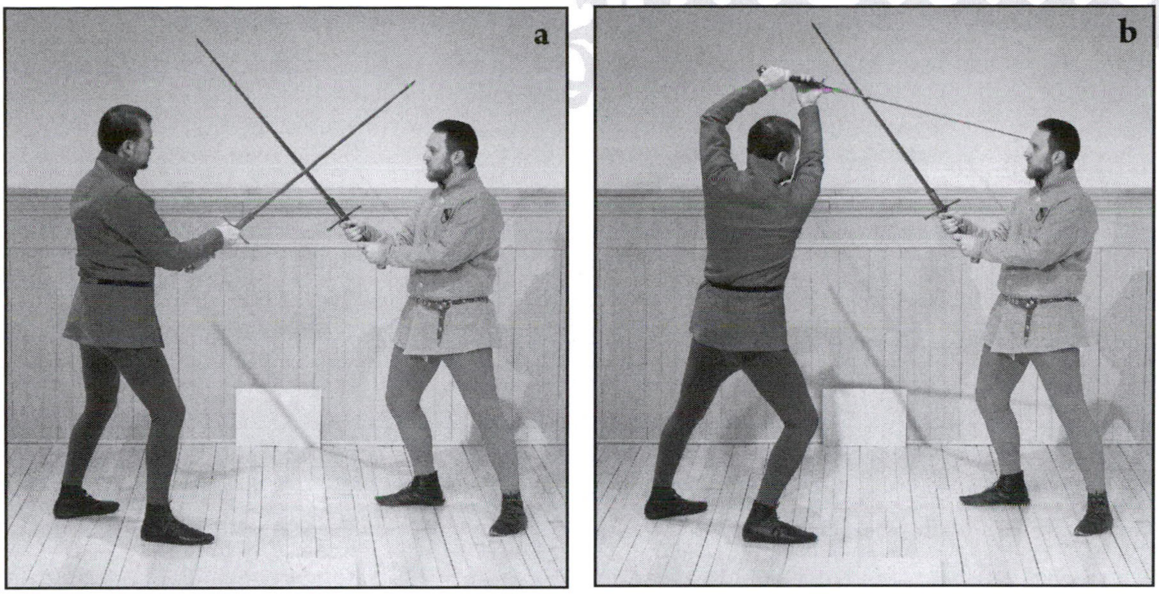

Fig. 8 Janusz answers Christian's counterattack by parrying conservatively, creating a threat of his own (a), so Christian winds into left Ochs to bring the strong of his sword onto the weak of Janusz's sword, thrusting to the face as he winds (b).

If this technique was instead performed as the result of a bind on the right side of the body, as if from the intersection of two backhand blows, then you would maintain contact with your long edge instead, remembering that while left *Ochs* presents the short edge outward, right *Ochs* presents the long edge.

Be sure that, as you wind your sword, you do not retract it into *Ochs*, but rather continue pushing forward. All of the motion here drives forward, continuing to menace your opponent.

Your opponent's natural "flinch response" will be to lift their hilt up to try to move your point away from their face. If this happens, remain in the winding by driving your hilt a little higher and letting your point sink down over their blade and into the chest. [Fig. 9] If instead, they drive up very high, drop your point under their hilt in a tight arc to thrust to your opponent's chest while pinning the arms high. [Fig. 10]

This is the most basic example of winding. *Winden* is one of Liechtenauer's *Hauptstücke*, however, and I will devote a full chapter to its various forms later in this volume.

Refer to the flow chart that closes this chapter for a concise guide to the proper response for each type of bind.

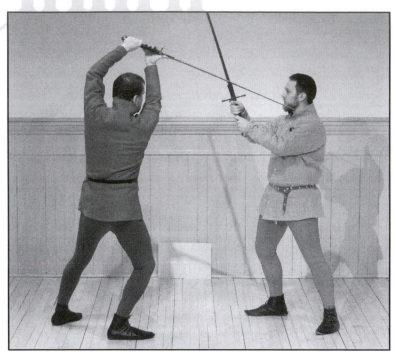

Fig. 9 Janusz lifts his hilt a bit to deny the thrust out of the winding from the previous technique, so Christian angles his sword to thrust down to the chest.

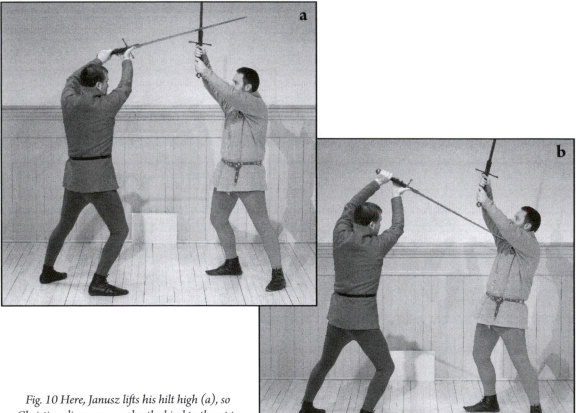

Fig. 10 Here, Janusz lifts his hilt high (a), so Christian disengages under the bind to thrust to the chest (b).

Drill 12: Developing *Fühlen* with the *Zornhau*

In each of the following steps, you and your partner begin in right *vom Tag*. Your partner strikes an *Oberhau* and you respond with a *Zornhau* to their attack.

- As the swords meet, your partner provides weak pressure. Perform the *Zornhau-Ort*: Thrust to their face or chest as the bind occurs.

- As the swords meet, your partner provides moderate pressure, slightly pushing your sword to your right. Perform the *Abnehmen*: Lift your sword out of the bind and strike their head on the other side of the sword, re-establishing contact between the blades.

- As the swords meet, your partner provides strong pressure, pushing your sword well to your right. Perform the *Zucken*: Pull your sword toward yourself and strike their head or body on the other side of the sword. Or, *Durchwechseln* with the pommel to hit them in the face.

- As the swords meet, your partner *strikes to your point*. Perform the *Durchwechseln*: Drop your point under and through the bind to thrust to them on the other side of their sword.

- As the swords meet, your partner applies *equal pressure* to your sword, with their point threatening you. Perform the *Winden Am Schwert*: Turn your short edge against their sword, up into the left *Ochs*, to thrust to their face or chest without breaking contact.

- Repeat steps 1 – 6, but with your partner randomly varying how much pressure they apply in the bind. Choose the appropriate action each time, based on this pressure.

- Repeat all steps with both partners beginning in left *vom Tag*.

Zornhau Decision Chart

Chapter 10: Breaking the Four Openings

If you want to avenge yourself,
break the four openings with skill:
double above,
transmute below correctly.

— Johannes Liechtenauer

Following the techniques for the *Zornhau*, Master Liechtenauer addresses methods optimized for attacking the four openings (*Vier Blössen*), "breaking the four openings with skill." These are *Duplieren* (Doubling) and *Mutieren* (Transmuting), two techniques derived from winding that are used from a bind. These are additional, and very sophisticated, methods for working with varying pressure and position as the swords cross.

Duplieren derives its name from the double attack that seems to occur during its execution; one doubles the attack by winding behind the opponent's sword, seemingly striking them by passing through the bind. *Mutieren* is so-called because one transmutes or changes which side of the opponent's sword is engaged by winding the blade over their sword. Both techniques may be used on either side of the body and from both the lower (*Pflug*) and upper (*Ochs*) binds. *Duplieren* should be used when an opponent is hard at the sword, *Mutieren* when they are soft.

If your opponent binds hard to your sword after you have both struck from your right sides, then move your pommel in a counter-clockwise arc so that your arms cross and strike or slice their face with your long edge. [Fig. 1] If you struck initially from your left side and your opponent binds hard to you, then move your pommel upward in a clockwise arc and strike or slice their face behind their sword with your short edge. The short edge is employed here so that the wrists remain straight.[43] [Fig. 2]

Duplieren is a very fast technique and need not necessarily be accompanied by footwork, although a turnout of the trailing heel will facilitate the turning of the hips and shoulders. While it might appear that this technique makes you vulnerable to their sword, remember that you are making use of their over-commitment in the bind, which makes their sword drive into your cross, and creating a threat to their face that they dare not ignore in favor of hitting you.

---

[43] The wrist is much more vulnerable to injury when it is bent. With the wrists straight, you can better withstand the stress of a powerful blow against your sword.

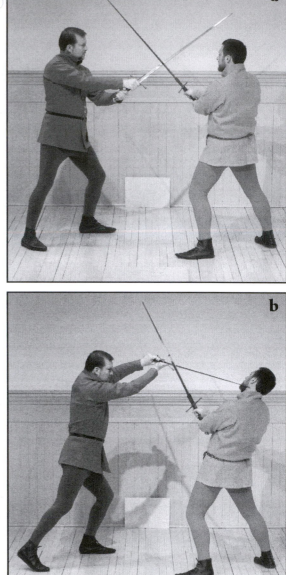
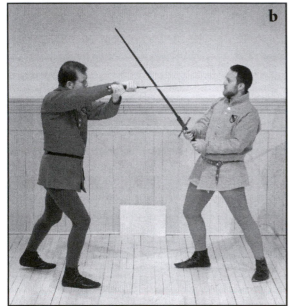

Fig. 1 Both fencers having struck from their right sides, Janusz is hard in the bind (a), so Christian pushes his pommel counterclockwise under his right arm to turn the sword behind his opponent's, slashing through the face with the long edge (b)

Fig. 2 Both fencers having struck from their left sides, Janusz is hard in the bind (a), so Christian pulls his pommel up clockwise to turn the sword behind his opponent's, slashing through the face with the short edge (b).

Mutieren is used when your opponent is soft at the sword or beginning to withdraw from the bind. This is a particularly good technique to employ if you have driven your opponent's blade well to the side so that your point is no longer in presence. In such a case, it is dangerous to reposition your point by releasing the pressure on their sword.

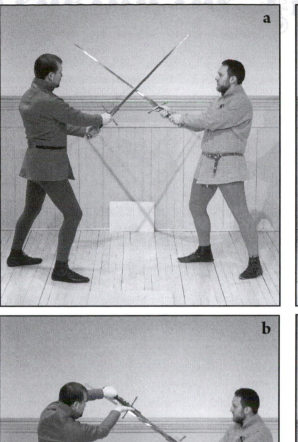

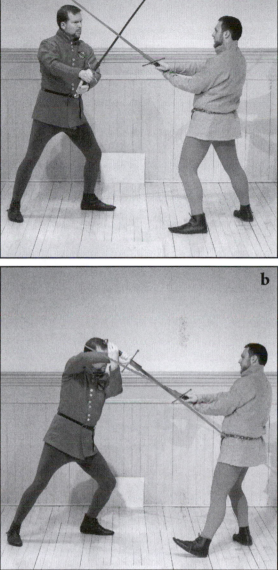

Fig. 3 Both fencers have struck from their right sides. Janusz is soft in the bind (a), so Christian winds his short edge, dropping his point down on the other side of Janusz's sword to thrust to the lower right opening (b).

Fig. 4 Both fencers have struck from their left sides. Janusz is soft in the bind (a), so Christian winds his short edge, dropping his point down on the other side of Janusz's sword to thrust to the lower left opening (b).

If you bind from a stroke from your right side, lift your hilt up into left *Ochs*, with your short edge against their blade, and allow your point to drop over and outside their blade and plunge down, thrusting to their lower openings. [Fig. 3] This action should constrain their blade, so do not relinquish the pressure at any time. When you have struck from your left side and bound to them, lift your hilt up into right *Ochs*, again controlling their blade with the short edge as you thrust low. [Fig. 4]

Drill 13: *Duplieren* and *Mutieren*

- You and a partner both begin in right *vom Tag*.

- Both of you strike right *Oberhaue*, meeting in a bind.

- Your partner strongly pushes your sword to your right.

- Perform a *Duplieren*, slashing their face or neck with the long edge behind their sword.

- Repeat steps 1 – 2, but with you now overwhelming your partner in the bind.

- Perform a *Mutieren*, winding into left *Ochs* and dropping your point over their blade to hit the lower right opening.

- You and your partner now form left *vom Tag*.

- Both of you strike left *Oberhaue*, meeting in a bind.

- Your partner strongly pushes your sword to your left.

- Perform a *Duplieren*, slashing their face or neck with the short edge behind their sword.

- Repeat steps 7 – 8, but with you now overwhelming your partner in the bind.

- Perform a *Mutieren*, winding into right *Ochs* and dropping your point over their blade to hit the left lower opening.

- Repeat all steps, reversing roles each time.

Chapter 11: Krumphau

Strike crooked with nimbleness,
throw the point at the hands.

– Johannes Liechtenauer

Krumphau means "Crooked Stroke" and indeed this stroke appears to be crooked to the observer. Another *Oberhau*, a stroke from above, the *Krumphau* is struck across the line of engagement. When you strike a *Krumphau* from your right side, the stroke looks "crooked" because it cuts across your path and strikes not towards your opponent's left side openings but toward their right. By traveling in this direction, the blow can reach your opponent's hands as they strike. [Fig. 1]

The *Krumphau*'s trajectory contains another aspect of its crookedness. A *Krumphau* struck from the right side can begin in the right *vom Tag* or *Schranckhut* and ends in the left *Schranckhut*. As the blow moves through its arc, the arms cross at the wrists and the blow lands with the long edge striking the opponent. If you find this crossing of the wrists unduly awkward in practicing the blow, you are likely holding your sword with too tight a grip. From the left side, the *Krumphau* can start in left *Schranckhut*, with the wrists crossed, and as the blow is executed the hands uncross, the sword now striking with the short edge.

The 4th and 8th response plays from Chapter 7 teach the *Krumphau* from the right and left sides respectively, and you should recall that they were performed with an especially deep pass. This is because one of the stroke's attributes is evasion. You step away from your adversary's stroke while hitting them with the part of your blade near the point, hence Liechtenauer's advice to "*throw the point on the hands.*" A deep pass, forward and out to the side, offers several advantages. It takes one away from the attack, angles the torso so that it is harder to reach, and allows one to better flank the opponent.

The *Krumphau* can target the hands, but can also bind against an opponent's sword. Here, though, the follow-on actions are a little different from those following the *Zornhau*, in that the point will not initially be in line against the opponent. So, if you strongly displace your opponent's sword, the action that follows the bind will be another stroke, but if they bind strongly

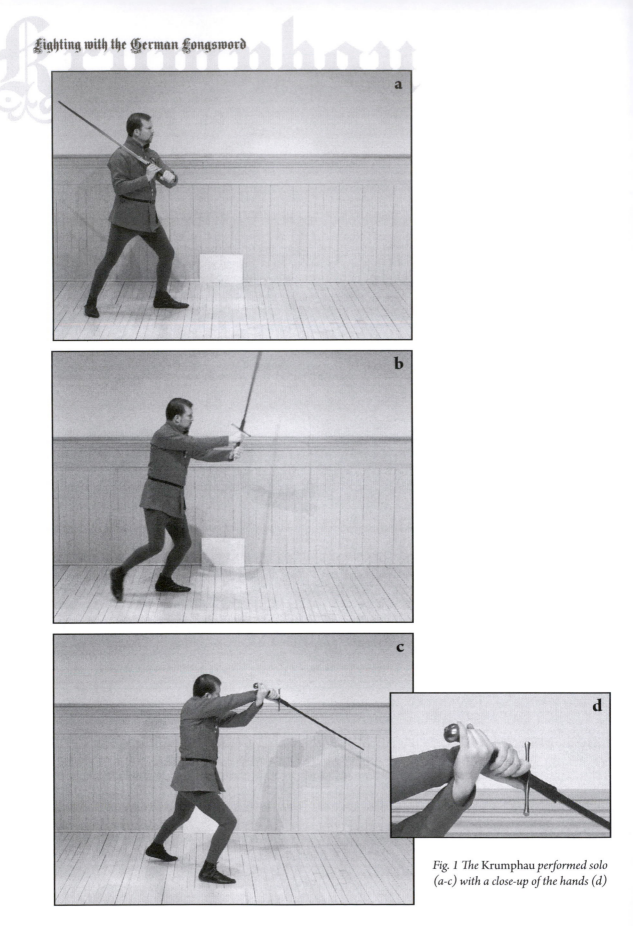

Fig. 1 The Krumphau *performed solo (a-c) with a close-up of the hands (d)*

against you, you must wind your sword to bring the point against them. Remember, everything that we learned about decision-making in the bind in the chapter on the *Zornhau* applies here too and will continue to apply whenever we bind swords.

When you strike a *Krumphau*, your body must work as a unit, as with striking any other blow. It is important that your weight move smoothly forward, particularly as this *Oberhau* requires a deeper pass than the others we have learned. Further, if you strike a *Krumphau* from your right side, your right hip must twist a bit more than when you strike a more typical *Oberhau*, because you need to reach a target that is far to your left with your point. Do not attempt to do this with just the hands. If you follow the above advice on where to aim your right foot, then your body will naturally orient for the blow. Of course, for a *Krumphau* from the left, these directions are reversed: you step with your left foot and your left hip must coil to help you reach a target to your right side.

It is very important to properly manage distance while striking the *Krumphau*. Do not, however, "think with your feet" and fixate on where to step. Rather, envision casting your point at your opponent's hands from a safe distance. When you do this, you will find that you step exactly where you need to every time. Keep your hilt high and relatively near your head. The hilt must remain high because, if you miss your opponent, you will need your blade to fall into the *Schranckhut*, protecting your body.

This stroke is also one of the *Vier Versetzen* ("Four Oppositions"), strokes used to attack one of the four primary guards in safety. This means that the stroke can close off a line of attack associated with a particular guard, but this may or may not involve actual blade contact, depending on how your opponent reacts. So think of them as strokes that can prevent an attack from a guard. Thus, the *Krumphau* counters *Ochs*: if you attack someone in this guard with the *Krumphau*, they will not be able to thrust against you from above, as we will see shortly.

> ## Drill 14: The *Krumphau*
>
> - Begin in right *vom Tag*.
> - Strike *Krumphau* from your right.
> - Repeat steps 1–2 several times.
> - Move to right *Schranckhut*.
> - Strike *Krumphau* from your right.
> - Repeat steps 4–5 several times.
> - Reset to left *Schranckhut*.
> - Strike *Krumphau* from your left.
> - Repeat steps 7–8 several times.
>
> This drill can be varied as you strike a series of *Krumphaue* from one side to the other. Begin in right *vom Tag*. Strike a *Krumphau* from the right (which terminates in left *Schranckhut*). From there, strike from one *Schranckhut* to the other with the *Krumphau*.

Countering an *Oberhau* or *Unterhau*

One of the best times to use the *Krumphau* instead of a more pedestrian *Oberhau*, such as the *Zornhau*, is when you aren't sure if your opponent's blow is coming from above or below, that is, whether it is an *Oberhau* or an *Unterhau*. As we learned in the drills of Chapter 7, the *Unterhau* is hard to defend from *Pflug* or *Ochs*, our binding guard, so stepping away from this stroke and casting the point at your opponent's hands is a safer bet. Then, if your adversary strikes to you and you're not sure of what's coming at you, step deeply away as you cast your point at their hands. If you are on guard in *vom Tag*, strike the *Krumphau* with a good deep passing step so that you defend yourself and offend them whether they strike an *Oberhau* [Fig. 2] or an *Unterhau*. [Fig. 3]

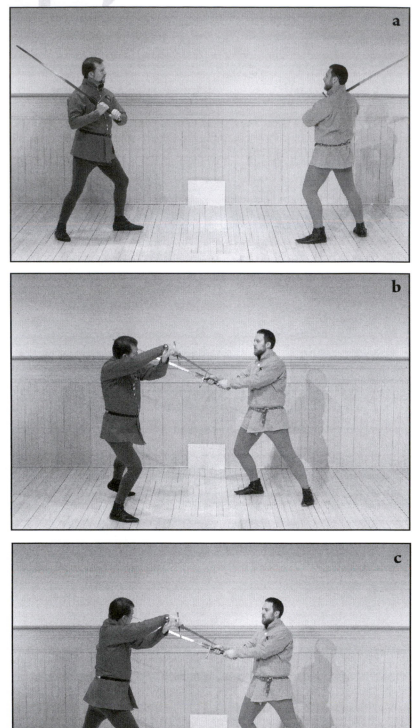

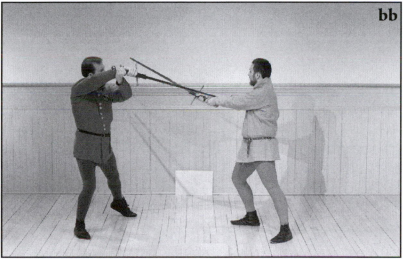

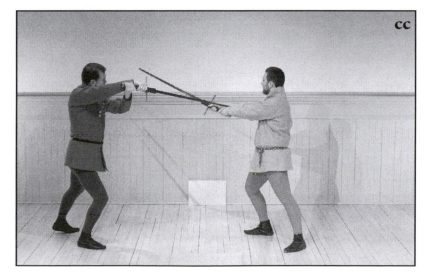

Fig. 2 The fencers begin in right vom Tag (a/aa). Janusz strikes an Oberhau, so Christian springs out to the right and then compass steps with his left foot as he strikes Janusz's hands with the long edge and with crossed hands (b/bb-c/cc).

Fig. 3 Janusz strikes an Unterhau, *so Christian springs out to the right and then compass steps with his left foot as he strikes Janusz's hands.*

The *Schranckhut* on either side of the body is also a good guard from which to launch a *Krumphau*. From the right *Schranckhut,* strike the *Krumphau* through a counter-clockwise arc so that the long edge hits their hands. [Fig. 4] From the left *Schranckhut,* strike the blow through a clockwise arc so that the short edge cuts their hands. [Fig. 5] You can also strike a left *Krumphau* from left *vom Tag,* but this is a bit more awkward than from the left *Schranckhut.*

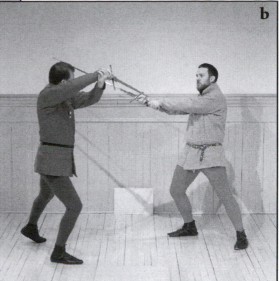

Fig. 4 Christian stands in right Schranckhut, with Janusz in right vom Tag *(a). Christian responds to Janusz's Oberhau by striking counterclockwise with crossed hands to Janusz's hands (b).*

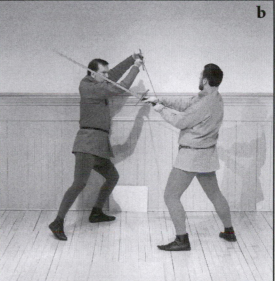

Fig. 5 Christian stands in left Schranckhut, with Janusz in left vom Tag *(a). Christian responds to Janusz's* Oberhau *by striking counterclockwise, by uncrossing his hands, to Janusz's hands (b).*

Binding with the *Krumphau*

You can commit more of your blade with the *Krumphau* to strongly bind against an incoming stroke. Because your point is offline from your opponent as you do this, you must immediately

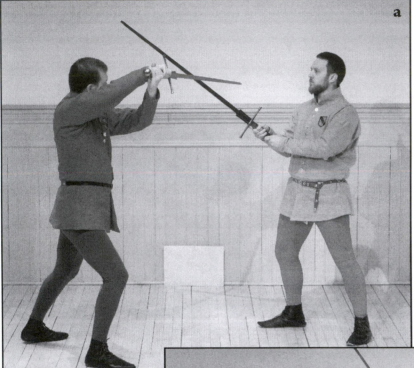

strike or thrust to them from the parry.

If your opponent is hard in the bind, wind your sword, with your short edge in contact with their blade, into the left *Ochs* to thrust to their face. [Fig. 6] If they are soft in the bind, snap your short edge back up hard against their head. [Fig. 7] A consequence

Fig. 6 Christian strikes a right Krumphau against Janusz's incoming sword (a). Encountering strong resistance, he winds his short edge against Janusz's sword into left Ochs to thrust (b).

of the *Krumphau's* angle of attack is that you will almost certainly bind against the flat of your adversary's blade, hence the Liechtenauer verse: *"Strike crooked to the flats of the Masters if you want to weaken them. When it clashes above, then move away, that I will praise."*[44]

Recalling that a *Krumphau* struck from the left side employs the short edge, rather than the long edge, note that the action following the bind is also reversed. If you wind against their sword, it will be with the long edge [Fig. 8]; and should you strike to the head from the sword, this too will be with the long edge. [Fig. 9]

Fig. 7 Christian again strikes a right Krumphau *against Janusz's incoming sword (a). Encountering weak resistance, he strikes to Janusz with his short edge (b).*

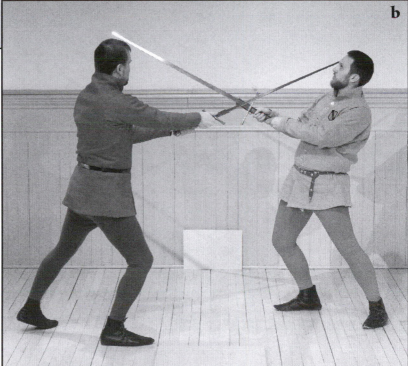

---

[44] Master Liechtenauer's verse, lines 87 – 90.

Fig. 8 Christian strikes a left
Krumphau *against Janusz's
incoming sword (a). Encountering strong resistance, he
winds his long edge against
Janusz's sword into right
Ochs to thrust (b).*

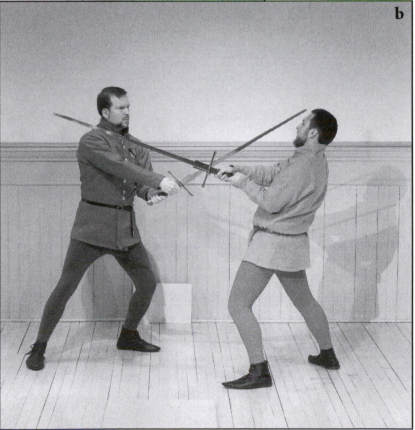

Fig. 9 Christian again strikes a left Krumphau *against Janusz's incoming sword (a). Encountering weak resistance, he strikes to Janusz with his long edge (b).*

Fighting with the German Longsword

Krumphau

Drill 15: The *Krumphau* against a Stroke

- You and a partner begin standing in right *vom Tag*.

- Have your partner strike an *Oberhau*. Respond by striking the *Krumphau* to their hands.

- Return to your guards. Have your partner strike an *Unterhau*. Respond by striking the *Krumphau* to their hands.

- Repeat steps 1 – 4, varying randomly between the two attacks.

- Return to your guards. Have your partner strike an *Oberhau*. Respond by striking the *Krumphau* to their sword. Have your partner respond with weak pressure against your sword.

- Strike from the bind to the head with your short edge powered only by a turn of the body.

- Return to your guards. Have your partner strike an *Oberhau*. Respond by striking the *Krumphau* to their sword. Have your partner respond with strong pressure against your sword.

- Wind your short edge against their sword to thrust to the face or chest.

- Repeat steps 5 – 8, with your partnering randomly varying the pressure applied in the bind.

- Repeat all steps with you beginning in right *Schranckhut*.

- Repeat all steps with you beginning in left *Schranckhut* and your partner in left *vom Tag*. Remember to now wind or strike with your long edge from the bind.

Consult the flowchart at the end of this chapter for a concise guide to your choice of actions as each encounter unfolds.

Breaking *Ochs*

In its role as one of the *Vier Versetzen*, the *Krumphau* is used to seize the initiative in the *Vor* to attack an opponent standing in *Ochs*. It is suited to this task because the deep passing step associated with the blow allows you to attack this guard from the side, away from the menace of the point, the horn of the Ox. If your opponent is in the right *Ochs*, and you are in right *vom Tag*, you can step deeply offline to your right as you strike to their upper left opening, avoiding their blade and point altogether. [Fig. 10] If, however, they are in the left *Ochs*, you should step deeply to your right, and away from the threat of their point, and hit their hands as they stand on guard. [Fig. 11]

If your stroke falls short when they are in the left *Ochs*, or if they slightly shift their sword to parry the *Krumphau*, then let your point drop under their sword. This is a Changing Through (*Durchwechseln*) and as soon as your point clears their sword, thrust under their sword to their face, neck, or chest. The *Krumphau* strikes with only the tip of the sword, making it very easy to deceive your opponent and drop under their blade. A compass step with the left foot affords even greater safety, allowing you to shift from right *Ochs* to left *Ochs* as the thrust is completed, maintaining defensive cover. [Fig. 12]

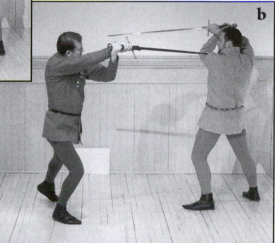

Fig. 10 Janusz forms right Ochs, so Christian strikes a
Krumphau *from right* vom Tag *to the upper opening*
(a-b).

Fig. 11 Janusz forms left Ochs, so Christian strikes a
Krumphau *to Janusz's hands (a-b).*

Fig. 12 Seeing Christian's incoming Krumphau, Janusz withdraws his hands, so Christian drops his point under Janusz's sword (a), compass stepping with the left foot to pivot his body, maintaining cover while he finishes the thrust beneath the sword (b).

Drill 16: The *Krumphau* against the *Ochs*

- Stand in right *vom Tag* and have a partner stand in right *Ochs*.

- Step deeply offline and strike their upper left opening with the *Krumphau*.

- Have your partner stand in left *Ochs*, while you remain in right *vom Tag*.

- Step deeply offline to strike their hands with the *Krumphau*.

- Have your partner stand in left *Ochs*, while you remain in right *vom Tag*.

- Step deeply offline and strike the *Krumphau* short. Durchwechseln under their blade and thrust.

Countering the *Krumphau*

If your opponent defends against your *Oberhau* or *Unterhau* by striking a *Krumphau* to your blade, then as soon as the swords meet, turn your point against them before they can wind their sword against you or strike to your head from the bind. [Fig. 13] This makes use of the fact that they need two fencing times to hit you with a *Krumphau* to your sword, which gives you the opportunity to regain the initiative.

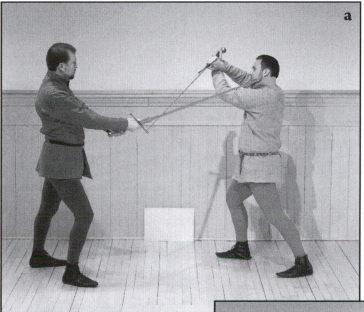

Fig. 13 Janusz strikes a Krumphau to Christian's sword (a), so Christian commands the weak of Janusz's sword by winding into right Ochs to thrust (b).

Krumphau Decision Chart

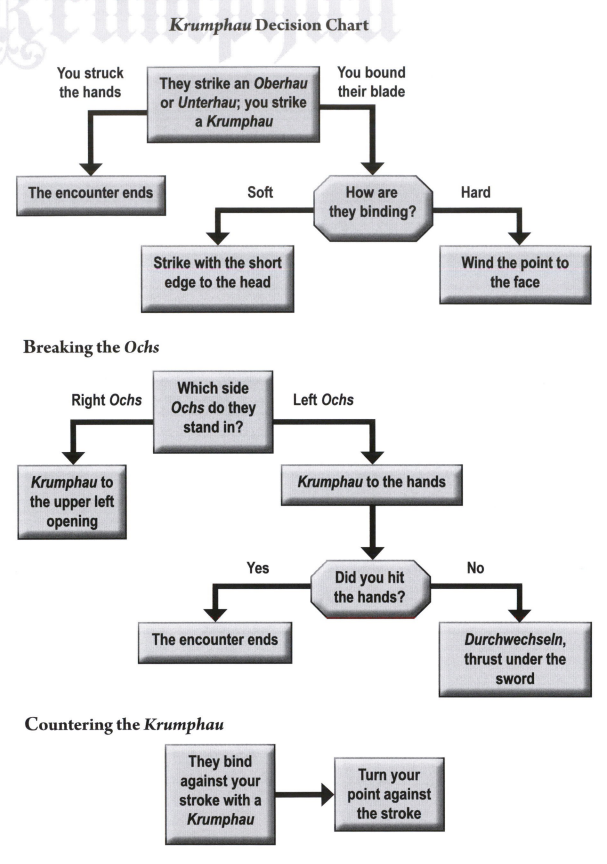

You struck the hands

They strike an *Oberhau* or *Unterhau*; you strike a *Krumphau*

You bound their blade

The encounter ends

Soft

How are they binding?

Hard

Strike with the short edge to the head

Wind the point to the face

Breaking the *Ochs*

Right *Ochs*

Which side *Ochs* do they stand in?

Left *Ochs*

***Krumphau* to the upper left opening**

***Krumphau* to the hands**

Yes

Did you hit the hands?

No

The encounter ends

***Durchwechseln*, thrust under the sword**

Countering the *Krumphau*

They bind against your stroke with a *Krumphau*

Turn your point against the stroke

Chapter 12: Zwerchhau

*The Thwart Stroke takes
whatever comes from the roof*
— Johannes Liechtenauer

The *Zwerchhau*[45] ("Thwart Stroke") is a high horizontal blow that can strike any of the four openings. It is similar to the *Mittelhau*, but sometimes partakes of aspects of the *Unterhau* as well, depending on whether the upper or lower openings are targeted. Unlike the *Mittelhau*, the *Zwerchhau* is not so easily parried. This is because the blow is struck with the hilt held high, protecting the head and creating a fulcrum at the intersection of the hilt and strong of the blade, should the blow meet an opponent's attempt to parry it. [Fig. 1]

This stroke is performed very similarly to the first response from Chapter 7. It is in essence a powerful movement between *vom Tag* to *Ochs* on the opposite side of the body. To execute a *Zwerchhau* from the right, you strike from right *vom Tag* and into left *Ochs*, but with your blade flattening out as you strike so that your short edge hits your opponent. From the left, strike the *Zwerchhau* by moving between left *vom Tag* and right *Ochs*. This will bring the long edge to bear against your opponent. In both cases, the edge orientation is dictated by whatever is mechanically stronger and does not require bending of the right wrist. On both sides, your right thumb should always be placed on the flat of your blade near the cross. This helps stabilize the sword and guide the *Zwerchhau* so that the edge is properly oriented toward your opponent as you strike.

The commentaries found in the Lew and Speyer codices offer a way to perform the *Zwerchhau* without having to rotate the hilt and flatten the blade when striking from *vom Tag* on the shoulder. Instead, they advocate 'pre-flattening' the blade by laying the flat on the shoulder. The only downside to doing this is that it more obvious to your opponent that you mean to strike a *Zwerchhau*.

---

[45] Some texts render the name as *Twerhau*, likely resulting from regional and dialect differences.

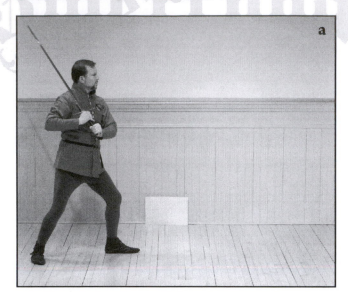

When you strike a *Zwerchhau* from your right side, be sure you tightly coil your right hip with the blow, because this charges the left hip for an even more powerful *Zwerchhau* from your left side, should you need it. The *Zwerchhau* is unique in this regard, because the follow-on stroke will start in *Ochs* and travel through an almost complete circle to strike their other side.

The aforementioned response plays taught us that a transition into *Ochs* allows one to safely answer a vertical blow from above while still threatening with the point or edge. Thus, the *Zwerchhau* is ideal for simultaneously defending against downward blows and hitting your opponent. This same quality is what gives it its role as one of the *Vier Versetzen*: The *Zwerchhau* breaks *vom Tag*, because it shuts down the line of attack from that guard.

In the following techniques, the binds ensuing from the *Zwerchhau* obey the same rules as those from the *Zornhau*. The same concepts of hard and soft, and their relationship to maintaining the initiative, apply. The only difference is that the *Zornhau* binds in *Pflug*, the lower bind, while the *Zwerchhau* binds in *Ochs*, the upper bind.

Fig. 1 The Zwerchhau *performed solo (a-c).*

Drill 17: The *Zwerchhau*

Repeat each step of this drill until the strikes flow smoothly.

- From right *vom Tag*, strike the *Zwerchhau* from the right.

- From left *vom Tag*, strike the *Zwerchhau* from the left.

- Starting in right *vom Tag*, strike a *Zwerchhau* from the right.

- At the end of the *Zwerchhau*, remain in left *Ochs* to strike a *Zwerchhau* from the left.

- Continue striking the *Zwerchhau* back and forth. Remember to alternate between targeting high with your blade, and dropping your tip to target low to reach each of the four openings.

Countering an *Oberhau*

You should disrupt an opponent's *Oberhau* with the *Zwerchhau* if it is coming more or less straight down to your head. Stand in *vom Tag* with your left leg leading. When your opponent strikes down, pull your hilt up, letting your point drop so that your blade is roughly horizontal, and strike into their stroke so that you catch their blade on the strong of your sword. As you do this, your short edge should hit the left side of their head. Attack and defense therefore happen within the same single fencing time. Be sure that your *Zwerchhau* is accompanied by a good pass forward with your right foot. [Fig. 2] You will succeed in hitting your opponent provided they do not bind too hard against your sword. Be sure your hips turn with the stroke to provide a powerful push against their *Oberhau* as you intercept it. Later, we will examine which techniques to use when they do bind strongly.

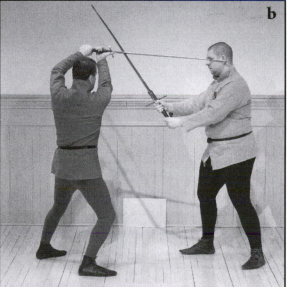

Fig. 2 Both fencers form right vom Tag, *with Christian allowing the flat to rest on his shoulder (a). Christian intercepts Chris' Oberhau with the strong of the short edge while the weak of the sword strike's Chris' head (b).*

Breaking *vom Tag*

The *Zwerchhau* is the stroke among the *Vier Versetzen* that breaks *vom Tag*. It does this by closing off the line of attack from that guard: *vom Tag* is held at the shoulder or above the head, so a high horizontal attack can keep blows from coming down "from the roof." This technique works the same way as the previous *Oberhau* counter. The only difference is that this technique is pre-emptive, while the other was in response to an attack; that is, this is used in the *Vor*, while the counter to the *Oberhau* was used in the *Nach*. So if your opponent is in *vom Tag*, strike a *Zwerchhau* at their head, taking care to be sure your hilt is held high so that it provides cover for you. [Fig. 3] If they respond by coming out of the guard and binding hard against your sword, then use one of the techniques that follow in the next section. Note that it is much easier to break their guard when they form the high version of *vom Tag*, rather than the shouldered variant.

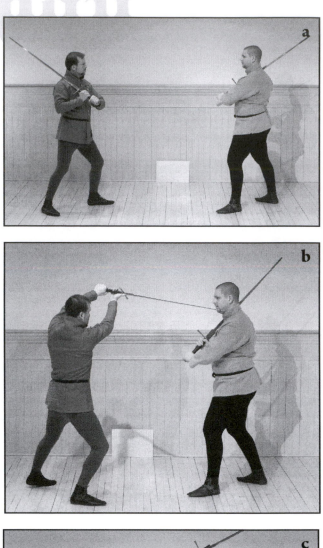

Fig. 3 From vom Tag *(a), Christian can attack to break Chris' right* vom Tag *(b) or, even more easily, high* vom Tag *(c).*

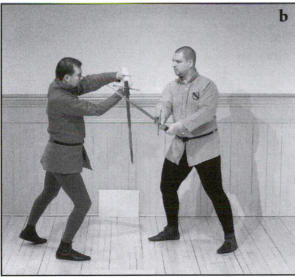

Fighting from a Strong Bind

When your opponent binds hard against your *Zwerchhau*, you should use the concept of *Zucken* ("Pulling") to withdraw from the bind and strike around to their other side. If you strike a *Zwerchhau* with the short edge from your right side, one option is to strike around to hit their right side with your long edge if they bind to you. Begin the action by using your sword's guard to hook their blade and take it offline to your right side. Continue this motion so that your blade swings around over your head to them with the long edge on the right side of their head. [Fig. 4] This follow-on *Zwerchhau* from the left should be accompanied by a pass forward with the left foot. Note that in this case, the second blow does not originate from *vom Tag*, but is instead a transition from left *Ochs* to right *Ochs* through a close to 360° arc. As stated above, this makes it very important that you coil your right hip, charging the left hip with potential energy for the second stroke.

Depending on how your opponent has stepped, you may find that you are too close to be able to hit your opponent with the second *Zwerchhau*. If the distance tightens up too much, then as you come around for the follow-up technique, let go of your grip with your left hand and grab your blade in the middle, so that you shorten your sword, and thrust to your adversary's face with the sword held thus. [Fig. 5]

Fig. 4 Chris binds against Christian's right Zwerchhau *(a), so Christian knocks Chris' blade aside and down with his cross (b) and strikes around with a left* Zwerchhau *to the head with the long edge (c).*

This type of grip on the sword is called *Halbschwert* ("Half-sword") or *Kurzen Schwert* ("Shortened Sword"). Half-sword fighting is a salient feature of the armoured combat we will see toward the end of this book and effectively turns your longsword into a short spear. It is also useful for those times when you run out of room for cutting blows. Be sure to clamp your blade in your left hand so that your own edges do not make solid contact with your palm or fingers. Pressure should be applied to the flats of the blade, not the edge.

Fig. 5 Chris again binds against the Zwerchhau *(a), so Christian, now closer, strikes around into a half-sword grip to thrust (b).*

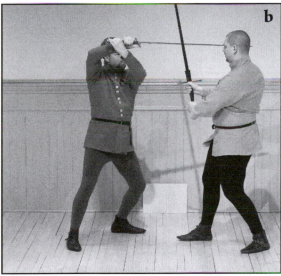

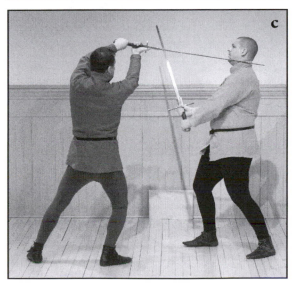

You can vary your targeting with the *Zwerch-hau*, by varying the angle at which your blade hangs to the side from your hilt. By letting the blade slope, you can hit a lower opening instead of an upper opening. You can throw a succession of blows, high and lower, to both sides, to keep your opponent scrambling to defend against each *Zwerchhau* that comes their way. [Fig. 6] This is called the "*Zwerch-hau* to the Four Openings"; it is described as alternating between striking to the Ox (*Ochs*) and the Plow (*Pflug*), because these guards defend the upper and lower openings on each side. Sigmund Ringeck says of this:

> *This is how you can strike to the four openings with the Zwerch-hau: When you close in with your adversary with the Zufechten, at the right moment, jump towards him and strike with the Zwerchhau to the lower opening of his left side. This is called "striking towards the plow." When you have attacked the lower opening with the Zwerchhau, immediately strike another Zwer-chhau to the other side, at his head. This is called "striking towards the ox." And then strike swiftly alternating the Zwerchhau towards the plow and the ox, crosswise from one side to the other.*[46]

You can rain down blows in rapid succession with this technique, pulling away from each of their parries, until at last they fail in their defense and are struck.

Fig. 6 Christian's right Zwerchhau to the lower left opening is bound by Chris (a), so he strikes around with a high left Zwerchhau, which Chris also parries (b). Christian then strike back around with a high right Zwerch-hau, hitting Chris in the left side of the head (c).

---

[46] Sigmund Ringeck, *Fechtbuch*, folios 28v – 29r.

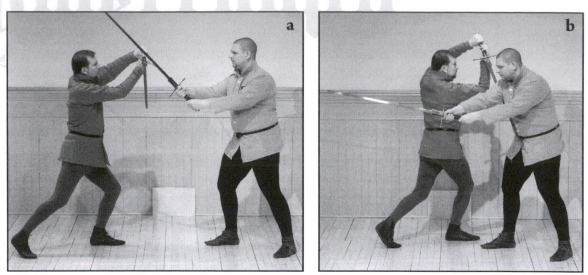

Fig. 7 Christian feints a high right Zwerchhau *(a), but drops his point as he passes across the line to strike the lower left opening instead (b).*

Feints with the *Zwerchhau*

The *Zwerchhau* can be used as a part of a particularly sneaky technique, the *Fehler*, which means "Failer," that is, "Feint," as the initial blow purposefully "fails" to hit the target. A feint must, however, have sufficient commitment that, should the opponent fail to take the bait, you may still hit them with authority. The skill required for finding the balance between commitment and the ability to pull and redirect your attack is one that requires considerable training.

To do this, strike either an *Oberhau* or a *Zwerchhau* to your opponent's upper left opening. If you opponent means to parry, then before they can bind, drop your point to strike the lower left opening with the short edge. For greater safety, this can be performed with a pass that crosses the line of engagement, which better removes your body from harm. [Fig. 7]

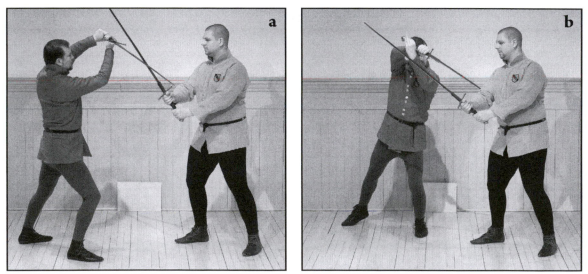

Fig. 8 Christian feint a high right Zwerchhau *(a), but pulls the blow to pass with the left foot and strike a left* Zwerchhau *to the lower right opening (b).*

Alternatively, you can also pull the first blow to strike a second *Zwerchhau* around to their lower right opening with the long edge. [Fig. 8] Here, if your opponent goes to parry, do not fully set your right foot down as you pull the first *Zwerchhau*, and immediately spring with left as you deliver the second blow to the other side.

In either case, be sure that you keep your hilt high before your head to provide cover. Also make sure to create the appearance that you are *intent* on hitting their upper left opening, or else the deception will not work. If they don't give you an obvious indication that they mean to parry high, simply finish your initial attack.

The masters also describe a technique with the *Zwerchhau* called the "Double Failer," for with it you can fool your opponent twice. As before, draw your opponent's parry by attacking the upper left opening with an *Oberhau* or *Zwerchhau*, again pulling the blow. Now strike around to their upper right opening with the long edge. If they manage to parry this, deceive them anew by performing a *Duplieren* with the short edge, striking them behind the sword. You can also slice down onto the arms, in lieu of the *Duplieren*, should you wish. [Fig. 9]

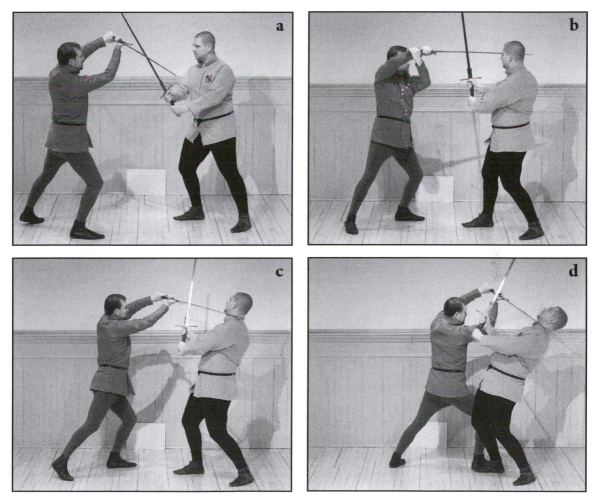

Fig. 9 Christian pulls his right Zwerchhau *before impact (a) to strike around with a left* Zwerchhau, *which Chris binds (b). Christian then uncrosses his hands to perform a* Duplieren *with the short edge (c), and knocks his opponent off his feet with a forward pass of the right foot (d).*

To complete any kind of Failer, you must observe your opponent committing their body to parrying the feinted attack. If they do not, you should finish that first action, rather than risking a double hit by attacking the next target. In short, if your opponent doesn't take the bait, *just hit them!*

Countering the *Zwerchhau*

You can defeat an opponent's *Zwerchhau* from their right side by binding down strongly against it from your right side. If you can push down their blade hard enough to gain position, angle your point toward them from left *Pflug*, and thrust while bound to their blade. Push their sword down with the entire body, including a turn of the hips as you come into *Pflug*. Do not attempt to drive their sword down with only your arms! [Fig. 10]

Fig. 10 Christian binds down Chris' right Zwerch-hau to place a thrust (a-b).

If you don't push their sword down, however, they will likely pull out of the bind to strike a second *Zwerchhau* to your other side. If this happens, then, using only a twist of the hips to propel it, strike a *Zwerchhau* of your own to the left side of their neck so that your blade comes under their sword, breaking the attack. [Fig. 11] This is an instance where footwork does not accompany a blow. As you've already struck from your right side to bind down their blade, you have already passed forward with the right foot and there is therefore no reason to step in this instance. A quick, but powerful, twist of the hips must power this stroke for it to succeed.

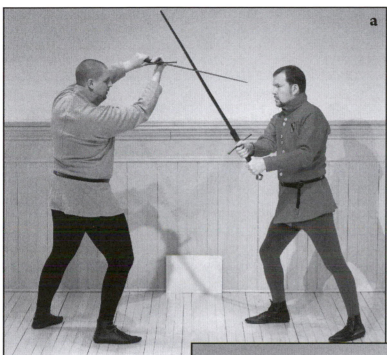

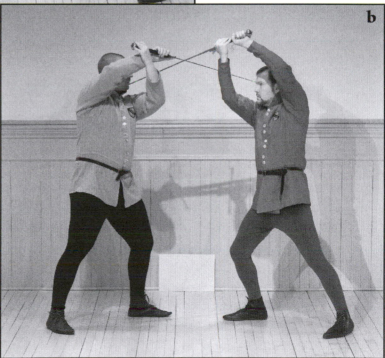

Fig. 11 Christian again binds against Chris' Zwerchhau from the right (a), so Chris attempts a left Zwerchhau, which Christian parries by striking a Zwerchhau of his own under it to the neck (b).

If your opponent strikes a second *Zwerchhau* around from your bind, you can also fall onto their arms with an *Oberschnitt*, a slicing cut from above. This is done by passing forward with the left foot to come into the right *Pflug* against their arms or wrists so that you push away their follow-on attack. Again, the entire body must be employed in making the slice. Remember that you are not only cutting them, you are strongly pushing the attack away from you. [Fig. 12]

Fig. 12 Chris' Zwerchhau is bound by Christian (a) so he attempts to strike a left Zwerchhau, but Christian falls upon his arms with a slice from above (b).

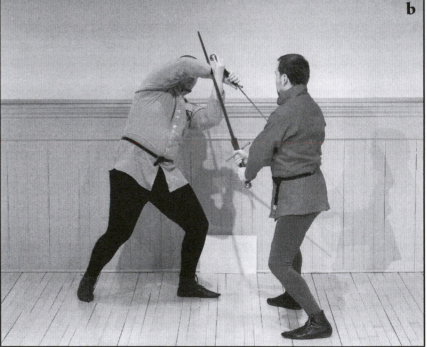

Drill 18: The *Zwerchhau* against an *Oberhau* or *vom Tag*

- You and a partner begin standing in right *vom Tag*.

- Seize the initiative by attacking your partner with a *Zwerchhau*.

- Both partners resume their guards.

- Have your partner strike down toward your head. Strike the *Zwerchhau*, parrying the attack and striking their head.

- Both partners resume their guards.

- Have your partner strike down toward your head. Strike the *Zwerchhau*, parrying the attack, but have your partner give you strong pressure. Hook aside their blade with your cross and strike a left *Zwerchhau* to their upper right opening.

- Both partners resume their guards.

- Have your partner strike down toward your head. Strike the *Zwerchhau*, parrying the attack, but have your partner give you strong pressure. Hook aside their blade with your cross and strike a left *Zwerchhau* to their lower right opening.

- Both partners resume their guards.

- Have your partner strike down toward your head. Strike the *Zwerchhau*, parrying the attack, but have your partner give you strong pressure. Hook aside their blade with your cross and thrust to their right side with the *Halbschwert*.

- Repeat all steps, switching which partner performs the *Zwerchhau*.

Zwerchhau Decision Chart

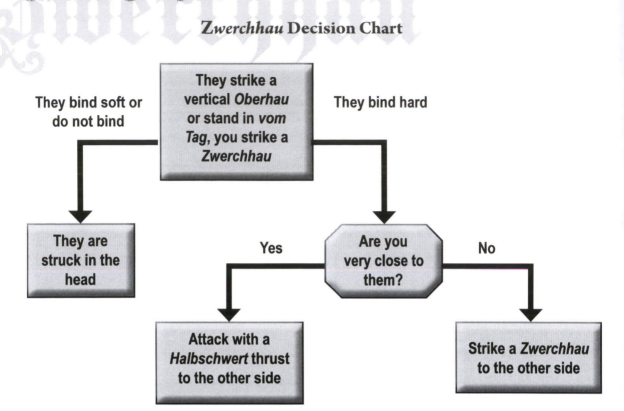

They bind soft or do not bind

They strike a vertical *Oberhau* or stand in *vom Tag*, you strike a *Zwerchhau*

They bind hard

They are struck in the head

Yes

Are you very close to them?

No

Attack with a *Halbschwert* thrust to the other side

Strike a *Zwerchhau* to the other side

Countering a *Zwerchhau*

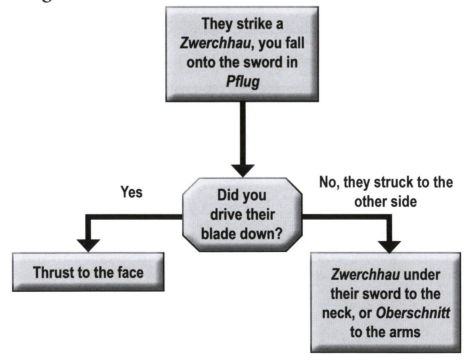

They strike a *Zwerchhau*, you fall onto the sword in *Pflug*

Yes

Did you drive their blade down?

No, they struck to the other side

Thrust to the face

Zwerchhau* under their sword to the neck, or *Oberschnitt* to the arms

Chapter 13: Schielhau

The Squinting Stroke breaks
Whatever a buffalo strikes or thrusts
– Johannes Liechtenauer

The *Schielhau*—the "Squinting Stroke" or simply the "Squinter"—is another stroke that begins in *Vom Tag* and terminates in *Ochs* on the opposite side of the body. In this regard it is identical to the *Zwerchhau* and therefore but another variation on the first response from Chapter 7. While the *Zwerchhau* strikes horizontally from *Vom Tag* to *Ochs*, the *Schielhau* comes down almost vertically from above to strike with the short edge, regardless of whether you strike from your right or left side. The *Schielhau* is aimed at the far shoulder or the top of the head so that it can both close off a line of attack from the guard *Pflug* and "jam" an attack from a crudely slogging fencer (a *Büffel* ("Buffalo") in Liechtenauer's parlance). This requires a more vertical trajectory as you must clear your opponent's head to get to their far shoulder. However, the trajectory is not perfectly vertical; the blow must be angled about 70 degrees (off the horizontal), so as to expel the opponent's sword down and out to your left side. [Fig. 1]

The stroke derives its name from the performer's appearance. To reach an opponent's right side when striking a *Schielhau*, you need to turn your hips and shoulders more as you step, bringing you into a position where you are "squinting" with one eye at them. The best way to strike the *Schielhau* is to strike as if delivering an ordinary *Oberhau*, but instead turn your right hand over as you strike, so that the short edge comes down against your opponent and their blade. This turning over the edge should happen smoothly throughout the course of the blow. Make sure you keep your movement compact as you strike the *Schielhau*. Do not allow your blade to swing out too far away from you, as you want to keep your point menacing your opponent as much as possible.

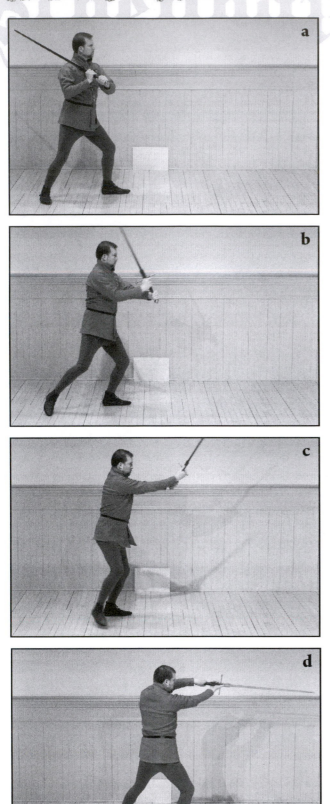

Just as with the *Zwerchhau*, you must coil the right hip when you strike a *Schielhau* from the right, and coil the left hip when striking from your left. The *Schielhau* needs to reach a far opening: the right stroke hits an opening on your opponent's right side and the left stroke must reach their left side. Without the hip twist, you cannot reach those targets. Also remember that you are countering a powerful, committed blow. Without the strong push imparted by the movement of your hips and shoulders, you will not be able to generate enough power to withstand the strength of their stroke.

Unlike the *Krumphau* or *Zwerchhau*, the *Schielhau* does not require a committed springing step outward to the right. Where the commentaries are precise, they do advise that one spring, but simply toward the opponent. This makes perfect sense, given this strike's greatest virtue is that of forestalling a powerful attack.

The trajectory and point orientation of the *Schielhau* make it very hard to defend against. I believe it is no accident that the masters of the 15th century do not include a counter-technique to this stroke in their commentaries. Any attempt to parry aside a *Schielhau* is likely to engage only the sword's point, which simply forces the striker to change through (*Durchwechseln*) and thrust against the defender. If someone strikes a *Schielhau* against you, your best bet is to simply step offline and/or pivot out of the way of harm, *if* you can do this in time!

Fig. 1 The Schielhau *performed solo (a-d).*

Countering a Buffalo

Liechtenauer's verse calls a cloddish, crudely slogging fencer who relies only on brute strength a *Büffel* ("Buffalo"). When such a fencer pulls back hard to charge a powerful blow against you, they waste a tempo by moving away from you. This gives you time to strike a *Schielhau* against them and jam their attack before they can strike. In doing this, you are essentially inserting a bar between their neck and sword to keep their stroke away. If your opponent strikes from their right side, then strike a *Schielhau* from your right so that your short edge hits their sword and their right shoulder at almost the same time. [Fig. 2] If they strike from the left side, then strike the *Schielhau* from your left so that your short edge hits their blade and left shoulder. [Fig. 3]

Fig. 2 Both fencers begin in right vom Tag, but Chris pulls back to charge a powerful blow (a). Christian deflects Chris' blow with the Schielhau, *striking the right shoulder with his short edge (b).*

Drill 19: The *Schielhau*

- Begin in right *vom Tag*.

- Strike the *Schielhau* from the right side. Be sure your point remains facing an imaginary opponent as you complete each stroke.

- Repeat the Drill from left *vom Tag*

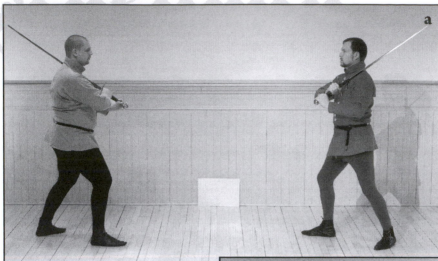

Fig. 3 From left vom Tag, *Christian strikes a left* Schielhau *against Chris' left* Oberhau *(a-b).*

Durchwechseln with the *Schielhau*

I mentioned earlier how *Schielhau* is very difficult to defend against. Your opponent may try to strike aside your point as you strike the blow or they may make incidental contact with it in an attempt to change through and set up their own thrust on the other side of your blade. If either of these happens, remember that the *Schielhau*'s angle of attack is such that the point is inherently in line against your adversary as it meets their blade. If they strike your sword or slide through the bind to chamber a thrust, then let your point change through and thrust at them before they can complete their technique. [Fig. 4]

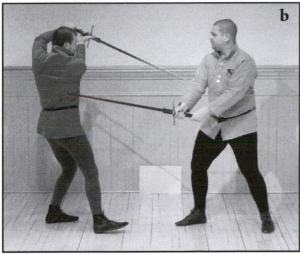

Fig. 4 Chris attempts to parry Christian's Schielhau (a), but Christian changes through with the point (b) and thrusts to the other side (c).

Drill 20: The *Schielhau* Against a Buffalo

- You and a partner begin in right *vom Tag*.
- Have your partner pull back hard, telegraphing their intent, to strike with strength.
- Strike the *Schielhau* against their stroke and their right shoulder or head.
- You and your partner reset to left *vom Tag*.
- Have your partner pull back hard to strike with strength.
- Strike the *Schielhau* against their stroke and their left shoulder.
- You and your partner reset to right *vom Tag*.
- Begin to strike the *Schielhau* against their stroke and their right shoulder or head.
- As you do so, have your partner meet your strike and set aside your sword.
- Change through to thrust to them as they do so.
- You and your partner reset to left *vom Tag*.
- Begin to strike the *Schielhau* against their stroke and their left shoulder.
- As you do so, have your partner meet your strike and set aside your sword.
- Change through to thrust to them as they do so.

Breaking *Pflug*

The *Schielhau* is the preferred stroke for attacking an opponent standing in *Pflug*, because it can close off that guard's likely attack, a thrust from below. However, this must be done in two fencing times. If you try to hit the opponent's shoulder while striking aside their sword while they are in *Pflug*, your blade will likely travel too high to either make contact with their sword or prevent them from thrusting.

Therefore, what you should do is strike the *Schielhau* against their sword and then thrust to their chest in opposition with their blade. You'll need to finish the blow with your hilt lower this time, in an extended *Pflug*, so that you don't lose control of their blade. You can attack the right *Pflug* in this way, [Fig. 5] but you can also do the same if they stand in the *Pflug* on the left side by stepping a little bit farther to your right as you hit the right side of their sword. When you break *Pflug* with the *Schielhau*, use the weight of your body to force open their centerline by turning your hips into the blow. [Fig. 6]

Fig. 5 Janusz is in right Pflug; *Christian in right* vom Tag *(a). Christian strikes a* Schielhau, *keeping the hilt low, to Janusz's sword (b), striking it to the outside to thrust to the chest (c).*

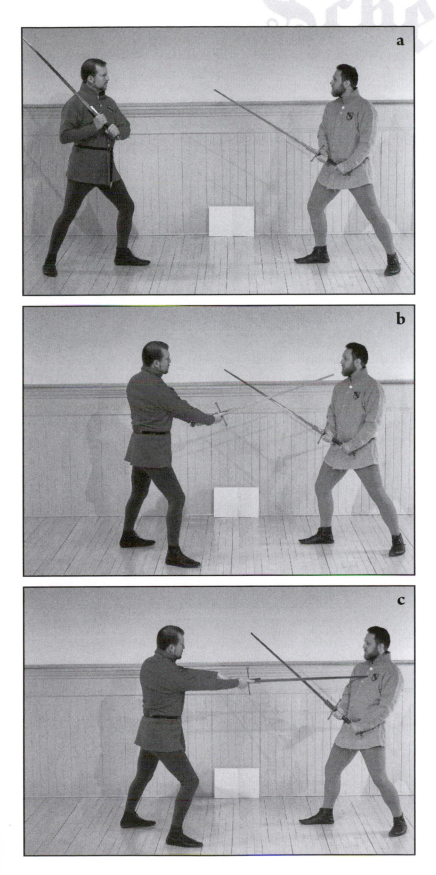

Fig. 6 Janusz is in left Pflug; *Christian in right* vom Tag *(a). Christian strikes a* Schielhau, *with the hilt low, to Janusz's sword (b), striking it to the inside to thrust to the chest (c).*

Breaking *Langenort*

The guard *Langenort* is just *Pflug* extended out forward, which makes the *Schielhau* also appropriate for attacking this guard. Here, however, you must use a bit of deception by appearing to be intent on striking your opponent's weapon aside with a simple *Oberhau*. The deception is important, as you need to cover more ground in attacking the *Langenort* than you do with the *Pflug*. Therefore, you must clear some room by moving their point aside a bit, so you can safely close without running onto their point.

Without moving your right foot, pretend you want to strike an *Oberhau* hard against their point. Instead, invert your sword to strike strongly with the *Schielhau* against their sword, knocking it down and aside to your left. Only when you see that you have driven their sword away is it safe to complete the action by stepping forward with your right foot to thrust into their neck. [Fig. 7] Alternatively, as Liechtenauer's verse has it, *Squint to the point and take the throat without fear.*

Fig. 7 Chris keeps Christian at bay by holding Langenort *against him (a). Christian strikes a* Schielhau *to Chris' sword (b), withholding his right foot until he sees the sword deflected aside. Only then does he pass in with the right foot to thrust the throat (c).*

Another way to break *Langenort* is to act as if you intend to strike an *Oberhau* to the opponent's head, but instead turn the stroke over and hit their hands with the *Schielhau*. [Fig. 8] This is a particularly good tactic to employ if your opponent is cagey and withdraws from your attempt to attack their throat, as in the technique above.

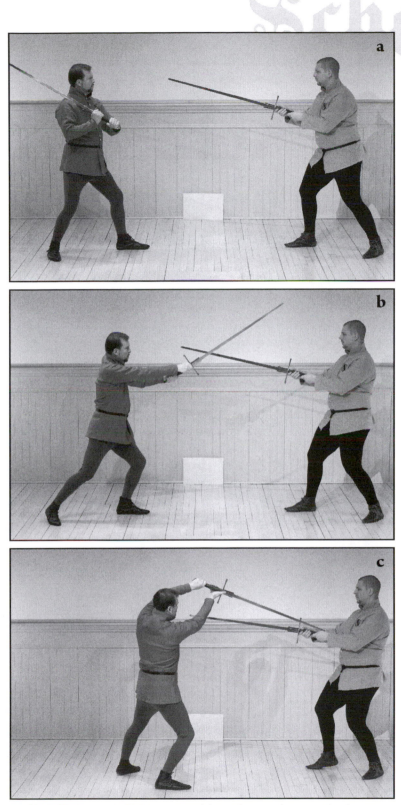

Fig. 8 Chris again holds Langenort *(a), so Christian feints an* Oberhau *to the head (b), but turns the blow over to strike down with the short edge to the hands (c).*

Scheilhau

Drill 21: The *Schielhau* Against *Pflug* and *Langenort*

- You begin in right *vom Tag*. Have your partner begin in right *Pflug*.

- Strike the *Schielhau* against their sword.

- Thrust to their chest.

- Reset to right *Vom Tag*. Have your partner reset to left *Pflug*.

- Strike the *Schielhau* against their sword.

- Thrust to their chest.

- Reset to right *Vom Tag*. Have your partner reset to *Langenort*.

- Begin as if to strike toward their point with an *Oberhau*, but then change to hit their sword with the *Schielhau*.

- Thrust to their neck or chest.

- Reset to right *Vom Tag*. Have your partner reset to *Langenort*.

- Begin as if to strike toward their head with an *Oberhau*, but then change to hit their hands with the *Schielhau*.

Schielhau Decision Chart

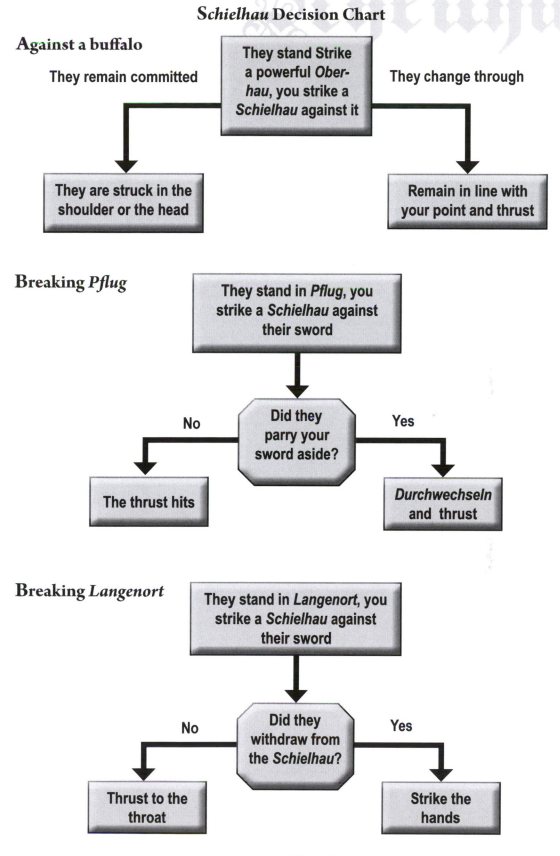

Against a buffalo

They remain committed

They stand Strike a powerful *Ober-hau*, you strike a *Schielhau* against it

They change through

They are struck in the shoulder or the head

Remain in line with your point and thrust

Breaking *Pflug*

They stand in *Pflug*, you strike a *Schielhau* against their sword

No — Did they parry your sword aside? — Yes

The thrust hits

Durchwechseln and thrust

Breaking *Langenort*

They stand in *Langenort*, you strike a *Schielhau* against their sword

No — Did they withdraw from the *Schielhau*? — Yes

Thrust to the throat

Strike the hands

Scheithau

Chapter 14:
Scheitelhau

The Scalp Stroke
is a danger to the face,
with its turn,
very dangerous to the breast.
— Johannes Liechtenauer

The *Scheitelhau* is the "Scalp Stroke" or "Parting Stroke" (as in parting the hair). It is a high vertical attack with the long edge, aimed at the top of the head or face. We saw this stroke first in the third response play in Chapter 7, where it was used to outreach an opponent's stroke to the leg using the principle of *Überlaufen* (Overrunning): high strokes and thrusts overreach low strokes and thrusts. The *Scheitelhau* employs this same principle in its role as the last of the Vier Versetzen – the Four Oppositions that disrupt the four guards – in breaking the guard *Alber*, a low-lying position. It is uniquely suited to this purpose, for the raised position of the arms narrows one's shoulders, allowing for maximum extension of the weapon.

The Ringeck and von Danzig commentaries describe the *Scheitelhau* as targeting the top of the head, while the Jud Lew manuscript, perhaps favoring the maintaining of a more cautious distance, advises that the stroke fall slightly short, so that the point can then drop against the face or breast:

> *When you come to him in the* Zufechten *and he stands in the guard* Alber, *then set your left foot forward and hold your sword with outstretched arms high above your head in the guard* vom Tag. *And spring to him with the right foot and strike with the long edge strongly from above down and remain with your arms high and sink the point down to his face or breast.*[47]

If an opponent is standing in the *Alber*, with their right leg leading, it is hard for them to simply lift their sword into left *Ochs* to intercept your *Scheitelhau*, as you may get inside their attempt to parry. Their most natural response will instead be to lift the hilt, point upward into the *Kron*, and intercept your blade. The techniques for the *Scheitelhau* are therefore mostly focused on how to deal with this parry.

---

[47] Jud Lew, *Fechtbuch*, folio 27r.

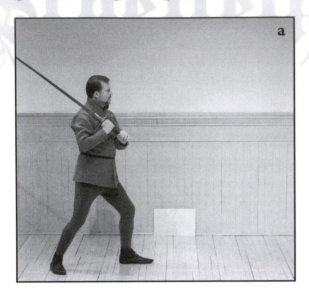

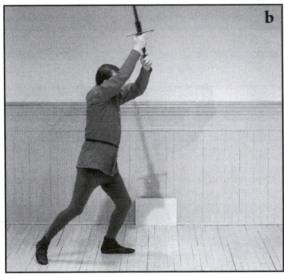

The *Scheitelhau* must be performed with the arms remaining high and the hands outstretched so that it can reach the top of your opponent's head. It should be struck with a casting motion. The hands should be driven high before the body is allowed to come forward. If you begin in the shouldered version of *vom Tag*, allow yourself to pass through the high variant as you strike. [Fig. 1] As the hands come up, let the sword suddenly move forward—imagine throwing the point on top of your opponent's head. This also allows your blade to rock over an opponent's parry to some extent, and you should keep your hands loose so that your stroke has an element of levering action to it.

The *Scheitelhau* does not require as much coiling of the hips as the *Zwerchhau* or *Schielhau*. If you turn them as much as you would one of the other *Meisterhaue*, you will change the trajectory of the cut and alter the technique. Rather, make a smaller turn of the hips and sink your weight straight down onto your lead leg. This should provide more than sufficient power to "part their hair."

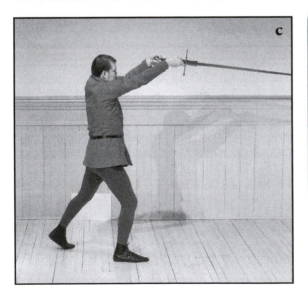

Drill 22: The *Scheitelhau*

- Stand in right *vom Tag*.

- Strike the *Scheitelhau*. Remember to cast your point forward with your arms high.

- Repeat the drill starting from the high variant of *vom Tag*.

Fig. 1 Christian begins in right vom Tag *(a), initiates the* Scheitelhau *by projecting the hilt upward (b), and casts the point forward with a pass of the right foot (c).*

Breaking *Alber*

As said previously, the guard *Alber* can be attacked by using distance to one's advantage. If you strike the *Scheitelhau* with outstretched arms, maximizing your reach, but without locking your elbows out, you can execute a stroke to their head or face without your adversary being able to lift up their sword against you in time. This is an application of *Über-laufen*: a high attack outreaches a low attack, or, in this case, a low guard. [Fig. 2] I've shown this attack from the version of *vom Tag* on the right shoulder, but it certainly works very well from the over the head version too, as the Jud Lew commentaries recommend. Note that, should your blow fall a little short, you have still broken the opponent's guard, and your point is now standing before their face!

Fig. 2 Christian assumes vom Tag, *confronting Janusz who stands in Alber (a). Christian lifts his hilt, without yet committing himself, provoking Janusz into prematurely lifting his sword (b). Exploiting this mistimed reaction, Christian casts the point at Janusz's head by springing forward (c).*

Circumventing the Crown

If your opponent has any reflexes at all however, they will lift up their sword into *Kron* to intercept your *Scheitelhau* before it hits their head. If they do this, you should work against their parry appropriately, depending on how they respond to your attack. If their *Kron* is too low, then allow your blade to rock over the fulcrum created by their hilt and hit them in the head anyway. [Fig. 3] If they form *Kron* correctly and catch your sword high enough so that this is impossible, then invert your sword into the *Ochs* against their sword so that your point plunges down into their face or chest. [Fig. 4]

The higher on your blade they catch you with the *Kron* however, the more likely they are to bind near your point, which puts them in danger of *Durchwechseln*, or "Changing Through". So if their Crown is too high, let your point drop under hilt in a tight arc and thrust to their face or chest under their hands. [Fig. 5]

Fig. 3 Janusz now defends Christian's Scheitelhau by lifting his sword into Kron (a). Christian levers his blade over this defense to strike the head (b).

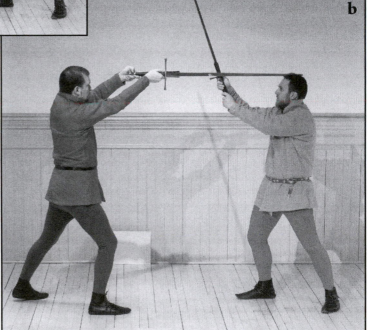

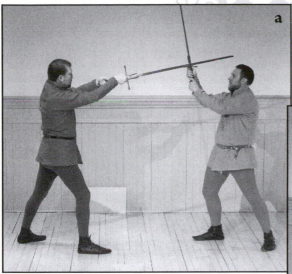

Fig. 4 *Janusz now defends the* Scheitelhau *with Kron held higher (a). Christian inverts his sword into a high left* Ochs *to thrust down to the chest (b).*

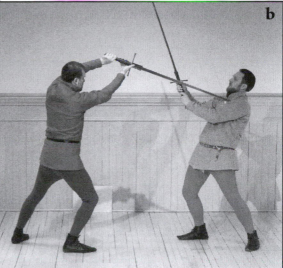

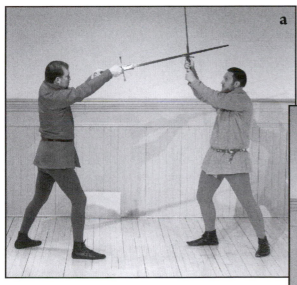

Fig. 5 *Janusz lifts his sword into an even higher Kron (a), so Christian forms left Ochs as he disengages his point under his opponent's hilt to thrust to the chest (b). Note how Christian also constrains Janusz's arms above as he completes the thrust.*

Slicing Through the Crown

Kron is a useful parry only when you do not remain in that position.[48] From it, you must either wind your point against the opponent or let your point collapse so you can close and apply one of the grappling techniques that we will see in the later chapters on wrestling. [Fig. 6] If your opponent begins to close against you from the *Kron*, you should turn your sword under their hands into left *Ochs* to slice through their wrists from below with the *Unterschnitt*, the slice from below. You can then continue to push aside their attack by compass pacing backward with your left foot while rotating your edge around their wrists and into the left *Pflug*. [Fig. 7] With both slices, you should employ the middle or strong of your blade. This is an example of *Hende Drucken*—the "Pressing of the Hands."

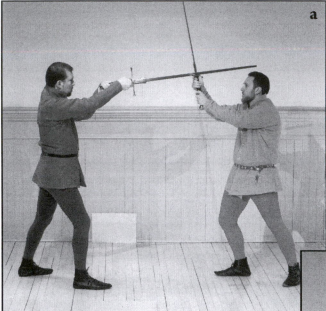

Fig. 6 Janusz now employs Kron *correctly (a), remaining in the position momentarily and then closing to fight at close quarters, applying both grappling and a pommel strike (b).*

---

[48] As we learned in chapter three, *Kron* is only a transitional position and not one to lie in.

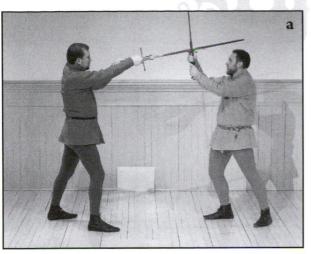

Drill 23: The *Scheitelhau* against the Alber

- Begin in right *vom Tag*.

- Have your partner stand in *Alber*.

- Strike the *Scheitelhau* against the top of their head.

- Repeat steps 1–5, but have your opponent catch the *Scheitelhau* in *Kron* with the cross at the correct (brow) height.

- Wind to *Ochs* to thrust over their cross.

- Repeat steps 1–5, again having your opponent catch the *Scheitelhau* in *Kron* with the cross at brow height.

- Your partner should close to grapple.

- Slice their hands as they close.

- Repeat steps 1–5, again having your opponent catch the *Scheitelhau* in *Kron* with the cross too low.

- Allow your sword to rock over your partner's cross to hit the head.

- Repeat steps 1–5, again having your opponent catch the *Scheitelhau* in *Kron* with the cross too high.

- Change through, with your sword in *Ochs*, to thrust under their parry.

Fig. 7 Christian prevents Janusz's attempt to rush in from Kron *(a) by slicing the arms with the short edge from below (b), and then continuing to press the hands from above with the long edge (c), compass stepping back with the left foot as he completes the action of forcing Janusz down and away.*

Scheitelhau Decision Chart

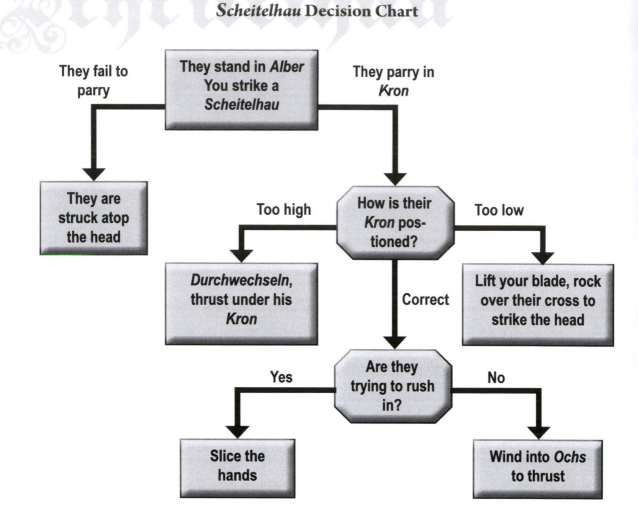

They fail to parry

They stand in *Alber* You strike a *Scheitelhau*

They parry in *Kron*

They are struck atop the head

Too high

How is their *Kron* positioned?

Too low

Durchwechseln*, thrust under his *Kron

Correct

Lift your blade, rock over their cross to strike the head

Are they trying to rush in?

Yes

No

Slice the hands

Wind into *Ochs* to thrust

Chapter 15:
Vier Versetsen

Four are the oppositions, which hurt the guards very much.
Beware of parrying. If it happens to you, it troubles you greatly.
If you are parried and when that has happened,
hear what I advise to you: Tear away and strike quickly with
surprise.

– Johannes Liechtenauer

The *Vier Versetzen*, as we have learned in the previous four chapters, comprise those four of the five "Secret Strokes" used to break the four guards. As we saw, these are not "parries" in the usual sense, but rather relatively safe offenses to be given when an opponent frames a particular guard. Liechtenauer also uses this chapter to caution us against defending without offering an offense (an "empty parry," as I like to call it), as well as offer advice on what to when you are parried by the opponent.

Breaking the Guards

Let us first review, as the 15th century commentaries do, the *Vier Versetzen* [Fig. 1]:

> The *Krumphau* breaks *Ochs*.
>
> The *Zwerchhau* breaks *vom Tag*.
>
> The *Schielhau* breaks *Pflug*. In addition, we know it can also break *Langenort*.
>
> The *Scheitelhau* breaks *Alber*.

Before presenting a Drill for breaking the guards (taught to me by my German colleagues Jörg Bellinghausen and Hans Heim) let me offer the following cautions and additional advice:

Reacquaint yourself with the methods for employing the above strokes in breaking the guards by reviewing the previous four chapters.

Breaking the shouldered version of *Vom Tag* can be tricky, as it is difficult to get one's *Zwerchhau* to come under their guard, so consider simply offering a very threatening *Zornhau* instead that they must defend.

Remember that breaking a guard is simply a matter of forcing them out of it by giving them two choices: parry or be hit.

You can break the other, secondary low guards, *Schranckhut* and *Nebenhut*, in the same way as breaking *Alber*: by striking a *Scheitelhau*. Only be prepared to change through, as their parries will be more powerful from those guards.

Drill 24: Breaking the Guards

- Stand just outside of wide measure, forming the shouldered variant of *Vom Tag*.

- Have your opponent stand in a neutral position, not forming any guard.

- Your opponent will now form a guard. At first, confine the choices to the four primary guards, until you develop proficiency.

- You have one second to attack their guard with the proper stroke. As soon as you see what guard they have formed, put your left foot forward and then spring at them with your attack.

- Step back out of measure and repeat, with your opponent at first going through a set pattern of guard choices, and then randomizing them.

- Repeat the Drill, now adding in the secondary guards of *Langenort*, *Schranckhut*, and *Nebenhut*.

- Repeat the Drill again, only now adding more incentive to strike quickly. Should you fail to act within the allotted one second, your opponent is now allowed to strike or thrust you!

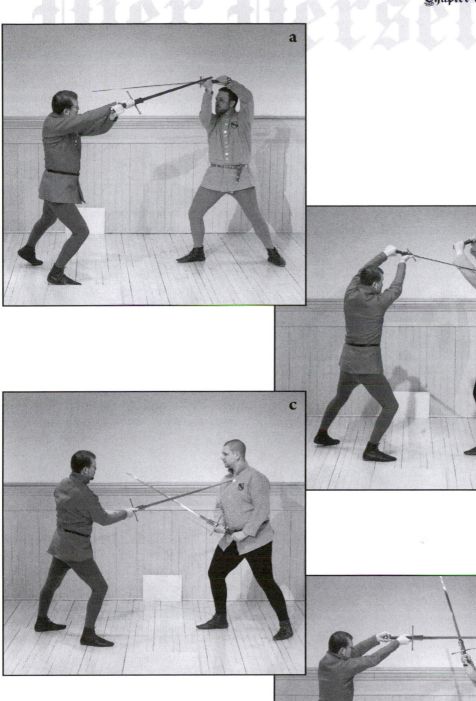

Fig. 1 Breaking the four guards.
The Krumphau breaks Ochs. (a)
The Zwerchhau breaks vom Tag. (b)
The Schielhau breaks Pflug (c)
The Scheitelhau breaks Alber (d).

Countering a Parry

We have seen many techniques in the preceding chapters for dealing with an opponent's parrying of your attack. In his chapter on the *Vier Versetzen*, Liechtenauer offers advice about parrying, and how not to do it. His disciple Sigmund Ringeck, in glossing this, puts it very well:

> And beware of all parries used by bad fencers. Note: Strike, when he strikes, thrust, when he thrusts. And in this chapter, and in the chapters on the five strokes, you shall find written down how you shall strike and thrust.[49]

In modern terms, we can safely say that Liechtenauer far prefers counter-attacking to parrying. Recall from Chapter 6 that a counterattack is a strike opposed to the attack that takes a single fencing time, in contrast to the parry-riposte, which takes two fencing times.

If you have been parried, an additional method is prescribed for very sneakily dealing with it. We are already familiar with the *Abnehmen* ("Taking Off"), described in the chapter on the *Zornhau*. Here, the masters describe dealing with the parry by acting as if you intend to take off of their blade, but instead of leaving their sword, go only part way up, and then drive right back down onto their head. This both fools them and allows you to "open the door" a bit by controlling the weak of their sword, moving it aside to give you their head as a target again. [Fig. 2]

Another technique for countering parries is called *Schnappen* ("Snapping"), so named from the way the sword snaps out of the bind. *Schnappen* is used when your opponent binds so strongly that your sword is forced down. In this case, your sword becomes pinned such that you have no room to pull it back out of the bind. You must instead free your sword by pushing your pommel forward until your blade comes parallel to your opponent's and thereby "snaps" out from the bind. As you snap out from the bind, you hit your opponent in the face with your edge.

If you bind when striking from your right side, then snap out and strike with the long edge to the face. [Fig. 3] If you strike from your left side and bind, you snap out and strike with the short edge. [Fig. 4] In each case, the edge employed is dictated by what flows kinesthetically best from the bind on each side. *Schnappen* is a good technique for countering powerful binds that limit your movement. It also works very well if you strike an *Unterhau* and are parried. [Fig. 5]

---

[49] Sigmund Ringeck *Fechtbuch*, f. 35r.

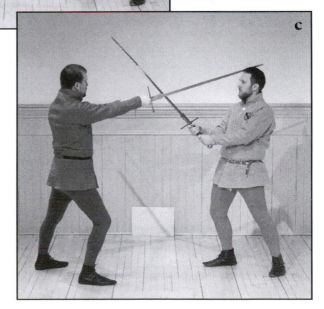

Fig. 2 From a bind (a), Christian slashes up as if he intends to move to other side of Janusz's sword (b), but instead then strikes down to the head (c).

Fig. 3 Janusz binds Christian's sword down hard
to his right (a). Christian drives his pommel
forward, bringing the blades parallel to each other
and snaps out of the bind to hit Janusz in the
head with the long edge while passing forward
with the left foot (b-c).

Fig. 4 Christian is bound down on his left (a), so he drives his pommel forward to free his sword and strike with the short edge, the blow accompanied by a pass forward of the right foot (b-c).

Vier Versetsen

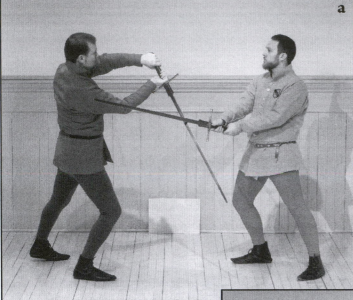

Fig. 5 Janusz binds down Christian's Unterhau (a), so Christian snaps out to strike with the long edge (b).

Chapter 16: Nachreisen

Chase twice, or slice in the weapon.
Two outer intentions. The work after that begins.
And test the attacks, if they are soft or hard.
— Johannes Liechtenauer

Liechtenauer and his disciples prized control of the fight. However, knowing how and when to seize the initiative isn't always easy. Quite the contrary, it ranks among the greatest of skills.

Nachreisen ("Chasing" or "Traveling After") is a fundamental principle of fencing, one that allows the swordsman to follow their opponent's actions, to the latter's detriment. As the anonymous Von Danzig commentary has it:

> *Chasing is diverse and manifold, and should be done with striking and thrusting with great foresight against combatants who strike free and long strokes, and will really observe nothing of the true art of the sword.*[50]

This principle is also lauded as one of the primary ways of seizing the initiative by attacking the four openings:

> *Now there are two attacks with which one should seek the openings. First, you should seek them from the Zufechten with the Chasing, and by shooting into the Longpoint. Secondly, you should seek them with the eight windings when one combatant has bound the other on the sword.*[51]

We, of course, have some experience now with the second method, and will return to it later.

Any time your opponent is moving away from you, it is relatively safe to follow them. Thus, if they lift their sword to attack *within wide measure* you have a tempo in which to attack them, because their sword is moving up and backward, not toward you, in this moment. So if your opponent lifts to strike or pulls the sword back to charge a thrust, strike to their head or chest

---

[50] Peter Von Danzig, *Fechtbuch*, f. 27v.

[51] Ibid., f. 15v.

while springing aggressively toward them. [Fig. 1] Of course, they may react before you complete your stroke, but now they must parry *your* attack, and the fencing continues from the bind, as we have learned before.

You can also pursue them as they lift their sword by falling onto their upraised arms to press them with your long edge. Do this by passing across the line with your right foot and then passing with the left to continue pushing them back as you form the right *Ochs*. [Fig. 2]

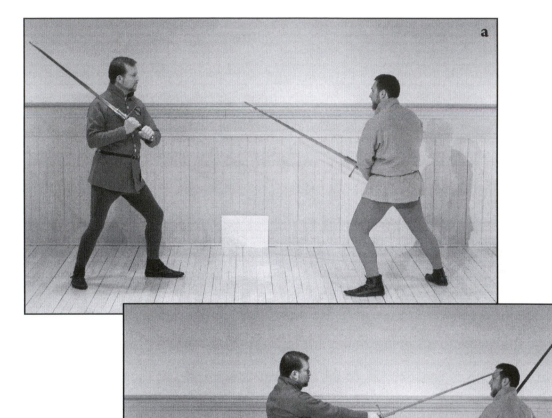

Fig. 1 As Janusz pulls back to charge a stroke, Christian follows after his motion, striking him (a-b).

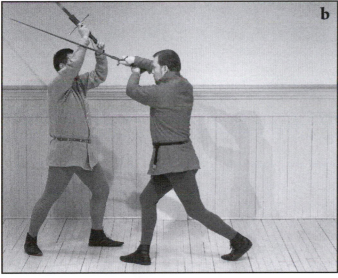

You can also chase after your opponent by inciting them to execute an over-extended stroke to you. Force them to miss by initially leaning forward a bit, fooling them into thinking you're standing closer than you really are, and then shifting your weight back so that your body is out of measure. Alternately, take a conservative step back with your left foot to void the blow.[52] Once their sword passes out of presence and heads toward the ground, thereby moving away from you, strike to their head with a big spring toward them. [Fig. 3]

Fig. 2 Janusz lifts his sword overhead to strike (a), so Christian passes across the line with his right foot to lay his edge onto Janusz's arms (b). He then passes with the left foot to continue pressing Janusz away (c).

---

[52] I have provided two evasive options, as the anonymous gloss only says, "*see that he doesn't reach you with the stroke*".

Fig. 3 Janusz strikes to Christian, who retreats with the left foot to let the blow pass harmlessly (a-b), and then springs forward with the right foot to counterattack (c).

Chasing on the Sword

Nachreisen can be employed on the sword as well. If you attack your opponent after they miss you, but they are able to bring their sword back up against yours, then step left with your left foot and hit the right side of their head with the *Zwerchhau*. [Fig. 4] Should they parry that, continue with the various techniques for dealing with binds and parries. This technique is known as an *Aussere Mynn* ("Outer Intention").

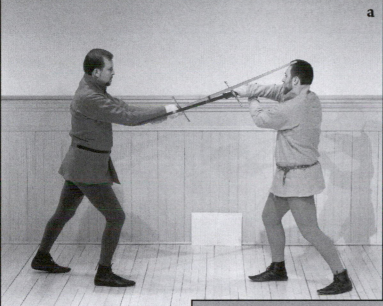

Fig. 4 Janusz now recovers quickly enough to parry Christian's counter-attack (a), so Christian passes with the left foot while delivering a left Zwerchhau *while in contact with Janusz's sword (b).*

Another option, should they lift their sword in time to prevent your counterstroke, is to leave their sword suddenly, either slicing hard into their neck, with a pass across the line with the right foot, [Fig. 5] or slicing down into their arms, with a left foot pass and compass step with the right foot. [Fig. 6] The first option will disrupt their structure, the second suppress their sword.

Whenever your opponent exposes an opening, either through mismanagement of time, measure, line, or initiative, you should chase after and hit them.

Fig. 5 Janusz again parries Christian's counterattack (a), so Christian steps across the line with his right foot to slice hard into Janusz's neck (b).

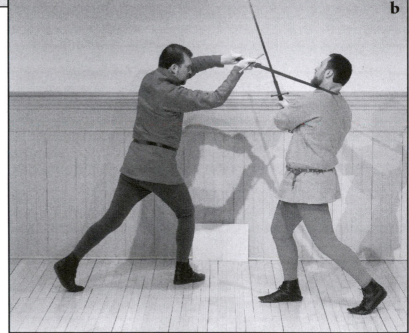

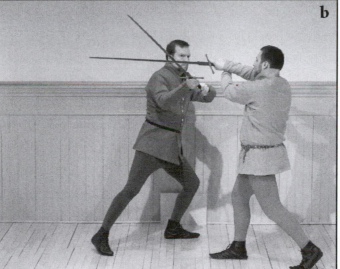

Fig. 6 Janusz once again parries Christian's counterattack (a), so Christian passes with the left foot and then compass steps back with the right to slice the arms (b-c).

Nachreisen

Drill 25: *Nachreisen*

- Stand in right *vom Tag*, with your partner in right *Pflug*.

- Your partner begins to lift their sword to right or high *vom Tag*.

- Spring and strike to your partner before they can complete their guard change.

- Repeat steps 1 – 2.

- Press your long edge to their forearms, with a right foot pass across the line, followed by a left foot pass, pressing them backward.

- Both partners now assume right *vom Tag*.

- Your partner makes a committed *Oberhau* with arms extended.

- Void the blow and spring to strike at them as soon as their blade passes before you.

- Repeat steps 6 – 8, but have your partner recover to bind against your attack.

- Spring with your left foot to their right side and strike a left *Zwerchhau*.

- Repeat steps 6 – 8, with your partner again binding your return attack.

- Slice the neck by passing across the line with the right foot, or down onto the arms with a left foot pass and right compass step.

Chapter 17:
Fühlen and Indes, an Interlude

Learn the feeling. The word "Indes" slices sharply.
                                    – Johannes Liechtenauer

In the middle of his chapter on *Nachreisen*, Liechtenauer pauses to remind us of the importance of the concept of *Indes*, the principle of acting *within the time of an opponent's action*. In this reminder segment, he also ties the notion of *Indes* with that of *Fühlen* ("Feeling"), the principle of sensing an opponent's intent through pressure, either at the sword or, when unarmed, at the body.

As I do no better than to present the *Von Danzig Fechtbuch*'s anonymous commentary on the matter, I quote it here in its entirety:

> *"Fühlen"* and the word *"Indes"* are the greatest and best of the art of the sword. And anyone who is or wants to be a master of the sword and does not understand the feeling, and has not also learnt the word "Indes," is not a master, but a buffalo at the sword. Therefore, before all else, you should learn these two things well so that you understand them truly.

> Here note a lesson on *Fühlen* and the word "Indes."

> Note when you come to him in the *Zufechten*, and one of you binds on the other's sword, then as soon as the swords clash together you should sense at once whether he has bound soft or hard at the sword. And as soon as you have felt that, then think upon the word "Indes," which means that as soon as you have felt, you should nimbly work on the sword; thus he will be struck before he is aware of it.

Here you should note that Fühlen *and* Indes *are one single thing, and that one cannot be understood without the other. Understand it thus: when you bind on his sword, then you must in the hand (at once) feel with the word "Indes" whether he is soft or hard on the sword. And when you have felt that, then you must instantly work according to the soft and hard at the sword. Thus the two of them are a single thing, and the word "Indes" is immanent in all techniques. And understand it thus:*

Indes *doubles,* Indes *transmutes,* Indes *changes through,* Indes *runs through,* Indes *takes the slice,* Indes *wrestles,* Indes *takes the sword.* Indes *does what your heart desires.*

"Indes" is a sharp word with which all masters of the sword are sliced, if they do not know or understand the word; it is the key to the art.[53]

As the passage makes clear, *Indes* and *Fühlen* inform every aspect of this fighting art: all that we have studied thus far in this volume, and all we can ever hope to learn of it. Be mindful of these two words, and the masters' advice on them, in all that you do.

---

[53] Peter Von Danzig, *Fechtbuch*, ff. 29r – 29v.

Chapter 18: Überlaufen

Who wants to strike below, overrun him, and he will be shamed.
When it clashes above, then strengthen: this I truly do praise.
Do your work, or press hard twice.

– Johannes Liechtenauer

We have seen examples of *Überlaufen* ("Overrunning") earlier in this book, in the 3rd and 7th response plays of Chapter 7. *Überlaufen* is the principle, rooted in simple geometry, which dictates that attacks (and defenses) made in the high line outreach those made in the low line. Hence, an attack to the legs is outreached by one to the head; the downward angle of an attack targeting the lower openings compromises its extension.

We are advised by the commentaries to avoid parrying an attack to the leg, instead voiding the opponent's blow and delivering a high counterattack. For example, if you stand in the high variant of *vom Tag*, and your opponent cuts to your leading leg, simply slip the leg backward (but conservatively!) as you cut straight down onto their head. [Fig. 1] This is even easier to execute than the similar play detailed in the previous chapter on *Nachreisen*, where you voided a blow and then stepped in for the counterattack. Because the opponent has squandered their measure by aiming low, it all happens in one tempo.

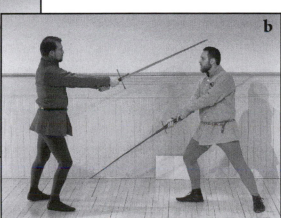

Fig. 1 Janusz attacks Christian's legs, so Christian voids the attack by retreating with his left foot and striking long to Janusz's head (a-b).

The texts also describe another consequence of the principle of *Überlaufen*: An *Unterhau* ("Stroke from Below") may be overreached by a counterattack above; the body mechanics of the former are such that it does not create as much extension as the latter. If your opponent attacks you with an *Unterhau*, then before they can come up all the way, shoot your point over their attack into *Langenort* ("Longpoint"), opposing their attack and thrusting them. If they try to parry this, continue to work against their sword with the winding or other techniques from the bind, familiar to us now in our travels. [Fig. 2]

> ### Drill 26: *Überlaufen*
>
> - You and a partner assume right *vom Tag*.
>
> - Your partner strikes to your left hip or leg.
>
> - Void the blow by passing back the left leg while striking an *Oberhau* to their head.
>
> - Both resume their guards.
>
> - Your partner strikes an *Unterhau*. Thrust into *Langenort* to forestall the stroke.

Fig. 2 Christian simultaneously suppresses Janusz's Unterhau *and counterthrusts by shooting his sword into* Langenort.

Chapter 19: Absetzen

Learn to set aside, to hinder stroke and thrust with skill.
Who thrusts at you, your point hits and counters his.
From both sides, hit every time if you want to step.

— Johannes Liechtenauer

Another of the *Hauptstücke*, Absetzen ("Setting Aside"), is the act of parrying a thrust or stroke by moving into one of the two hangings – the upper hanging, corresponding to the guard *Ochs*, or the lower one, *Pflug*. The parry ends with your point thrusting them. We briefly touched on this concept when training with the response drills of Chapter 7, for any counterstroke that falls short may transform into a thrust. Here we will see Absetzen employed as a technique in its own right.

Whether performed above or below, *Absetzen* provides swift defensive cover – provided you definitively move the sword first. The accompanying step is used to complete the action by driving the point home.

Both of the examples cited in the major manuscript glosses[54] begin in right *Pflug*. This provides your opponent with a tempting opening on the left side of your body.

In the first example, your opponent is also in right *Pflug*, and thrusts against you. You respond by strongly transitioning into left *Pflug*, setting aside their thrust by driving it down and away with your short edge. With a step forward of your right foot you then thrust to them, maintaining opposition against their sword, hitting them in the face or chest. [Fig. 1] All of this happens in one smooth motion, but the sword must move well before your body advances.

The second example finds you again in right *Pflug*, tempting your opponent to attack your left side. This time however your opponent attacks the left side of your head with a stroke, so you respond by forcefully moving into left *Ochs*, parrying their blow with your short edge. A step forward with the right foot then delivers your thrust. [Fig. 2]

These actions can be performed on the other side of the body, beginning in left *Pflug*, in answer to attacks from the opponent's left. The only difference is that you should now engage your long edge in the parry, whether low [Fig. 3] or high. [Fig. 4]

---

[54] By this I mean those found in the Ringeck, Von Danzig, Lew, and Speyer *Fechtbücher*.

Fig. 1 Both fencers face each other in right Pflug (a). Janusz thrusts, so Christian passes into left Pflug to set off the thrust and land a thrust of his own (b).

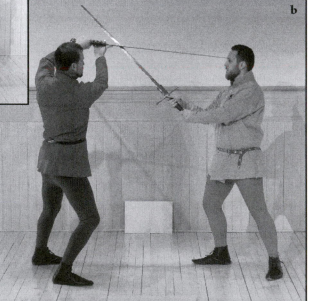

Fig. 2 Christian forms right Pflug, with Janusz in right vom Tag (a). As Janusz strikes an Oberhau, Christian passes into left Ochs, setting aside the blow and counterthrusting (b).

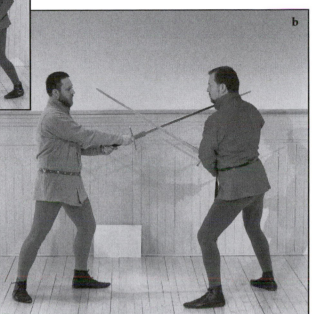

Fig. 3 Both fencers face each other in left Pflug (a). Janusz thrusts, so Christian passes into right Pflug to set off the attack and counterattack with a thrust (b).

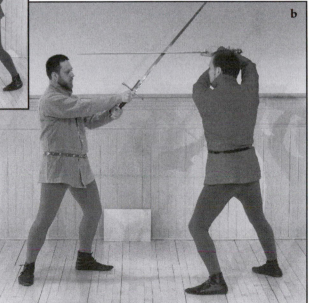

Fig. 4 Christian forms left Pflug, with Janusz in left vom Tag (a). Janusz strikes an Oberhau, so Christian passes into right Ochs, setting aside the blow to counterthrust (b).

Absetzen

Drill 27: *Absetzen*

- Assume right *Pflug,* with your partner in right *vom Tag.*

- Your partner attacks with an *Oberhau.*

- Move to left *Ochs,* with a pass forward of the right foot.

- Both partners now assume right *Pflug.*

- Your partner attacks with a thrust.

- Move to left *Pflug,* with a pass forward of the right foot.

Chapter 20:
Durchwechseln and Zucken

Learn the changing through from both sides, thrust with intent.
Whoever binds to you, change through and find him exposed.
[...]
Step close in bindings. The pulling provides good finds.
Pull - if he meets, pull more.
Work to find: that will hurt him.
Pull in all encounters with the Masters, if you want to fool them.
                                                        – Johannes Liechtenauer

Durchwechseln ("Changing Through") and *Zucken* ("Pulling") are closely related concepts; we saw examples of each in the earlier chapters on the five strokes. They are also given their own short chapters by Liechtenauer that serve to remind us of these ideas and broaden their scope.

Both are means for escaping or avoiding a bind where the opponent is fighting your sword and not the openings of the body, bringing your sword to the other side of their blade. The difference between the two is simple: When you change through (*Durchwechseln*), you drop your sword under the bind to circumvent it. When you pull (*Zucken*), you withdraw your sword to strike or thrust around and over the bind to the other side.

In our earlier foray into using *Durchwechseln* (in the chapter on the *Zornhau*), we let our sword's point come through under the bind when the opponent attempted to strike our point aside. However, this idea can be applied with even greater deceit by not allowing them to even make contact with the sword. If you can bait your opponent into striking at your point, you can drop it under their attempt to parry and come into the *Ochs* to thrust at them unopposed on the other side of their weapon.[55] This can be performed with a step across the line of engagement. Once the thrust hits, however, you should immediately come back into cover, striking their head and/or arms with a left foot pass, followed by a compass step of the right foot. This allows you to safely flank them. [Fig. 1]

Beware: You may change through safely only when your opponent has moved their point out of presence in their attempt to parry!

---

[55] I am indebted to Hans Heim and Alex Kiermayer for this interpretation, presented in their instructional DVD *The Longsword of Johannes Liechtenauer: Part I* by Agilitas TV.

Fig. 1 The fencers each begin in right vom Tag (a). Christian attacks, so Janusz tries to strike down Christian's point, but Christian drops his point under the potential bind, stepping pass across the line to thrust on the other side of Janusz's sword (b-c). Christian completes the action by passing with the left foot and compassing backward with the right to cut down onto the arms (d-e).

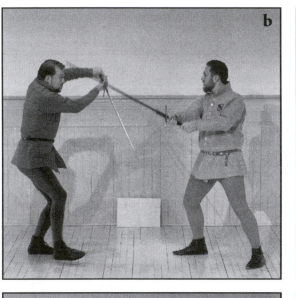

We saw earlier that *Zucken* could be used to leave a bind and strike around to the opponent's other side. Other exemplar techniques of the German masters make clear that the follow-on blow can also be a thrust, rather than a hewing stroke. Here is an elegant example of doing just that: Strike a right *Oberhau* to your opponent's upper left opening. Before they can bind against you, pull your sword back and around so that your come into the right *Ochs*, on the other side of their sword, and thrust to their face or chest. [Fig. 2]

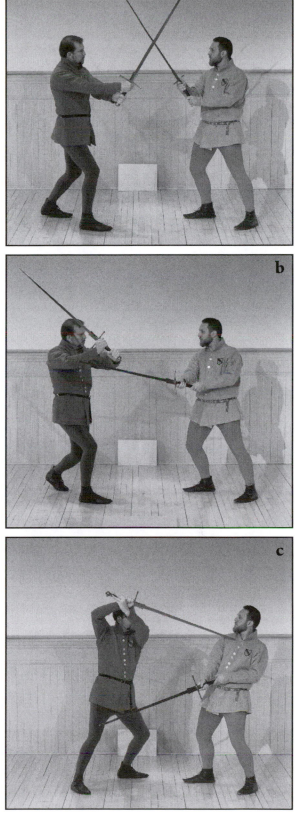

Fig. 2 Janusz moves to parry Christian's Oberhau (a), but Christian pulls back before the bind can ensue (b) to thrust on the other side of Janusz's sword (c).

Zucken may also be used to deceive your opponent. Rather than fully withdraw your sword, pull your sword only halfway out of the bind, and then immediately thrust back in at them in left *Ochs*. [Fig. 3] This works much like the feinted *Abnehmen* (itself a kind of *Zucken*) that we saw in the chapter on the *Vier Versetzen*, because the partially withdrawn blade naturally gains the weak of their blade, moving their sword aside and opening the door for your renewed attack. Remember the previous advice regarding feints: The opponent must believe that you are going to attack the other side of their sword for this to work. If they do not take the bait, then strike or thrust around to the other side.

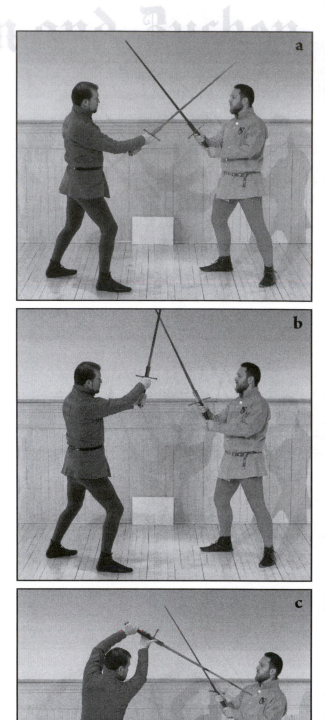

Fig. 3 From a bind (a), Christian pulls his sword partly back as if to leave the bind (b), but then thrusts back into Janusz in Ochs (c).

Durchwecheln and Zucken

Drill 28: *Durchwechseln* and *Zucken*

- Both partners assume right *vom Tag*.

- Attack your partner with an *Oberhau*.

- Your partner attempts to parry aside the tip of your sword.

- Change through under their parry to thrust in left *Ochs*.

- Pass left and compass step right to strike the head and arms.

- Both partners assume right *vom Tag*.

- Both partners strike *Oberhaue*.

- Before the bind ensues, pull back and into right *Ochs*, on the other side of their sword, with a pass of the left foot.

- Repeat steps 9 – 10, but now allow your opponent to strongly bind you. Pull your sword halfway up and out of the bind. Thrust back down immediately in left *Ochs*.

Chapter 21: Ringen

Be a good grappler in wrestling;
lance, spear, sword and messer
handle manfully,
and foil them in your opponent's hands
— Johannes Liechtenauer

The fighting arts of the Middle Ages were integrated systems of combat. Grappling or wrestling techniques were an important part of these arts. In fact, these disciplines appear to provide the foundation of all of the combat we find in the late medieval fighting treatises. Two of the four extant copies of the northern Italian master Fiore dei Liberi's treatises begin with wrestling stances and techniques, afterwards layering work with various weapons onto that foundation, while the earliest manuscript in the Liechtenauer tradition (*Hs. 3227a*) relates the aphorism "all fencing comes from wrestling."[56]

"Wrestling" is, unfortunately, an imperfect translation of either the Italian word Abrazare found in Fiore dei Liberi's treatises or the German word *Ringen*, at least in their medieval sense. Much like the word Fechten and its translation "fencing," the word *Ringen* encompasses much more than the word "wrestling" connotes today. In addition to the techniques one might see in today's collegiate wrestling, the art of wrestling in the Middle Ages included various striking techniques, joint destructions and throws, in addition to the takedowns, locks, and holds associated with wrestling today.

---

[56] Hs. 3227a, folio 86r.

The Jewish master Ott, who was "wrestling teacher to the noble Prince of Austria," wrote an influential treatise specifically on wrestling. He opens his work with a discussion on the general tactics of wrestling, wherein he employs the same notions of initiative that Master Liechtenauer considers so important:

> *In all wrestling, there should be three things. The first is skill. The second is quickness. The third is the proper application of strength. Concerning this, you should know that the best is quickness, because it prevents him from countering you. Thereafter you should remember that you should wrestle a weaker man in the Before, an equal opponent simultaneously,[57] and a stronger man in the After. In all wrestling in the Before, attend to quickness; in all simultaneous wrestling, attend to the balance; and in all wrestling in the After, attend to the crook of the knee.[58]*

There's much to be gleaned from this short prologue. If someone is weaker than you, you should simply seize the initiative and act in the *Vor* to quickly dispatch them. If they are stronger, you should respond in the *Nach* by waiting for a moment where they commit themselves and then pulling out their knee. When you face an equal opponent, you must keep your balance while working *Indes* ("Simultaneously") to unbalance them.

Ott's prologue could be read very literally. We might be tempted to conclude that we should simply gauge our opponent's overall physical strength at the outset and fight accordingly thereafter. I think, however, that there is more at play. While that simple meaning may also be there, a deeper one may be read from it.

The interplay of strength and leverage in a wrestling encounter can change rapidly. Therefore, it seems likely that one of the prologue's implications is that you should adapt your approach to the fight as it evolves, that is, as your opponent's ability to bring their strength to bear waxes and wanes with the progress of the encounter. In this regard, the decision-making process is guided much by the sense of *Fühlen* that we learned of in our study of the binding of the swords. As you feel your opponent's intent, you should use what tactics are appropriate based on that input.

Wrestling provides not only the kinesthetic foundation of Liechtenauer's art, but a tactical option in fencing with any weapon whenever one comes into close range with one's opponent. When you fight this way with the longsword, it is known as *Ringen Am Schwert* ("Wrestling at the Sword"). *Ringen Am Schwert* may be performed on foot or on horseback, in armour or out of it, and its principles can be applied while fencing with any weapon.

It is important for you to understand *Ringen Am Schwert* because it is an option whenever you bind swords, for you or your opponent. Before we learn to wrestle at the sword however, it will be helpful to learn some basics without a sword in our hands. In this chapter, we will turn to several unarmed techniques that will serve us well in many fighting scenarios. This will prepare us for the wrestling at the sword of the following chapter.

---

[57] The German word used here is *Geleichen*, which carries similar meaning to *Indes*.
[58] Peter von Danzig, *Fechtbuch*, folio 100v.

First, Some Safety Concerns

Although it may seem counter-intuitive, unarmed combat practice is often more dangerous than practice with a weapon. Everyone *knows* a sword is dangerous; after all, it is a sharp deadly weapon. However, the human body is a dangerous weapon too. If you practice grappling arts without the proper respect for what the body can and cannot do, you or your partner may be injured.

The techniques below include throws and takedowns, so you must prepare yourself properly if you want to train them in earnest. Simply working on a wrestling mat is not a sufficient precaution. You must train yourself to fall safely and work with a partner who has done the same. There are a number of good books on the market teaching the aikido and judo discipline of *Ukemi* ("Breakfalling") that are excellent sources for training this skill. However, I recommend the training presented by my student Jessica Finley in her book *Medieval Wrestling*, where she presents falling skills within the context of late medieval German fighting arts.

Until you have learned how to fall, I must strongly caution you to not follow the techniques of this section to their completion. Follow them only to the point where one combatant has the advantage and could fell their opponent. Practice these techniques slowly and carefully. In addition to the perils of falling incorrectly, the techniques involve joint locks and dislocations. No training should carry the price of permanent debilitation because of a destroyed joint, or death from a spinal injury or skull fracture. Whether you learn to fall correctly and can carry these techniques further or limit yourself to practicing them slowly, please train sensibly and safely.

Now that we have established some parameters for safety, let us explore some wrestling techniques and see the system's basic grappling concepts in action.

---

[59] Jessica Finley, *Medieval Wrestling*, Freelance Academy Press, 2014.

Measure

Early in this book, we saw the importance of measure, of managing the distance between yourself and your opponent. This is true even when there is no weapon in your hand. The German masters describe three measures, and associated techniques, for unarmed *Ringen*:

Zulaufen Ringen ("Wrestling in the Approach") – This is the distance, and phase of the fight, where you are coming toward your opponent. It is analogous to the term *Zufechten*, used in the techniques for the sword. [Fig. 1]

Arme Ringen ("Wrestling at the Arms") – At this distance, you and your opponent have seized each other by the arms. This means that you have grasped them with one hand inside the opposite bicep, with the other hand outside the opposite arm. Your opponent mirrors your position. [Fig. 2]

Leib Ringen ("Wrestling at the Body") – At this measure, you and your opponent have seized each other at or around the body. Each wrestler has a hand high, either at or over the shoulder, and the other hand low, at or around the hip or waist. [Fig. 3] At very close range, the two hands may clasp behind the back of the opponent. [Fig. 4]

Fig. 1 Two open guards for approaching the opponent, low and high.

Fig. 2 Grips for wrestling at the arms, with each wrestler placing one hand inside the opponent's bicep and the other outside the other arm.

Fig. 3 Shallow grips at the body, with each wrestler grasping the other by the shoulder and hip.

Fig. 4 Deeper grips at the body, with each wrestler clasping the hands together around the opponent's back.

Mordstöße – Murder Strikes

Despite the colorful name, these techniques would rarely cause death on their own. Instead, in *Ringen* they are used to either soften up an opponent as you start to grapple, or to work them over once you've established a joint lock or hold. The *Kunst des Fechtens* is a medieval combat art, suitable for use on the battlefield and in the lists in a judicial duel and, like all such arts, includes techniques for both grappling and striking. Although there are usually more techniques for grappling, striking techniques figure importantly in the medieval German fighting manuscripts. Such strikes are often called *Mordstöße*, or "Murder Strikes." As you learn about the wrestling techniques that follow, you will see opportunities where one of these strikes might be employed to make an opponent more cooperative in being taken to the ground.

The mid-15th century manuscript attributed to Master Sigmund Ringeck includes a section on these strikes. It includes a strike over the heart with the fist, a knee strike to the groin, a blow with the fist to the temple, a strike with both fists to the neck, a technique for driving the thumbs into the cheeks and a punch to the stomach. After the description for each of these techniques follows the admonition *"and then wrestle."*[60] The implication here is that the techniques are meant to stun or distract the opponent and thus create an opportunity to contain them with grappling techniques proper. We read in other texts of techniques where the opposite is done: An opponent is contained with a takedown or joint lock of some sort and this allows one to strike them in relative safety.

Mordstöße, like strikes or kicks from any martial art, must be performed with the whole body working together, not just the hands or legs. The hips, shoulder, and the connecting muscles of the torso must all work in harmony to deliver the blow powerfully while keeping your balance.

Drei Ringen – The Three Wrestlings

Nestled within the cornucopia of grappling techniques found in the "Ringeck *Fechtbuch*" are three techniques grouped together and named only as *Drei Ringen* ("Three Wrestlings"). At first glance, these do not seem to be of special significance. I have found, however, that these three techniques offer a key to all takedowns and throws that can be performed with or without a weapon in hand. I therefore teach them as fundamentals.

The three wrestling techniques contain key concepts for taking an opponent to the ground. These concepts all employ the idea of push-pull leverage: If you push someone above their center of gravity while pulling below it, or pull someone above their center of gravity while pushing below it, they will fall down or at the least lose their balance, which gives you the advantage.

The basic principles that appear in the *Drei Ringen* are:

- You can use one of your hands to push one part of your opponent's body while the other hand pulls.

- Creating forward pressure against the back of your opponent's knee while creating backward pressure against their neck or upper body will cause them to fall backward.

---

[60] Sigmund Ringeck, *Fechtbuch*, folios 73r–74r, 76r–77v.

- Conversely, creating backward pressure against the front of your opponent's leg while creating forward pressure against their neck or upper body will cause them to fall forward.

- Should your opponent thwart your attempt to throw them with one hand high and the other low, you can reverse which hand holds them above and which holds them below.

- All three wrestlings may be used interchangeably. When one fails, another may be brought to bear.

- All three wrestlings may be used in countering each other. They comprise a very tidy and self-referential sub-system within the Kunst des Fechten.

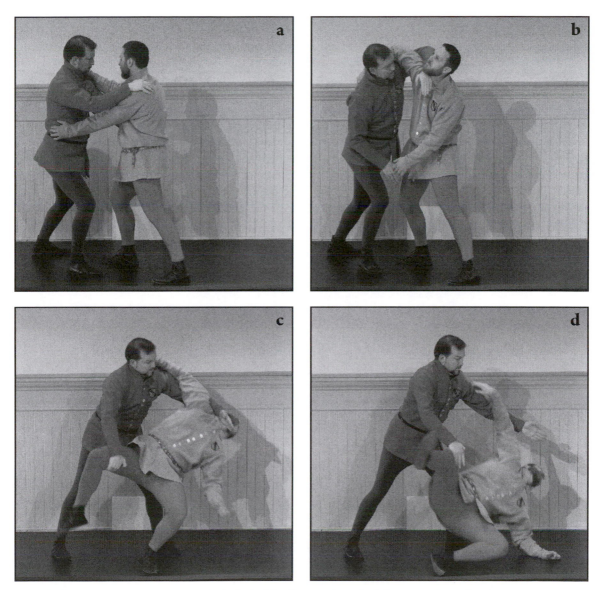

Fig. 5 The First Wrestling. From a grip at the body (a), Christian drives his left arm over Janusz's right upper arm to the neck, breaking the latter's structure (b). As Janusz begins turning and losing his balance, Christian grabs Janusz's right leg and passes forward with his left foot, completing the throw (c-d) by pushing the upper body while pulling on the leg.

As in the original manuscript, I will present them starting from a clinch at the body (*Leib Ringen*). Also, each technique will begin with the wrestlers leading with their right leg, but note that the techniques can be performed on the opposite side of the body by reversing the role of each hand, with the left leg leading, as well.

The First Wrestling

The technique begins with you and your opponent in a clinch. Like all of the Three Wrestlings it has a left and right variant, so the technique is based on which hand is higher or lower in that moment. They grasp your waist with the left hand and your shoulder or collar area with the right. You in turn mirror their hand positions with your own.

From this position, you drive your left hand up and across their right arm, the one they are using to hold your upper body. As you do this, you must apply inward pressure with your left arm to the part of their arm that is just above the elbow. This is a control point for containing their upper body's movement and is an important leverage point in many wrestling techniques. As you move your left hand across their arm and upper body, turn your hand so that your thumb is up and press across their neck.

As you are doing this, reach down with your right hand to grab their right leg. Grab just above and behind the knee. Then, pass directly forward with your left foot. In one motion, bring your entire body to bear with a twist of the hips to throw them by pushing their neck while pulling out their leg. By applying push-pull leverage, and employing very little strength, you are able to

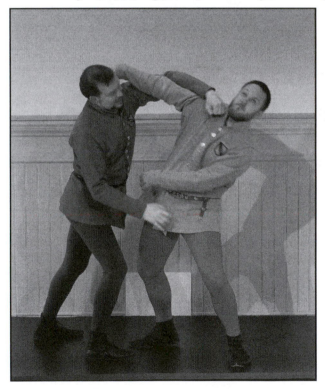

Fig. 6 A strike to the face or throat can be employed to "soften up" an opponent as their upper body is brought under control in this alternate start to the First Wrestling.

throw your opponent backward. The forward movement of your weight, focused at their neck, coupled with the backward pull at their knee, moves their center of gravity backward, causing them to fall. [Fig. 5]

You may notice that the motion of your left hand from low to high to reach their neck is very much like driving your sword from *Pflug* through *Ochs* and then to *Langenort*. This should be no surprise, for the system's core principles are universal, regardless of the weapon.

A strike (one of the *Mordstöße*) can easily be incorporated into the technique to stun your opponent as you go to throw them. Before pressing their neck, strike their face first or slam your hand hard into their windpipe as you move to grab them for the throw. Of course, for safety's sake, this step can only be simulated in practice. [Fig. 6]

The Second Wrestling

This technique is nothing more than switching which hand is employed at the neck with the one that is at the leg. If you attempt to throw your opponent with the first wrestling, they may respond by preventing you from grabbing their neck.

This is tactically very similar to the situation where, in a bind with the longsword, your opponent commits strongly to defending one part of the body and thereby exposes another. The response here is much the same. If someone strongly defends one opening of the body, attack the opening they expose.

Thus, if your opponent pushes aside your left hand as you reach for their neck, bring your right hand up from below to press their neck. Let the left hand now drop down to grab behind the knee. Using the same push-pull action as in the First Wrestling, push their neck while pulling out the leg and throw them backward to the ground. By switching the hand above with the one below you follow the force and direction of their reaction and continue to press the offensive. Your hips must follow along with this motion; you must use the opposite hip rotation when you switch from the First Wrestling to the Second Wrestling. [Fig. 7]

Fig. 7 The Second Wrestling. Christian begins the First Wrestling, but Janusz prevents it by striking aside Christian's arm (a). Christian responds by exchanging the hand he has above with the one below, pushing Janusz's chest and throat with his right hand and grabbing the right leg with his left hand (b). Christian clears Janusz's leg by compassing back with his left foot (c).

The Third Wrestling

The third and last technique addresses the situation where your opponent, either initially, or in response to your attempt to throw them backwards, is moving their center of gravity forward. The correct thing to do here is therefore to go with the flow of their momentum and instead throw them forward. In our overview of basic principles earlier, we learned that if one is to throw an opponent forward, one should push the leg backward while pulling the upper body forward.

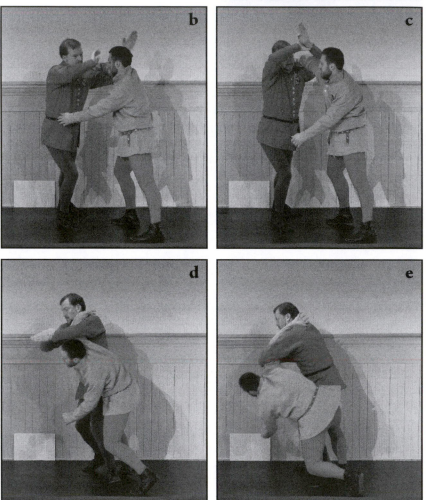

Fig. 8 The Third Wrestling. From the grip at the body, Christian once more drives over Janusz's upper right arm with his left arm (a-b), but now grasps his own left wrist with his right hand (c). Christian then steps with his left foot inside of Janusz's right foot and pulls Janusz around his left hip to throw him down (d-e). Christian's compass step backward with his right foot facilitates the throw.

Just as in the First Wrestling, move the left hand up and over their right arm. Only this time, rather than going for their neck, you should encircle their upper arm and then grab your left wrist with your right hand to tightly trap their arm. This will allow you to pull their upper body forward. Backward pressure against their right leg is created by stepping in front of it with your left foot.

Now, swing your right leg around backward with a compass step, pivoting on the left foot you have in front of their leg, while your hips and shoulders twist in the same rotational motion as your backward compass step to provide power for the takedown. Your weight must be focused forward and downward, creating further momentum. The arms do not provide much of the power or motion for this action. They primarily secure the opponent's upper body, but it is your torso and the bracing of your skeleton against theirs that does the actual work. [Fig. 8]

Another variant of this technique is useful to know should things go slightly awry. If your opponent denies you their arm as you try to entrap it, continue with your left hand to grab around their neck. You can, and should, still bring the right hand to grab your own wrist, "tightening the noose." From there, the action continues the same as before. Swing backward with the right foot while the left bars their right leg and bring them to the ground. [Fig. 9]

Fig. 9 In this alternate execution of the Third Wrestling, Janusz denies Christian's attempt to control his right arm (a), so Christian seizes him about the neck instead (b).

Applying the Three Wrestlings

As noted earlier, all Three Wrestlings can be mirrored to work on the opposite side of the body from the one we have illustrated here. Look for which arm your opponent has forward as you approach and move your hand over it to seize the throat with the First Wrestling, or seize it with both hands as in the third technique.

The Three Wrestlings all work together. If you try to use the First Wrestling, and they set off your arm, you can use the Second wrestling, as we saw earlier. If they move to counter it by moving forward, switch to the Third Wrestling. [Fig. 10] In the same way, should you attempt to use the Third Wrestling and they pull back, go with the flow, and release the trap around the arm, pushing their neck while dropping your other hand to the knee. [Fig. 11]

Fig. 10 Christian attempts the First Wrestling, but Janusz pitches his weight forward (a), so Christian switches instead to the Third Wrestling (b-c) to capitalize on Janusz's direction of movement, casting him down forward.

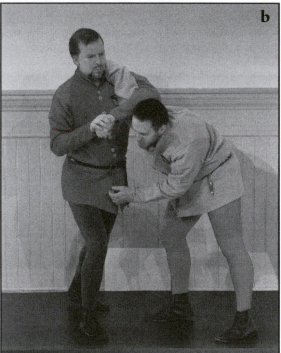

The key to knowing which technique to employ is *Fühlen* ("Feeling"). This is the same concept so important in binds with the longsword. Here, you must feel your opponent's intention through direct contact with their body, rather than the pressure applied through their sword. That sense of intention will tell you if they mean to shift their weight forward or back, or if they want to move their arms to prevent you from grabbing them. Their intent must inform your choice of which wrestling technique to use.

The three wrestling techniques can also be used to counter each other. For example, if someone attempts to use the First Wrestling against you, you can capitalize on their forward momentum and employ the Third Wrestling against them. And, although we have started each of these techniques from a clinch, you can use these techniques, and variants based on them, as you approach to grappling range as well. We will now see that concept at work as we add the longsword into our repertoire of grappling techniques.

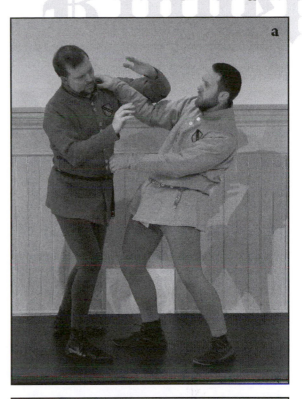

Fig. 11 Christian attempts the Third Wrestling, but Janusz leans away backward (a), so Christian follows after him, switching to employ the First Wrestling to throw him backward and down (b).

Ringen

Drill 29: *Drei Ringen*

- Both partners lead with the right leg. Approach to grasp at the body.

- Grasp your partner at the left shoulder with your right hand and at the right hip with your left hand. Have your partner do the same to you.

- Begin the First Wrestling: Drive your left hand up and over their right arm and to the neck.

- Begin turning your left hand so the thumb is up, turning their head and pushing their neck.

- Grab their right knee with your right hand as their balance begins to fail as you pass forward with your left leg to thrown them backward.

- Resume grabbing each other at the body.

- Begin to do the First Wrestling, driving your left hand over their arm.

- Your partner pushes your left hand away with their arm.

- Drive your right up to their neck while dropping your left hand to their right knee.

- Pull the leg up while pushing the neck, without stepping, to push them over backward.

- Resume grabbing each other at the body.

- Drive your left hand up and over their right arm.

- Bring the right hand to grab your left wrist.

- Step with your left foot in front of their right foot.

- Swing back and around with your right foot to throw them forward.

- Repeat all steps with a left leg lead, reversing the roles of the hands and arms.

Chapter 22:
Durchlaufen

Run through, let hang
with the pommel. Grasp if you want to wrestle.
Who comes strongly at you,
the running through then remember.
— Johannes Liechtenauer

The techniques for wrestling at the sword are grouped in Liechtenauer's treatise under the chapter heading of *Durchlaufen*, or "Running Through," which contains methods for bypassing a rushing attack. By running through under your opponent's arms, you can close and either throw them or take their sword. The commentaries on *Durchlaufen* usually include three families of methods: the wrestling at the body, where you literally run through the attack to grip the body and bring your opponent down in the process; wrestling at the arms, which are techniques for taking down an opponent while grasping their arms; and *Schwert Nehmen* ("Sword Taking"), which are methods for disarming an opponent.

All of these methods are related in that all involve coming into range where contact with the arms or body is likely.

Wrestling at the Body

The wrestling at the body is performed when your opponent attempts to rush or bear down on you in such a way that they keep their hands, and thereby their sword, high.

If you and your opponent come to a bind by each striking from the right side, and the swords are high, they may try to rush your right side. If they do, you can gain their flank by stepping with either of your feet. Depending on the space between you, it may be more advantageous to step with your left foot or your right. Below are descriptions for both scenarios. If you do not step where you initially intend, you can adapt to either a forward or backward takedown easily just by altering where you grab. Note that in these examples, it is always the rotation of the body that powers these throws, not muscle power from the arms.

When stepping with the right foot, step across such that your foot lands behind their right foot. Let go of your sword with your right hand, letting the sword hang behind your back for cover. Now use your right hand to grab around their midsection to the left side of their body. Grab-

bing higher up will allow you to better constrain their arms from coming down on you. Pull your opponent *around* your right hip to throw them onto their back. [Fig. 1] This is an application of the First Wrestling, seen in the previous chapter.

If you are unable to step deeply enough to land behind their right foot (i.e., your right foot lands in front of their foot instead), grab all the way around their back with your right hand. Then pull them around your right hip, so that they fall forward, face first, behind you. [Fig. 2] This is an application of the Third Wrestling.

Fig. 1 From a bind, Janusz presses Christian (a), who responds by letting go of his sword with his right hand to seize his opponent under the arms while cross-stepping behind Janusz's right leg and casting him down over the hip (b). The left hand continues to hold the sword, creating cover at all times.

Fig. 2 Here, Christian steps instead before Janusz's right leg and grabs the latter around the back, throwing him forward over the hip.

You may instead step with your left foot. This is particularly advantageous if their right leg is easily accessible. Taking care to use your hilt to contain their sword to your right, now let go of your sword with your *left* hand. Step such that your foot lands behind theirs. Then, grab under their arms around their chest. Pull them around your left hip, throwing them onto their back. [Fig. 3] This is another application of the First Wrestling.

If you are unable to step deeply enough to land behind their left foot (i.e., your left foot lands in front of theirs instead), then grab around their back, throwing them forward by pulling them around your left hip. [Fig. 4] This is another application of the Third Wrestling.

The above techniques are shown from a right-side bind, but reversing the actions will easily accommodate a bind formed when both parties have struck from their left.

Fig. 3 Janusz again presses Christian in a close bind (a). Christian lets go of his sword with his left hand and passes behind Janusz's right leg with his left while grasping beneath Janusz's arms to throw his opponent over the hip backward (b). Here the right hand wields the sword to both create cover and threaten with the pommel.

Fig. 4 Christian now steps before Janusz's right leg, so he grabs around the latter's back to cast him forward over the hip instead of backwards.

Drill 30: Wrestling at the Body

- Begin in a bind with your partner, as if each had struck from the right side.

- Your partner presses down on your sword with their arms high.

- Let your sword hang down with your left hand. Cross step with your right foot behind their right foot, while grabbing them about the body, under their arms, with your right hand. Throw them onto their back over your right hip.

- Re-form the bind. Your partner again presses down on your sword with their arms high.

- Let your sword hang down with your left hand. Step with your right foot in front of their right foot, while grabbing them around the back with your right hand. Throw them onto their face over your right hip.

- Re-form the bind. Your opponent now drives toward your right with their arms high.

- Let go of your sword with your left hand. Use your hilt to press their sword and arms to your right.

- Step with your left foot behind their right foot while grabbing around their body, under their arms, with your left hand. Throw them onto their back over your left hip.

- Re-form the bind. Your opponent again drives toward your right with their arms high.

- Let go of your sword with your left hand. Use your hilt to press their sword and arms to your right.

- Step with your left foot in front of their right foot while grabbing around their back with your left hand. Throw them onto their face over your left hip.

- Repeat all steps, but with each partner now coming to the bind from wide measure by striking.

Wrestling at the Arms

The wrestling at the arms is used when your opponent rushes you with their arms presented low and forward. It is now impractical to simply run through their attack, so the arms are grappled instead.

When they start to press forward, stepping with their left foot, with their hands low, then let go of your sword with your left hand. Invert your free hand and grab their right wrist with your thumb facing down. Now pull their hand, and thereby their sword, strongly to your left. This opens the door for you either to deliver a single-handed blow to their head, or to step behind their left foot with your right, pressing their neck to throw them over your right knee. [Fig. 5] This throw is another application of the First Wrestling.

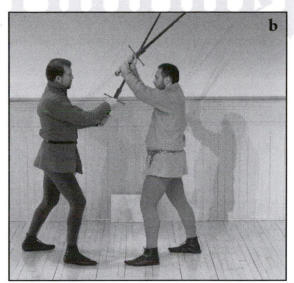

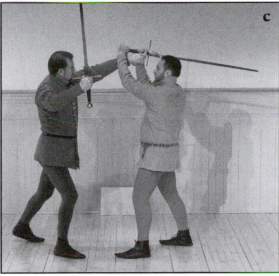

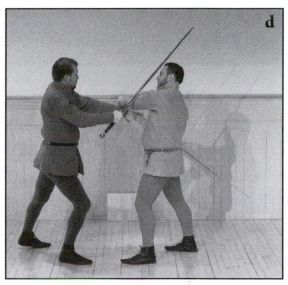

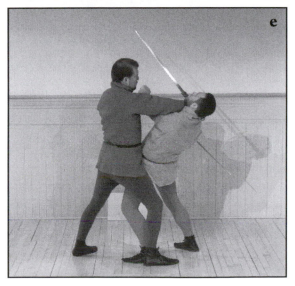

Fig. 5 From bind, Janusz passes in with his left foot to press Christian above (a-b). Christian seizes Janusz's right wrist with his left hand, pulling it to his left, while threatening with his sword (c). From here, Christian can either strike Janusz in the head (d) or step behind him to hook him with the pommel and throw him down (e).

As with the wrestling at the body, you can also use your *left* foot as a prop for the opponent's downfall. As they press you with their hands low and leading with their right foot, let go of your sword with your left hand. Use your right hand to hook your pommel over their right wrist, while employing your left hand to push their right elbow up and inward toward their center of balance.[61] Only as you gain control of their arm should you step in front of their right foot with your left. Finish the action by pulling their wrist down and toward you as you press the elbow, pulling them around your leg and down onto their face. [Fig. 6] This is another application of the Third Wrestling.

Fig. 6 Janusz is strong in this bind (a), so Christian hooks the wrist with his pommel and grabs the upper arm, and then steps before Janusz's right foot, throwing him forward over the hip (b). This is done with a push up and over at the upper arm, a strong pull at the wrist, and a compass step back and around with the right foot.

---

[61] This technique appears often throughout the Liechtenauer tradition corpus, across the entire spectrum of knightly weapons. It is sometimes given the name "The Elbow into the Balance."

Drill 31: Wrestling at the Arms

- Begin in a bind with your partner, as if each had struck from the right side.

- Your partner presses your sword with their arms low, stepping with the left foot.

- Let go of your hilt with the left hand. Invert your left hand and grab inside their right hand, between the hands.

- Pull your partner's hands and sword to your left, while striking their head with your sword using your right hand.

- Repeat steps 1 – 3.

- Again pull your partner's hands to the left. Step with your right foot behind their left foot while bringing your right arm to their neck. Throw them backward over your right knee.

- Re-form the bind. Your partner presses you, but remains leading with their right leg.

- Release your left hand. Drive your pommel over their right wrist.

- Grab their right elbow with your left hand. Step with your left before their right foot.

- Pull with the pommel while pushing up and over with the left hand. Throw them over your leg onto their face.

- Repeat all steps, but with each partner now coming to the bind from wide measure by striking.

Schwert Nehmen – Sword Taking

Disarming techniques, or *Schwert Nehmen* ("Sword Taking"), are usually included among the commentaries for Liechtenauer's *Durchlaufen*, and with good reason: anytime you or your opponent close to grappling range, you may have an opportunity to grab your opponent's sword. Here are several sword disarming techniques addressing various situations.

One simple sword taking starts from a bind in *Pflug*. If your opponent binds against your sword after striking from their right side, let go of your sword with your left hand, grab their sword grip or pommel (whichever you can grasp), with

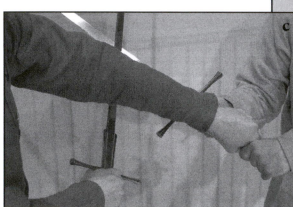

your left arm against both blades. While keeping up pressure with your arm, pull your left hand to your left with a counterclockwise rotation to disarm them. [Fig. 7] This will work even if you miss grabbing their grip: Just use the back of your hand to press their sword's grip instead.

Fig. 7 From an equal bind (a), Christian releases his left hand from his sword to grab Janusz's sword grip while using his arm to keep pressure on both blades (b-c). A counterclockwise pull with the left hand wrenches the sword out of Janusz's hands (d).

If it is hard to reach your opponent's pommel with your left hand, then instead clamp your sword blade against your opponent's where the swords cross, using your inverted (thumb facing down) left hand. While holding the blades tightly together, move your pommel clockwise and forward over their right hand and then towards your right side, with a rowing action, to pull their sword away from them. Rotate your shoulders and hips back to the right to employ your whole body in disarming them. [Fig. 8]

If your opponent strikes a *Zwerchhau* from their left side and you bind against it in right *Pflug*, then let go of your sword with your left hand and seize their pommel or grip. Push their blade toward them with your right hand while pulling with your left to disarm them. Your hips must turn to your left to power this push-pull motion. [Fig. 9]

Should your opponent lift up their sword from *Alber* into the *Kron* to answer an attack of yours from above, they may try to rush in to wrestle with you, as we discussed in the last chapter. As they close, grab their pommel with your inverted left hand and push it upward and to the left to break their grip from their sword while driving forward with your weight, so that the strength of the body is opposed to the strength of their hands. [Fig. 10] A similar action will work if things get too close in the *Krieg* and your opponent lifts their sword to overwhelm you from above. If they do, reach over their right arm with your inverted left hand, grab their grip or pommel and push upward to your left to take their sword. [Fig. 11]

Drill 32: *Schwert Nehmen*

- Begin in a bind with your partner, as if each had struck from the right side.
- Release your left hand from the hilt. Grab their grip or pommel.
- Keep your left arm against the bound swords. Move your left hand in a counter-clockwise motion to disarm the opponent.
- Re-form the bind. Release your left hand and use it to clamp the blades together in the middle.
- Drive your pommel clockwise over their hands with a rowing motion to disarm them.
- From wide measure, both partners form left *Vom Tag*.
- Your partner strikes a left *Zwerchhau*. Bind against this in right *Pflug*.
- Release your left hand. Keeping pressure with your sword against theirs, grab their pommel or grip. Pull with the left hand to disarm them.
- Have your partner assume *Alber*. Attack them with a *Scheitelhau*.
- Your partner parries in *Kron* and rushes in with the pommel.
- Release your left hand. Grab with this hand inverted to their pommel.
- Drive forward and left with your hand to disarm them.
- Repeat all steps, adding in an approach before the bind ensues.

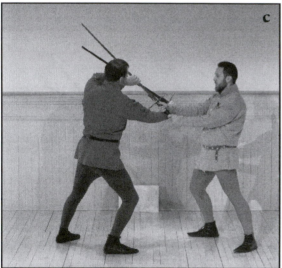

Fig. 8 From an equal bind (a), Christian lets go of his sword with his left hand, inverts it, and clamps both blades together (b). He then drives his pommel, using a tight, clockwise rowing motion (c), over Janusz's right arm to pull the sword away from him (d), passing backward with the right foot to retreat while creating menace with both sword points (e).

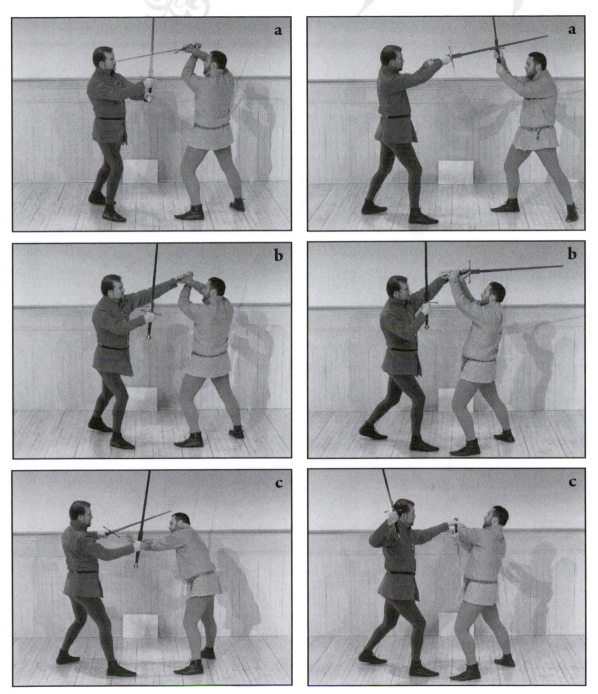

Fig. 9 Christian parries Janusz's left Zwerchhau (a), grabs Janusz's pommel with his left hand (b), and, pushes with his blade and pulls by the pommel, relieving his opponent of his sword (c).

Fig. 10 Janusz parries Christian's Scheitelhau in Kron (a) and steps forward to rush him, so Christian grabs Janusz's pommel (b) and wrenches it to the left while threatening with his sword (c).

Durchlaufen

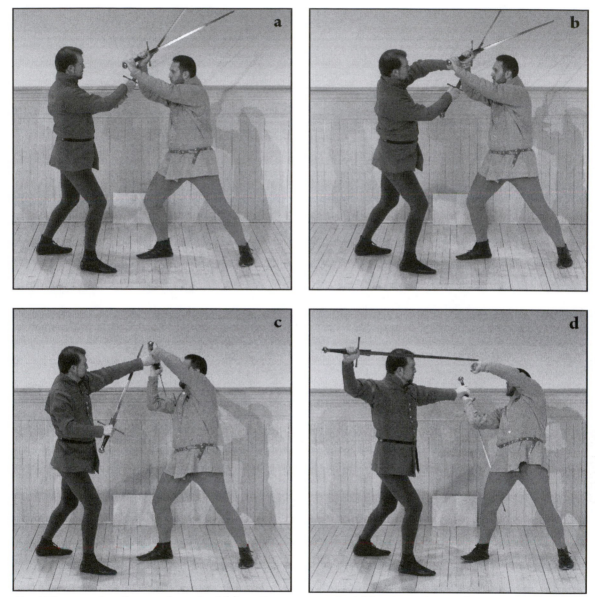

Fig. 11 Janusz rushes Christian from a bind (a), so Christian inverts his left hand to grab Janusz's right wrist, wrenching it to the left (b-c), and drops his point under and through to threaten a thrust (d).

Chapter 23: Sprechfenster

Execute the Speaking Window;
stand freely and look at his actions.
Strike him until he is defeated
when he withdraws from you,
I say to you truthfully:
no one protects himself without danger.
If you have learned this, he will scarcely manage a blow.

– Johannes Liechtenauer

*L*angenort ("Longpoint") is a very old guard. It appears in several forms in the oldest extant European fighting manuscript, the so-called *Tower Fechtbuch*, Royal Armouries Ms. I.33. We have learned that the *Langenort* is also a very important position; attacks, whether strokes or thrusts, often terminate in or pass through this position. However, it is also a position of provocation, for if the *Langenort* is held against an opponent's face or chest, they must address this concern before attacking you.

Langenort appears in Liechtenauer's verse through its epithet, the *Sprechfenster* ("Speaking Window"). It is called this because when you have bound against an opponent's blade, you can stand with your arms outstretched, using *Fühlen* ("Feeling") to sense their actions through their blade. Their intent "speaks" to you through the "window" created by the bind. Thus, the *Sprechfenster* may be thought of as an *application* of the guard *Langenort*. The von Danzig commentaries laud this guard and connect the *Sprechfenster* and *Langenort* rather nicely:

> Note, you have learned before how, when you are before your opponent, you should position yourself in the four guards from which you are to fight. Then you should also now know the Speaking Window, which is a guard that you can stand well in. And this guard is the Longpoint, and this is the noblest and the best. Whoever can truly fight from it at the sword can coerce his foe so that he must be hit whether he likes it or not, and cannot manage to strike or thrust before your point.[62]

The use of the *Langenort* in this context is quite sophisticated, for it brings together many of the concepts of initiative and tactile sensitivity that we have seen in the preceding techniques. This sophistication is reflected in the above commentary: When you know how to use the *Langenort/Sprechfenster*, you can coerce your opponent into doing something disadvantageous.

---

[62] Peter Von Danzig, *Fechtbuch*, folios 36r, 36v.

The *Sprechfenster* can result in two scenarios, one where you have crossed swords and stand bound with your opponent, and the other where you hold the *Langenort* directed against them so that they must try to get around it to attack you.

The *Sprechfenster* at the Sword

You can employ the *Sprechfenster* as a probe once you have bound to an opponent's sword. If you strike to them, adjusting your extension so that your point is before their face or chest in the bind, you can remain in this position until you sense what they want to do. Let us examine what happens if both combatants have bound after striking from their right sides. You should remain in the bind with your arms moderately outstretched and use *Fühlen* to determine the proper response to your opponent's actions.

If you sense that your opponent is soft in the bind, you can simply thrust to one of their open-

ings, just as in the first technique of the *Zornhau* in Chapter 9. If you sense them departing from your blade so that they can strike around to your right side with an *Oberhau*, you should follow their movement by passing with your left foot and binding to their blade with your long edge as it comes around, hitting them in the head as you bind. [Fig. 1] However, if they strike around high and horizontally with the *Zwerchhau*, then pass with your left foot, bind against their arms and slice their arms with the *Oberschnitt*. [Fig. 2]

Fig. 1 In a bind, Christian provokes Janusz with the Sprechfenster *(a). As Janusz attempts to strike around from the bind, Christian suppresses his stroke with one of his own, stepping with the left foot (b).*

Fig. 2 Janusz now attempts to strike a Zwerchhau *around from the bind, so Christian falls upon his arms with the* Oberschnitt.

Your opponent may also try to strengthen against your sword so they can align their own point for a thrust from below while removing the threat of your point. If they do this, use the *Nachreisen* to follow their actions by bringing your hilt high into the left *Ochs* so that you command their point. In this way, you can prevent their thrust while chambering one of your own. [Fig. 3] Make sure you provide enough pressure against their point as you do this so that they cannot align their point correctly against you while you move up with your hilt. Otherwise, there is risk to you as their point is moving across your body. Do not do this with just your hands; turn your hips as you move into *Ochs* to bring your body into the action.

Fig. 3 Janusz attempts to force Christian's sword aside, so Christian winds into left Ochs to counter.

You can also use the *Duplieren* if they provide strong pressure against your sword. [Fig. 4] A small advancing step of the right foot may be needed to facilitate this.

If your opponent tries to beat your *point* aside, this affords you the perfect opportunity to change through and thrust along the other side of their blade as they expose themselves. As they push your point aside, let it slide free as you set your weight back onto your trailing foot (the left foot, in this case) to chamber a thrust of your own. Shift your weight forward again once you have cleared their blade and thrust anew into the *Langenort* against them. [Fig. 5]

Fig. 4 From the bind (a), Janusz applies strong pressure, so Christian performs a Duplieren (b).

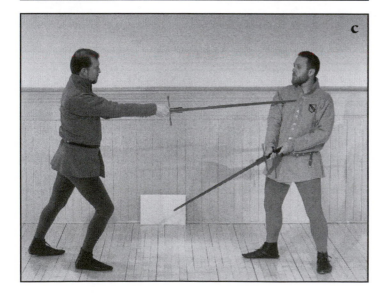

Fig. 5 Janusz strikes aside Christian's point (a), so he performs a Durchwechseln to thrust on the other side of the sword (b-c).

The *Sprechfenster* Disengaged

You can also probe an opponent's intent with the *Sprechfenster* without even touching their blade. If you extend your sword into the *Langenort* against them, they must try to get past your blade before giving you offense. It requires two fencing times for them to do this, as they are not quite in wide measure, while you are. As the von Danzig commentaries say:

> *…when you have come almost to him in the Zufechten, then set your left foot forward and hold your point long from your arms against his face or breast before you bind to his sword and stand calmly to observe what he will execute against you.*[63]

This tricky manipulation of distance, of not quite coming to them in the Zufechten, forces your opponent to give you the advantage of timing, provided they go for the bait.

Your opponent may try to step deeply around your point and deliver an *Oberhau* from their right side against you. If they do, simply wind your sword upward into left *Ochs* and thrust against them in opposition with their blade, a common tactic that we have seen before. [Fig. 6] If, however, they strike from their left side against your sword, use this to help propel a *Zwerchhau* against their left side. [Fig. 7]

As was the case with the *Sprechfenster* at the sword, the same tactic is employed if your opponent beats aside your point: Change through. Let the point drop under and through the bind and thrust against them, as before. [Fig. 8]

Drill 33: The *Sprechfenster* at the Sword

- You and a partner begin in right *vom Tag*.
- Both partners strike *Oberhaue*. Be sure your stroke binds theirs, with your point threatening the face or chest.
- Your partner provides weak pressure in the bind. Thrust to the face or chest.
- Repeat steps 1 – 2.
- Your partner leaves the bind to strike an *Oberhau* to your right side. Bind their sword while hitting the head.
- Repeat steps 1 – 2.
- Your partner leaves the bind to strike a left *Zwerchhau*. Slice their arms.
- Repeat steps 1 – 2.
- Your partner strengthens somewhat in the bind. Wind into left *Ochs* to thrust.
- Repeat steps 1 – 2.
- Your partner strengthens more in the bind. *Duplieren* behind their blade.
- Repeat steps 1 – 2.
- Your partner attempts to displace your point. *Durchwechseln* and thrust to them on the other side of the sword.

---

[63] Peter von Danzig, *Fechtbuch*, folios 36v-37r.

Fig. 6 Christian provokes with the Sprechfenster *from wide measure (a). Janusz attempts to strike long to the head, so Christian steps into the left* Ochs *to set the blow off and thrust (b).*

Fig. 7 From left *vom Tag, Janusz strikes to Christian's sword (a-b), so Christian uses this impulse to propel a* Zwerchhau *to Janusz's head.*

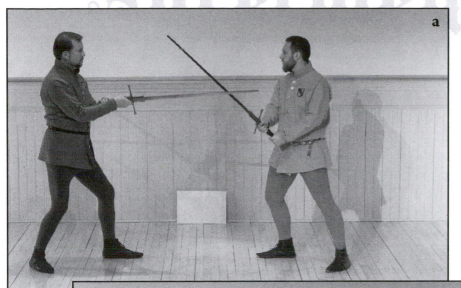

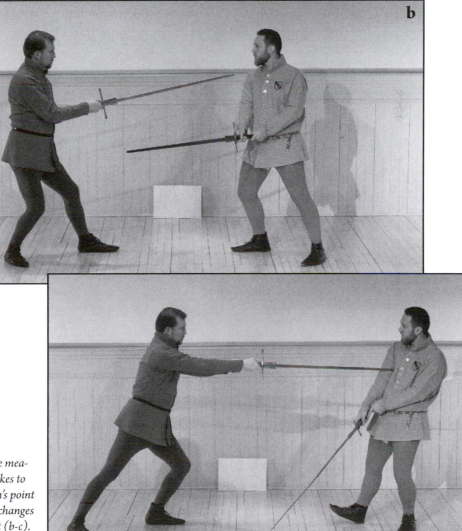

Fig. 8 From wide measure, Janusz strikes to displace Christian's point (a), so Christian changes through to thrust (b-c).

An interesting variant of the simple changing-through technique appears in the earliest Liechtenauer manuscript, *Hs. 3227a*. This is called the *Pfobenzagel* ("Peacock's Tail"). This involves a circular motion around the opponent's blade (doubtless an allusion to the fan-like tail of the peacock), essentially changing through without necessarily making contact with their blade. The idea is to occupy your opponent's attention while you seek an opening and opportunity to thrust to them:

> *One fighting technique is called the Peacock's Tail and comes from the point and goes with the point around his sword before the eyes like a wheel or compass directly around until one sees where one can come in and reach him.*[64]

A similarly described method, whose name, *Das Redel* ("The Wheel"), resonates with the description of the earlier *Pfobenzagel*,[65] appears in the Ringeck manuscript:

> *This is called the Wheel*
>
> *Item: When you fight with one, then extend your arms long from you so that your thumb remains above the sword, and turn your sword before you with the point around directly like a wheel from below to your left side nimbly and walk thereby to your opponent. And from this you can change through to whichever side you wish or bind. And when you have bound, then you can use whatever technique you wish – whichever you think is best – as before.*[66][67]

This technique will either land a thrust against your opponent or force them to bind against you, either of which is favorable for you. From the *Langenort*, move the point around their sword, from one side to the other with a circular motion beneath their hilt, until you feel you have an opportunity to thrust. [Fig. 9] Should they bind against your sword, defending against the thrust, keep working toward their openings with your point as we have seen in the earlier techniques of the book. Remember, you have gained the initiative; you have forced them to act, so take advantage of this.

The *Sprechfenster*, whether applied at the sword or disengaged, is a potent technique, one that draws upon much of what we have already learned. It is at once an excellent method to have in one's repertoire and a valuable tool for exploring the concepts it encompasses.

---

[64] Hs. 3227a, folio 47v.

[65] These two techniques are almost certainly one and the same; a modern German phrase for a peacock fanning its tail is *ein Rad schlagen*. *Rad* is the modern German word for "wheel."

[66] Sigmund Ringeck, *Fechtbuch*, folio 52r.

[67] Readers of my earlier title *Secrets of German Medieval Swordsmanship* will note that I have radically re-interpreted the Wheel in Ringeck based on the earlier manuscript evidence, refinement of my translation, and further experimentation.

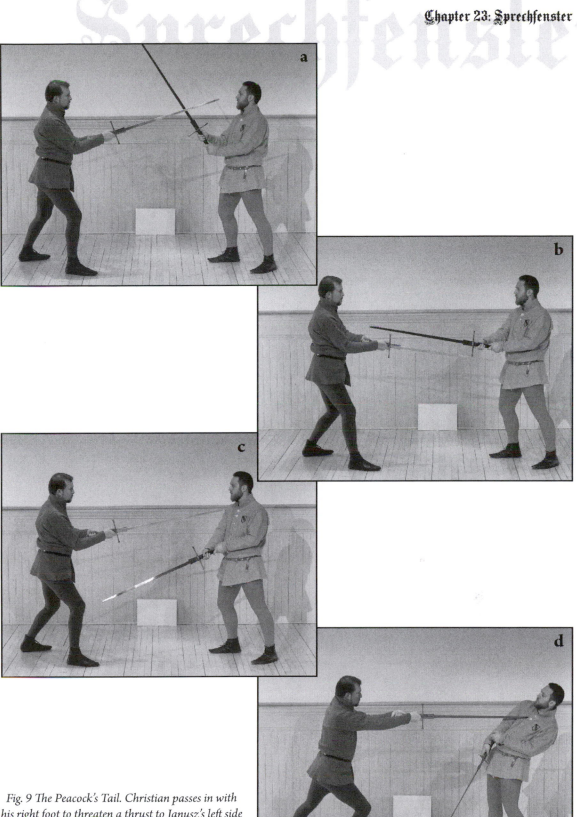

Fig. 9 *The Peacock's Tail. Christian passes in with his right foot to threaten a thrust to Janusz's left side (a). Janusz takes this bait (b), so Christian changes through to the other side in a circular motion to attack the right side (c-d).*

Drill 34: The *Sprechfenster* Disengaged

- Have your partner stand in right *vom Tag*. Approach your partner in *Langenort*, with your left leg leading. Threaten them with the point.

- Your partner attempts to flank you by striking an *Oberhau*.

- Wind to left *Ochs* with a pass of the right foot to thrust them.

- Resume *Langenort*. Your partner assumes left *vom Tag*.

- Your partner strikes a left *Oberhau* to your sword.

- Strike a *Zwerchhau* to their left side.

- Resume *Langenort*. Your partner resumes right *vom Tag*.

- Your partner attempts to strike aside your point.

- *Durchwechseln* and thrust with a step of the right foot.

Chapter 24:
Zwei Hengen, Acht Winden

Eight windings learn with stepping.
And test the bind
no more than soft or hard.

          – Johannes Liechtenauer

Winden ("Winding") is perhaps the most distinct element of Liechtenauer's art of the long-sword. As we saw in the techniques for the *Zornhau* in Chapter 9, *Winden Am Schwert* ("Winding at the Sword") is useful for achieving superior leverage in the bind and re-angling your point to thrust. This is but one example of such a winding technique, however. There are eight in total, the *Acht Winden* ("Eight Windings"), four from the "upper hanging" of the sword, which is *Ochs*, and four from the "lower hanging" of the sword, which is *Pflug*. Half of these windings are from the left side, half are from the right.

Fighting with the *Winden* involves a fierce struggle for leverage and angle of attack in the *Krieg*, the close combat phase of the fight. In addition to knowing the windings, you should know when not to use them. There's no need to remain at the sword if your opponent parries you too aggressively so that their point is no threat to you. If that happens, do not wind, but leave the bind to seek another opening to attack. While we will see some exceptions, in general a wind should be executed when your opponent's point stands before you and you need to mitigate the strength of their bind. You also must step properly as you wind or you will become vulnerable to your opponent because of your poor positioning. As the von Danzig commentaries say:

> *You cannot use the eight windings unless you step from both sides and first, before even that, test no more than the two dangers; that is, whether he has bound soft or hard to your sword. Then wind and work to the four openings as was previously described. Also know that if you fight with the winding at the sword and don't use the* Fühlen *at the sword, you will be hit while winding. This is why you should well remember the application of the feeling and the word* Indes, *for from these two things comes the whole of the art of fencing.* [68]

---

[68] Peter von Danzig, *Fechtbuch*, folio 38v.

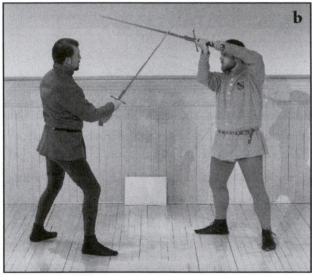

In this chapter, we will begin by learning how one can move from one hanger to another to respond to an opponent's lifting of their sword. We will then move to the eight windings, which will be presented in pairs, grouped by which guard and on which side of their sword they happen. When one winding is parried slightly by your opponent, you use its companion to get your point back in line. Then we will see how each of the *Drei Wunder* ("Three Wounders") works with winding before concluding with a couple of specialized winding techniques.

Zwei Hengen – Two Hangings

The *Zwei Hengen* ("Two Hangings") are the extended versions of *Pflug* (the lower) and *Ochs* (the upper). These are places that the swords can cross and they appear on both the left and right sides. Thus, there are actually four hangings altogether. If you meet your opponent's sword so that both of you bind in left *Pflug*, and they lift their hilt to prevent your thrust to their face, you can circumvent this action by lifting up your sword into the left *Ochs*, that is, into an upper hanging, to thrust to them over their sword. [Fig. 1] This can be viewed as changing from a lower winding to an upper winding.

Fig. 1 Christian meets Janusz's sword in the lower hanging (a). Janusz lifts his hilt (b), so Christian moves into the upper hanging to thrust (c).

Acht Winden – Eight Windings

As said above, there are four windings on the left side of the opponent's sword and four on the right. It may also be said that there are four above and four below; that is, four in the *Ochs* on both sides, and four in *Pflug* on both sides. The *Acht Winden* are:

1st Winding:	Left *Ochs*, on the right side of the their sword
2nd Winding:	Right *Ochs*, on the right side of their sword
3rd Winding:	Right *Ochs*, on the left side of their sword
4th Winding:	Left *Ochs*, on the left side of their sword
5th Winding:	Left *Pflug*, on the right side of their sword
6th Winding:	Right *Pflug*, on the right side of their sword
7th Winding:	Right *Pflug*, on the left side of their sword
8th Winding:	Left *Pflug*, on the left side of their sword

The windings are applied in pairs. Thus, if you come into the first winding, but your opponent pushes your sword aside to your right to parry it, you turn into the second winding to keep the point before them.

Note that the eight numbered above are windings at the sword. The term 'wind' also appears as a means of describing the turning action entailed in moving from one of the eight *Winden* to another.

The First and Second Windings

The first two windings happen in *Ochs* and are initiated from the right side of your body. The winding we practiced with the *Zornhau* was in fact an application of the first winding. Begin in the *Zufechten* facing your opponent in *Ochs* on your right side. If they strike an *Oberhau* from their right side to you, pass forward with your right foot into the left *Ochs* to catch their stroke on your short edge and thrust to their face, which is the first winding. If, however, they manage to counter the first winding by parrying your thrust to your right, pass forward with your left foot and continue to wind your short edge against their sword so that you come into the right *Ochs* (and thus the second winding) and again direct your point against them. [Fig. 2]

As you move from left to right *Ochs*, keep your movement tight so that your point stays directed against your opponent at all times. Otherwise, they can seize your blade or rush in to wrestle. Do this by moving your pommel in a small counter-clockwise arc as you make the guard transition.

This technique could easily end, of course, with the first winding. The second winding is there only if that doesn't quite come off, so make sure you attempt to strike your opponent as you perform the first winding. Note that although you moved from one *Ochs* to the other to move

from the first to second winding, you remained on the same side of their sword and your short edge remained in contact. Should your opponent *dramatically* push your point aside while you are winding (and this applies to any of the windings); remember that this involves their sword moving more towards your point. If they do this, you can easily employ the technique of *Durchwechseln*, as we saw in the chapter on the *Zornhau*.

Fig. 2 Christian begins in right Ochs, Janusz in right vom Tag (a). Janusz strikes to Christian's left side, so he passes into left Ochs (b), the 1st winding, thrusting to the face. Should Janusz parry this, Christian then passes into the right Ochs – the 2nd winding (c-d).

The Third and Fourth Windings

The second set of windings begins on the left side, with your standing in the left *Ochs*. If your opponent strikes from their left side, pass forward with your left foot into the right *Ochs* to set aside their stroke with your long edge and thrust to their face. This is the third winding. If they move your point aside to your left a bit, preventing your thrust, then pass forward with your right foot to come back again into the left *Ochs* with your long edge still in contact with their sword and thrust to them; that is the fourth winding. [Fig. 3] The object here, as in the first pair of windings, is to stick to their sword, remaining in the *Vor*, in spite of their attempts to parry you. Your pommel should move in a small clockwise arc during the transition from the third to the fourth winding.

Fig. 3 Janusz forms left vom Tag; Christian is in left Ochs (a). Janusz strikes a left Oberhau, so Christian passes into right Ochs – the 3rd winding (b). If Janusz parries this, Christian passes again, into the left Ochs – the 4th winding (c).

The Fifth and Sixth Windings

Having done all four of the upper windings, we now move to the lower windings, those done from *Pflug*. Begin in *Pflug* on your right side. When your opponent strikes an *Oberhau* from their right side at you, pass forward with your right foot into the left *Pflug* to set aside their stroke, with your short edge against their blade, and thrust to their face. That is now the fifth winding. If they prevent the thrust by pushing your sword toward your right side, then pass forward with the left foot to come back into right *Pflug*, that is, the sixth winding. [Fig. 4] Once again, the edge in contact with their sword does not change from one winding to the other.

Fig. 4 Christian stands in right Pflug; Janusz is in right vom Tag (a). Janusz strikes to Christian's left lower opening, so Christian passes into left Pflug – the 5th winding (b). If Janusz parries this, Christian passes into right Pflug – the 6th winding (c).

The Seventh and Eighth Windings

The last pair of windings begins with left *Pflug*. When your adversary strikes from their left side, pass forward into the right *Pflug*, and the seventh winding, with your long edge against their sword, and thrust up into their face. If instead they set that off to your left, follow the movement by passing forward with your right foot into left *Pflug* and the eighth winding to thrust to them. [Fig. 5] The pommel should travel from right to left across your body as you move from the seventh winding to the eighth.

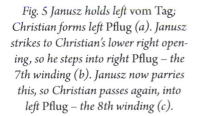

Fig. 5 Janusz holds left vom Tag; Christian forms left Pflug (a). Janusz strikes to Christian's lower right opening, so he steps into right Pflug – the 7th winding (b). Janusz now parries this, so Christian passes again, into left Pflug – the 8th winding (c).

The Three Wounders and the Eight Windings

Master Liechtenauer says in his verse that the *Drei Wunder* can each be used from all eight windings of the sword. Of this, Master Ringeck says:

> *And it follows that you can apply stroke, thrust and slice from each winding, so that one can execute all together twenty-four techniques from winding.*[69]

In each of the eight windings, you can use any of the three types of attack, as appropriate. If your point is in line, you can thrust from a winding. If your point is past them, but your edge is a few inches away from their person, you can strike them while in contact with their sword (or strike around to another winding). If your point is past them, but your edge is very close to them, then place the edge upon them and slice. [Fig. 6] You must decide which to use based on the feeling and your sword's position.

---

[69] Sigmund Ringeck, *Fechtbuch*, folios 48r – 48v.

Fig. 6 All three wounders are possible in any of the windings. For example, from the 1st winding, Christian can perform a thrust (a), a stroke (b), or a slice (c), as the situation demands.

Zwei Hengen, Acht Winden

Drill 35: *Acht Winden*
Part A – From the Upper Hangings

- In wide measure, assume right *Ochs*. Have your partner assume right *vom Tag*.

- Your partner attacks with an *Oberhau* to the left side of your head.

- Pass with the right foot to come into the 1st *Winden* (left *Ochs*).

- Thrust, strike, or slice your partner's head with your short edge in contact.

- Repeat steps 1 – 3. Your partner now displaces your sword to your right.

- Pass with the left foot to come into the 2nd *Winden* (right *Ochs*).

- Thrust, strike, or slice your partner's head with your short edge in contact.

- Resume wide measure. Assume left *Ochs*. Have your partner assume left *Vom Tag*.

- Your partner attacks with an *Oberhau* to right side of your head.

- Pass with the left foot to come into the 3rd *Winden* (right *Ochs*).

- Thrust, strike, or slice your partner's head with your long edge in contact.

- Repeat steps 8 – 10. Your partner now displaces your sword to your left.

- Pass with the right foot to come into the 4th *Winden* (left *Ochs*).

- Thrust, strike, or slice your partner's head with your long edge in contact.

Drill 35: *Acht Winden*
Part B – From the Lower Hangings

- In wide measure, assume right *Pflug*. Have your partner assume right *Vom Tag*.

- Your partner attacks with an *Oberhau* to your left side.

- Pass with the right foot to come into the 5th *Winden* (left *Pflug*).

- Thrust, strike, or slice your partner with your short edge in contact.

- Repeat steps 1 – 3. Your partner now displaces your sword to your right.

- Pass with the left foot to come into the 6th *Winden* (right *Pflug*).

- Thrust, strike, or slice your partner with your short edge in contact.

- Resume wide measure. Assume left *Pflug*. Have your partner assume left *Vom Tag*.

- Your partner attacks with an *Oberhau* to your right side.

- Pass with the left foot to come into the 7th *Winden* (right *Pflug*).

- Thrust, strike, or slice your partner with your long edge in contact.

- Repeat steps 8 – 10. Your partner now displaces your sword to your left.

- Pass with the right foot to come into the 8th *Winden* (left *Pflug*).

- Thrust, strike, or slice your partner with your long edge in contact.

Chapter 25: Nebenhut

Here note how to fight from the Side Guard, that is, from the slashings: Know that it is good to fight from the slashings. Although they are not named in the Zettel, yet the techniques with which one executes them arise from the Zettel. And one should execute the slashings from the left side, since they are not as sure from the right side as from the left.

– The "Ringeck Fechtbuch"

The Ringeck *Fechtbuch* features additional techniques once its commentary on Liechtenauer's longsword verse concludes. One of these sections, influential enough to appear in other compendia, treats the use of the guard *Nebenhut* ("Side Guard"). This short collection of techniques, which its author assures us, derives from the principles of the *Zettel* (Liechtenauer's verse treatise), describes how one can slash upward from the left *Nebenhut* with the short edge of the sword to address an opponent's attack from their right side by meeting it *outside*, rather than head on.

This "Slashing" (*Streichen*) is none other than the rising short edge *Unterhau* that we learned early in this book. Such a strategy enjoys the benefits of redirecting a foe's energy, rather than attempting to stop them cold. The following techniques are in the main from the Ringeck collection, with one technique culled from Master Hans Talhoffer's works. Also note that the Ringeck *Fechtbuch* cautions us that these methods are only effective from left *Nebenhut*, likely because on the right the hands would be crossed were the short edge presented forward.

Counterattacking from *Nebenhut*

The simplest application of this tactic is to assume the left *Nebenhut*, with your short edge facing up, as your opponent moves to strike down from right or high *vom Tag*. Slash upward against their stroke, redirecting it to your right. As you do this, begin to step forward and outward with your left foot, and then strike down directly to their head. [Fig. 1]

If your opponent reacts to your attempt to beat their attack aside and strike down, you are now right back to the sort of decision-making we learned early on in the chapter on the *Zornhau*, that is, how hard are they parrying you? If they turn their intention toward your threatening sword, but modulate their strength, wind against their sword by moving into the right *Ochs*. [Fig. 2] If they parry harder, employ the *Duplieren* with your short edge. [Fig. 3] If they are really strong, snap (*Schnappen*) out of the bind and strike their head with the short edge. [Fig. 4]

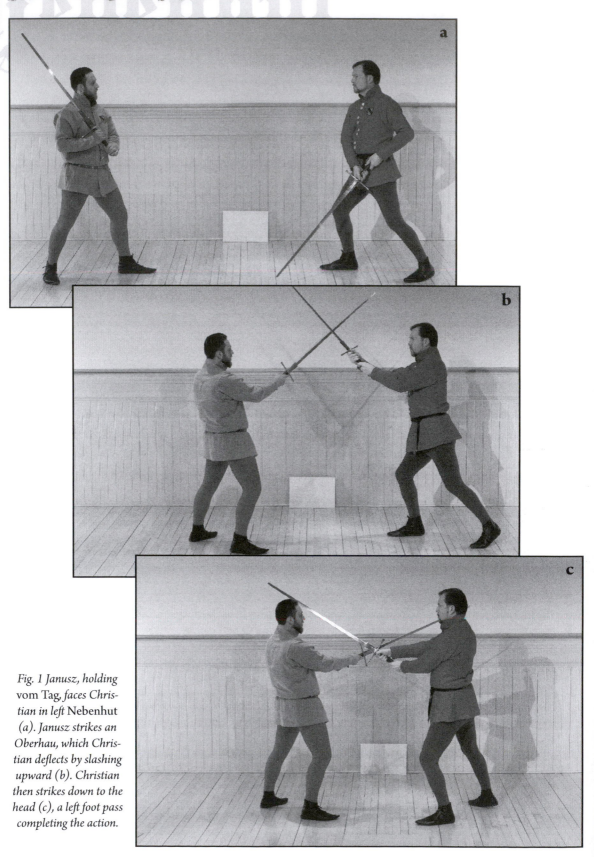

Fig. 1 Janusz, holding vom Tag, *faces Chris-tian in left* Nebenhut *(a). Janusz strikes an Oberhau, which Chris-tian deflects by slashing upward (b). Christian then strikes down to the head (c), a left foot pass completing the action.*

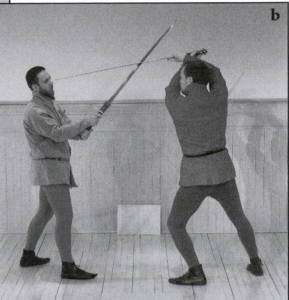

Fig. 2 Christian again slashes upward, but Janusz changes priorities, abandoning his attack to turn his sword to parry (a), so Christian winds into right Ochs to thrust (b).

Fig. 3 A stronger parry by Janusz (a) prompts Christian to employ a Duplieren (b).

Your opponent may try to strengthen their parry by winding into the right *Ochs* to attain the advantages of position and superior leverage provided by this guard. As they begin to move their sword upward, slash their right mid-section with a *Mittelhau*, compass stepping backward quickly with your right foot. [Fig. 5]

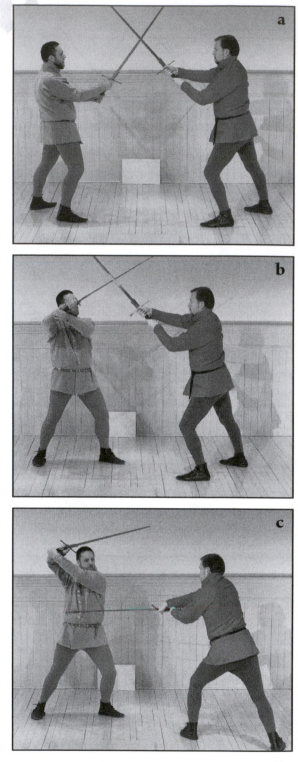

Fig. 4 In response to a very strong parry (a), Christian snaps out of the bind to strike with the short edge (b).

Fig. 5 Janusz binds Christian's slashing counterattack (a) and steps to begin winding into right Ochs (b), so Christian compass steps backward with the right foot, pivoting away, while striking a Mittelhau to Janusz's right side (c).

Should you not be quick enough to prevent their winding into *Ochs*, you must apply strong pressure against their sword to keep their point away from you. While this will give you no offensive advantage, as your own point is now facing away from them, it will force them to seek another avenue of attack. The most obvious one would be for them to strike around to the other side, in this case, using the *Zwerchhau*. As they go to leave the bind, pass backward with your left foot, slashing their left mid-section as you step. [Fig. 6]

Should your counterstroke from *Nebenhut* take your point far to your right, you can recover control by remembering the *Mutieren*. However, here you will not be able to easily thrust because you now lead with your left foot and they lead with their right, making their lower left opening inaccessible. So, instead we will draw upon a technique illustrated by Talhoffer: Once you have dropped your point over their blade, let go of your hilt with your left hand and grab your own mid-blade below. Complete the counter-clockwise rotation of your sword's point to trap their sword beneath your armpit. You now have the option of either thrusting to them, their sword safely contained, or turning your body to wrest their weapon from their grip, disarming them. [Fig. 7]

Fig. 6 Janusz now successfully winds into Ochs, so Christian binds strongly (a). Janusz now leaves the bind with a Zwerchhau, so Christian passes back with the left foot to strike a Mittelhau to Janusz's left side (b).

Fig. 7 Christian slashes up against Janusz's attack, driving it far towards Christian's right (a-b). Christian then drops his point over Janusz's sword (c), grabs his own blade with his left hand (d), and rotates his point upward to trap the opposing sword between his blade and armpit. Christian's sharp turn of his body to his right relieves Janusz of the sword (e).

Drill 36: Counterattacks from *Nebenhut*

- Assume left *Nebenhut* with the short edge facing forward. Have your partner assume right *vom Tag*.

- Your partner strikes an *Oberhau*. Slash up to deflect it to your right. Strike down to their head.

- Resume your guards. Your partner strikes an *Oberhau*. Slash up to their sword. Your partner binds your sword moderately. Wind to right *Ochs* and thrust.

- Resume your guards. Your partner strikes an *Oberhau*. Slash up to their sword. Your partner binds your sword strongly. *Duplieren* behind their sword.

- Resume your guards. Your partner strikes an *Oberhau*. Slash up to their sword. Your partner binds your sword very strongly. Snap out of the bind, strike with the short edge.

- Resume your guards. Your partner strikes an *Oberhau*. Slash up to their sword. Your partner parries in right *Ochs*. Strike a *Mittelhau* to their right side, compass stepping with the right foot.

- Resume your guards. Your partner strikes an *Oberhau*. Slash up to their sword. Your partner begins winding toward right *Ochs*. Strike a *Mittelhau* to their right side, compass stepping with the right foot.

- Resume your guards. Your partner strikes an *Oberhau*. Slash up to their sword. Your partner succeeds in winding to right *Ochs*. Bind their sword hard.

- Your partner reacts to your pressure, striking around with the *Zwerchhau*. Strike their left side with a *Mittelhau*, passing back with the left foot.

- Resume your guards. Your partner strikes an *Oberhau*. Slash hard up to their sword. Their sword and your point are driven far to your right.

- Drop your point to encircle their blade. Grab your blade in the middle, trapping their sword under your arm. Turn your body to control their weapon.

- Thrust to them or wrench their sword free.

Provoking from *Nebenhut*

The next three techniques assume that your slashing upwards is performed as an attack or provocation, rather than in response to their attack.

Slash up from left *Nebenhut* with your short edge at them. If they parry this with their sword across them, simply continue your attack up under their arms. You can strike into their arms or thrust to their chest. [Fig. 8]

Fig. 8 Christian provokes Janusz into falling across the line with his sword by slashing up from left Nebenhut *(a-b), but Christian continues to motion to strike the underside of Janusz's arms and thrust to the chest (c).*

A more reasonable response to your slashing attack would entail the opponent parrying your sword with their hands low. If they do this, drop your point through the attempted parry so your sword comes to the other side of their blade, obviating their defense. This is the *Durchwechseln* ("Changing Through") that we have seen repeatedly earlier in this book. Once you've changed through, thrust to their chest. [Fig. 9]

The cunning opponent will note your changing through and move to parry your sword on the other side. If that happens, brace your sword hard against theirs, lift your blade onto the side of their neck, and pass deeply with your right foot behind their left foot. A small advance of the left foot may be necessary before the pass of the right in order to adjust the measure. Now, use your blade to pull them by the neck, throwing them over your right leg and onto the ground. [Fig. 10]

Fig. 9 Janusz now tries to defend Christian's slashing attack by moving into right Pflug (a-b), so Christian changes through to thrust on the other side of Janusz's sword (c).

Fig. 10 Countering the previous technique, Janusz sets aside Christian's thrust to the other side (a), so Christian begins winding his sword to both set aside Janusz's sword (b) and bring his long edge to Janusz's neck, stepping behind his opponent's left foot with his right, to execute a takedown (c).

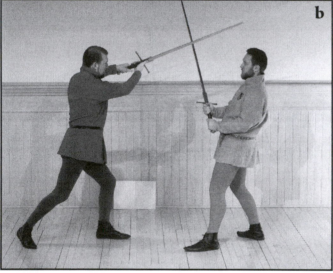

Drill 37: Provocations from *Nebenhut*

- Assume left *Nebenhut* with the short edge facing forward. Have your partner assume right *vom Tag*.

- Slash up toward your partner. They parry by dropping their point down and to their left. Strike below onto their sword and hit their arms or thrust to the chest.

- Resume your guards. Slash up toward your partner. They parry in right *Pflug*. *Durchwechseln* and thrust them.

- Resume your guards. Slash up toward your partner. They parry in right *Pflug*. You *Durchwechseln*, but they move to parry your thrust.

- Strengthen the bind, hook their neck with your blade, and pass with the right foot behind their left to throw them.

Chapter 26: Fence!

Here note that constant motion overcomes your opponent in the beginning, middle, and end of all fencing according to this art and teaching.

– Hs. 3227a

Fighting is about much more than knowing how to execute techniques. In the previous chapters, we have studied footwork, timing, distance, the guards, and various methods for attacking and defending. Before we take our leave of unarmoured combat, let us review this knowledge and see how we can use it to approach a fight both tactically and strategically.

When you begin a bout with an opponent, you must be observant. Assume a guard, remembering that guards such as *Ochs* and *Pflug* are good places to thrust from; *Alber* and *Langenort* good places to bait an opponent; and *vom Tag*, *Schranckhut*, and *Nebenhut* good places from which to strike. Be aware of the distance between you and your opponent. Remember that once you come into measure either you or your opponent can reach the other by taking only one step, so be careful about how you approach!

As you employ gathering and/or passing steps in the *Zufechten*, note what guard your opponent has assumed. You can seize the initiative—that is, fight in the *Vor*—by attacking any of the four primary guards *Ochs*, *Pflug*, *Alber* or *vom Tag* in relative safety by employing the Master Strokes *Krumphau*, *Schielhau*, *Scheitelhau* or *Zwerchhau*, respectively. You can also seize the initiative by simply striking or thrusting to whatever opening they have exposed, thereby forcing them to defend it, particularly if they draw back slightly to charge a stroke or thrust of their own; the principle of *Nachreisen* will serve you well at such times. Remember to keep the point before the opponent as you enter, maintaining a constant threat.

Should your opponent act first, you must respond in the *Nach*. Intercept a stroke from above with a *Zornhau*, *Krumphau*, or *Zwerchhau*, as appropriate, remembering that the *Zwerchhau* is particularly good at defending nearly vertical attacks. If they pull back obviously to strike from above with great strength, then jam their attack with the *Schielhau*. If, however, they strike an *Oberhau* down to your leading leg, slip that leg away from their attack and bring the *Scheitelhau* down on their head. If they strike from below with an *Unterhau*, strike the *Krumphau* against

c

their hands. If you cannot gather sufficient momentum to bring about one of these strokes, at least pass forward into the guard *Ochs* or *Pflug* on the opposite side you started from and set aside their attack; this is an *Absetzen* and you should thrust as you set aside their stroke or thrust.

Regardless of whether you seize the initiative in the *Vor* or regain it by responding in the *Nach*, your primary strategy is to *control the fight*. So if your attack or defense meets with their blade, do not automatically retreat but keep working against them from the binding of the swords. Look for where their sword's point is now. Is it a threat to you? How strong are they in the bind? Let the feeling (*Fühlen*) be your guide. Use both pieces of information to determine whether you should stay and work against them with the winding (*Winden*) or depart from the bind and attack some other opening with striking, thrusting, slicing or wrestling. As long as you keep up the onslaught of attack, your opponent "… *cannot defend himself without danger; if you have correctly learned, to striking he will barely come.*"[70]

Approaching an opponent can be done quite elegantly too. Our (likely) earliest surviving record of the Liechtenauer tradition, *Hs. 3227a*, describes one way to approach an opponent when engaging in *Schulfechten* ("School Fencing"), fencing for practice or fun. It gives some idea of how one might approach an opponent, albeit spiced up a bit so that one can show off on the way in! I'll let the master's words speak for themselves, with some annotation:

> If you want to go to your opponent in school fencing for fun and you want to do this nobly, then begin by shaking your sword bravely and come into the Schranckhut to both sides, and seek that position widely from one side upwards to the other with steps. Thereafter, come into the Lower Hanging to both sides with steps and, after that, the Upper Hanging to both sides with steps. After that, perform the Zwerchhau to both sides with steps. Thus, when you perform the techniques named here to one side you must therefore step: if you move to the left side, then set your right foot forward, and vice-versa on the other side.
>
> If you do this as you come to him then do something that is suitable in play.
>
> And aim for the upper openings rather than the lower ones, and drive in over his hilt. And remember the lessons already described: that above all else you should win the Vorschlag (Before Stroke) and as soon as you have then do the Nachschlag (After Stroke) without hesitation, as if you were trying to do them at the same time. And always perform one thing after another quickly and bravely, so that if one misses the other hits, so that your adversary cannot come to strokes.[71]

Translation by Thomas Stoeppler

---

[70] Liechtenauer's verse, lines 80 – 82.

[71] *Hausbuch*, Hs. 3227a, f. 52v.

If you want to do justice to this art and the masters who created it, focus your energies more on correct movement by trying to work the techniques you have drilled from this book, rather than simply rushing headlong into a contest of speed to "win points." This is not, however, an admonishment to be timid. Remember always that *your sword is your shield*. When you attack from behind its protection, you can well afford to be bold in attack and defense. Courage is one of Master Paulus Kal's fencing virtues; it is also one of the chivalric virtues, and this is a knightly art of combat. The best technique in the world is worth nothing without bravery. To this end, let me close this chapter, not with my own words, but with the infinitely better counsel of Master Sigmund Ringeck, whose words first inspired me to study Master Liechtenauer's teachings:

> *Princes and Lords learn to survive with this art, in earnest and in play. But if you are fearful, then you should not learn to fence, because a despondent heart will always be defeated, regardless of all skill.*[72]

Translation by Jörg Bellinghausen

---

[72] Sigmund Ringeck, *Fechtbuch*, folio 16v.

Chapter 27:
Armoured Foot Combat

Leather and gauntlets
Under the eyes seek the openings correctly
— Johannes Liechtenauer

The *Kunst des Fechtens* of Johannes Liechtenauer includes a discipline called *Harnischfechten*, fighting in harness, which is to say, armour. More specifically, this branch of the art is a body of techniques for overcoming and dispatching foes in armour on foot. This sub-discipline is also sometimes tellingly called *Kampffechten* ("Duel Fighting"), here specifically on foot. A duel on foot might be the agreed upon combat, or a duel that began on horse might progress to one where both combatants have dismounted.

Judicial duels and trials by combat were encounters fought to resolve legal matters, sometimes by the antagonists, other times through champions fighting for them. In some cases, these encounters could be fought to the death, effectively making them even more dangerous than fighting an armoured opponent on the battlefield, where there was at least a possibility of being captured and ransomed. The dueling techniques of *Kampffechten* are not geared toward subduing and capturing an opponent, but injuring and then killing them. Killing an opponent in armour efficiently requires a different set of techniques from those we have previously seen in this book. However, the overarching principles of time and timing, measure, and initiative all continue to apply.

During the years that Master Liechtenauer is likely to have lived, the mid to late 14th century, the armour of the medieval knight was changing. The defenses of the 13th century and earlier, composed almost exclusively of mail armour, were giving way to a new hybrid, transitional style. Plate armour elements began appearing on late 13th century harnesses, and this process accelerated as the 14th century began.

Swords had never been particularly effective at breaching knightly armour. During the High Middle Ages, the age of mail armour, a stroke of the sword would be unlikely to severely compromise a knight's hauberk, or long tunic of mail. However, due to mail's flexible nature, it provided limited protection against the blunt trauma of a particularly mighty blow, and a thrust through the rings of mail with an acutely tapered sword could cause injury.

Fig. 1 The author in a reproduction late 14th to early 15th-century armour. An abbreviated mail shirt – a haubergeon – provides much of the coverage for the torso, but plate armour covers most of the body, including full arm and leg harnesses, a simple breast-plate, steel gauntlets, and sabatons covering the feet. A bascinet helmet, fitted with a mail aventail for the neck and collar areas, defends the head.

Fig. 2 The author in a late 15th-century German armour, termed 'gothic armour' by antiquarians in the 19th century. Such armours, with much more complete plate defenses than 14th-century armours, still include some mail, particularly where the armour has gaps such as at the armpits, elbows, and groin.

The addition of plate defenses in the late 13th –14th centuries made the sword even less useful against armoured opponents. There is a negligible chance of hacking through plate armour defenses with a sword's edge. So if one wanted to kill an armoured opponent with a longsword, they would thrust into the gaps between pieces of armour, places where there was no protection or only the porous protection of mail. [Fig. 1] By the 15th century, plate armour was very complete in its coverage of the body, making an understanding of the harness' vulnerabilities even more important. [Fig. 2]

We learned earlier about how Liechtenauer divided the body into four target areas, the *Vier Blössen* ("Four Openings"). The openings for an armoured opponent are quite limited, however. The von Danzig commentaries describe these openings and how to seek them:

> Note, this tells where the best places are to attack an armored man through the harness. These are under the face, under the armpits, in the palms of the hands, on the arms from behind into the gauntlets, into the hollows of the knee, or below on the soles of the feet, in the insides of the elbows, between the legs, and anywhere the harness has its articulations. And you should seek the openings such that you do not work or thrust to a more distant opening when you can reach a closer one.[73]

These openings can be exploited with the point of a sword, spear, or dagger. [Fig. 3] Another way an armoured opponent can be attacked is to hit them with a staff weapon or one designed purely for delivering blunt trauma injuries: a poleaxe, halberd, mace, or war hammer.

Fig. 3 Two armoured combatants in late 14th or early 15th-century armour thrust into the gaps of each other's harnesses.
Codex Wallerstein, *folio 106v.*

---

[73] Peter von Danzig, *Fechtbuch*, folio 58v.

The longsword can be used in this capacity as well: If you swing the sword by its blade so that you strike with your pommel or hilt, you are essentially wielding a small poleaxe or war hammer. Such a stroke with the pommel is known throughout the corpus of German manuscripts by several names: the *Mortschlag* ("Murder Stroke"), the *Donnerschlag* ("Thunder Stroke"), and, Liechtenauer's own name for it, *Schlachenden Ort* ("Battering Point"). The von Danzig commentaries describe the three weapons of armoured dueling, the sword, the spear, and the dagger, in this passage:

> *Note, this is a lesson that with all the weapons appropriate for dueling you should always plant upon an armored man with the point, wherever you can most readily reach an opening, and you should know how to seek the openings correctly with the point; for there are three weapons, having four points. The first weapon is the lance, which has one point. The second weapon is the dagger, which also has one point. The third weapon is the sword, which has two points: one is the tip of the blade, the other is the pommel. And how you should work with the points you shall find all described in the commentaries from one end to the other.*[74]

Harnischfechten includes techniques for directing these "four points" against the vulnerabilities in the opponent's harness. It also includes armoured wrestling techniques (Kampfringen) comprising variations on the *Drei Ringen* seen earlier in this book, plus sundry joint locks and methods for pinning your opponent on the ground (*Unterhalten*, or "Holding Down"). Unless you get a very lucky thrust into your opponent's face through their eye-slots or raised visor, you are more likely to simply weaken your opponent with your sword. Ultimately, an armoured duel is likely to end with wrestling on the ground with one antagonist pinned down and their foe stabbing them with their dagger. This would have often been the conclusion of such a grim dueling encounter. Here, the anonymous author of the von Danzig commentaries speaks of this, and how you should secure your opponent first before thrusting with the dagger:

> *Now you should know that, for the most part, all fighting in single combat in harness comes in the end to dagger fighting and to wrestling. Therefore note, when you close with an opponent, then attend to nothing else but the wrestling and let your dagger stay in its scabbard, because you cannot hurt him through the harness as long as he is standing before you and hinders your hand. When you secured him with the wrestling or have thrown him and have overcome him, then work with the dagger to the openings that you will find explained hereafter, and that have already been explained.*[75]

---

[74] Ibid., folios 61r – 61v.

[75] Peter von Danzig, *Fechtbuch*, folios 71v – 72r.

The footwork for armoured combat with the spear or half-sword is different than the passing footwork used in striking with the sword's edge. This is because, in general, you will want to keep your point directed against your opponent. A pass will change which leg leads, and as both the sword and spear are held with the hands apart in this context, such a step would bring the point backward away from the enemy. Therefore, whenever thrusting attacks are used, always lead with the left leg and use gathering footwork to control distance and compass pacing to change the direction of your attack or void an opponent's thrust. The exceptions to this rule are when you strike with your sword's pommel, close to wrestle with the opponent, or need to void an attack by retreating quickly; here you may use passing footwork. If you do retreat with a pass, you must do so conservatively:

> Know that in dueling combat it is appropriate to take no more than one step away and one step towards the opponent; and otherwise stand fast so that you do not become tired in your harness. Understand this thus: if he has rushed upon you so that you can come to no parrying with your sword or otherwise, then step quickly backward with your forward foot, and look to plant upon him promptly again, or grasp him with wrestling with a step forward on the same foot that you stepped back with.[76]

This general limitation in the footwork raises the question of how you can keep your weapon, whether sword or spear, between you and your opponent, as I have recommended repeatedly in the unarmoured fighting syllabus. The answer is that you do not do this and do not need to. You are wearing armour: Your chief concern is to keep the point away from the gaps in your harness and you need not worry about a sharp edge traveling in an arc toward you. In this way, armoured combat is considerably simpler.

When you are fighting in armour, you must take special care to keep your weight low and centered. This is because wearing a late medieval harness raises your center of gravity by several inches. Helmets and breastplates were made proportionately thicker than armour for the legs and there is more armour above the waist than below. Be aware of your center of gravity and be sure you do not do anything to throw off your balance. Once lost, it is much harder to regain when you are in harness.

Liechtenauer's armoured combat has certain constraints and features that distinguish it from the unarmoured longsword combat we have studied thus far. Do not be overwhelmed by these distinctions, because the basics of timing, distance, and initiative all still apply. Even the guards we are about to explore should seem familiar, for they are no more than adaptations of those we have already learned, and we will continue to see that performing the techniques usually involves no more than moving from one guard to another.

---

[76] Ibid., folio 68v.

Chapter 28:
Fencing with the Spear

Spear and point
Thrust the Before Thrust without fear
Spring, wind, set truly upon
If he defends, pull, that will defeat him
— Johannes Liechtenauer

While the focus of this volume is the longsword, we begin our study of armoured fighting techniques with the spear. The spear is a very basic weapon, and the techniques for its use provide a distillation of Liechtenauer's core concepts. Its length also makes it an excellent training tool for developing sensitivity, *Fühlen*, when the weapons cross. The long moment arm of the spear's shaft amplifies small changes in your opponent's pressure. Lastly, fighting with the spear is very similar to fighting with the half-sword, but simpler still. Spear fencing has much to offer, whether or not you intend ultimately to focus on armoured combat.

One of the oldest weapons, the spear has been wielded in hunting and war for millennia. It is also one of the knightly weapons and figures in the armoured dueling of the Liechtenauer tradition. Where the sword and spear are both carried into a duel, the spear is used first and the sword is drawn only once the spear has been lost or become impractical if the range of the fight tightens. It can be wielded with both hands for thrusting against your opponent, or it can be cast at them. A cast spear would require a very lucky shot to seriously injure a fully armoured opponent, but it certainly would create a distraction that would allow the thrower to advance upon their enemy. The casting of the spear may also be a holdover from the early judicial combats on foot practiced by the Germans as early as the 5th or 6th centuries, the so-called "Migration Period." [Fig. 1]

Fig. 1 A judicial duel scene from one of Hans Talhoffer's 1459 Fechtbücher. *The combatant at left has cast his spear, which his enemy at right parries away with his longsword held at the half-sword, that is, with one hand on the grip and the other holding the middle of the blade; he also clasps his sword and spear together. The caption reads "Here the throw is parried." f 86r.*

Historical techniques from the late medieval period appear to treat two different sized spears: a roughly six-foot-long "short spear," which was used exclusively on foot, and a long spear, which could be anywhere from nine to thirteen feet in length and might do double duty as a light lance when the warrior was mounted. Some manuscripts, such as Paulus Kal's, show what appear to be heavy cavalry lances.

The techniques for spear found in the Liechtenauer commentaries of the 15th century seem to favor a long spear. In some manuscripts, the section for fighting on foot in armour comes immediately after that for fighting on horseback, and the commentaries make it clear that the long weapon that was your lance while mounted is your footman's spear once you have dismounted. A long spear is an unwieldy weapon for striking blows, and this most likely explains why those techniques do not appear here, the manuscripts instead focusing on the spear's thrusting abilities. Other treatises more or less connected to the Liechtenauer School do, however, include methods for fighting with short spears.

It's likely that some of these spears would have been equipped with the small acutely tapered heads of a cavalryman's lance. This is just what some of them seem to be, after all. Others would feature the more diamond-shaped heads shown in Talhoffer's judicial dueling illustrations. These would be affixed to an ash shaft, usually lacking any metal reinforcement at the butt of the spear.

Two spear guards are described explicitly in the commentaries on Liechtenauer's art appearing in the Ringeck and von Danzig manuscripts, with a third guard that is implied. [Fig. 2] These are called the High and Low Guards. They will look very familiar, for they are variations on the longsword guards *Ochs* and *Pflug*, only with the hands held widely apart on the spear's shaft. That these should appear here should be no surprise: The spear is a thrusting weapon, and these are thrusting guards.

A third guard is described with the spear shaft tucked under the right armpit, much the way a lance is couched there on horseback. This position is used to bring the entire strength of the body to bear against an opponent once you have set your point into a vulnerable part of their harness. It is similar to the longsword guard *Langenort*, in that it is the conclusion of a thrust.

There is perhaps yet *another* guard that can be inferred as well. In the chapter following this one there is a guard for the half-sword (the *third* guard with that weapon) where the weapon is held across the leading left knee. With a relatively short spear (perhaps 6 feet long or less), there is no reason why this guard could not be used practically for spear fighting. In essence, half-sword fighting is simply the use of the sword as a very short spear, so if the student wishes they can reference the techniques for the third half-sword guard and apply them to the spear.

The three spear guards explicitly described in the Ringeck and Danzig treatises are framed only on the right side of the body, with the left leg leading. While they can also be assumed on the left side of the body, the guards are not symmetrical in the same way that the longsword guards are. This is because a long spear's shaft cannot pass through the body. Passing from a right side guard to its left side version would require that the point turn away from your opponent, removing the threat. Otherwise both hands must hold the butt of the spear so it can clear the body while maintaining the threat with the point, which over-extends the weapon and allows little leverage for binding the opponent's spear. Therefore, the techniques do not include switching

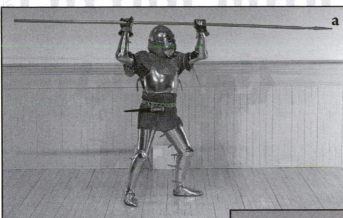

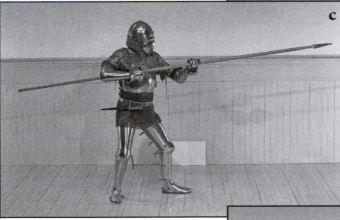

Fig. 2 Guards for fighting with the spear:
High (a), Low (b), and Couched in the
armpit (c). The last (d) is a guard held Over-
The-Knee, useful with shorter spears, but
impractical with longer ones.

from one side to another or passing footwork. Instead, footwork with the spear is confined to gathering steps, for advancing and retreating, and compass steps, for voiding and for redirecting the angle of attack.

The techniques for the spear are simple and elegant, and I highly recommend their practice, as they distill some important concepts of the system in a readily understandable way. Understanding the fight with the spear also paves the way for mastering the half-sword techniques of the next chapter.

Attacking and Pulling with the Spear

The simplest technique with the spear is to seize the initiative and attack your opponent with the point. Liechtenauer's verse calls this the *Vorstich* ("Before Thrust" or "Initial Thrust"). This is best initiated from the Low Guard. The Ringeck commentary says:

> *If you do not want to throw your spear, then hold it apart from your right side in the lower guard and go in such a way to him. And thrust it courageously from below to his face, before he does the same.*[77]

> ### Drill 38: Thrusting with the Spear
>
> - Thrust from the High Guard.
>
> - Thrust from the Low Guard.
>
> - Thrust from the High Guard, compass stepping forward with the right foot.
>
> - Thrust from the Low Guard, compass stepping forward with the right foot.
>
> - When each of these steps begins to feel natural to you, begin couching your spear under your arm to complete each thrust to strengthen it, coupling this with gathering steps.

If your opponent parries your thrust to the side, then you should pull your spear out of the bind and attack them again on the other side of their spear. This is an application of *Zucken*, the pulling from the bind done with the longsword. This can be done by pulling the spear back with both hands, or, as Master Peter von Danzig recommends in his own commentary, "*with your right hand, and with a light touch let your spear go in the left hand,*"[78] that is, much like the action of drawing back a pool cue. Once you successfully find purchase with your thrust into a vulnerable area of the opponent's armour you should gather yourself forward and tuck your spear under your arm into the third guard and drive the thrust into them. [Fig. 3]

Note that if you want to remove your spear from the bind efficiently, you can incorporate several elements. As described above, there should be a pulling action, but you can also let your point drop down and under the bind as you pull. This is combining the concept of *Durchwechseln* with that of *Zucken*, a circular disengagement paired with a strong pulling back of the haft. In addition, shifting your weight back can facilitate a speedy withdrawal of your spear from the bind.

---

[77] Sigmund Ringeck, *Fechtbuch*, folios 91r – 91v.

[78] Peter von Danzig, *Fechtbuch*, folio 109r.

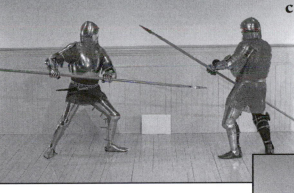

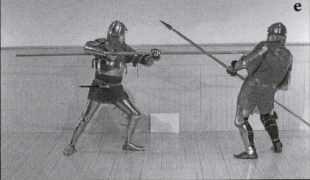

Fig. 3 *The two spearmen come into measure (a). Christian thrusts his spear, which Rob sets aside to his left (b). Christian changes through under the bind to thrust anew to Rob's mail-protected armpit (c-d) and then couches his spear for added power once he has hit the target (e).*

Winding at the Spear

It may happen that you and your opponent bind spears, whether through their parrying your thrust or you parrying theirs, in such a way that their spear point remains directed against you. In this case, as with the binding of the sword, you must not pull out of the bind, as they will simply thrust to you as you do so. Instead, as we have learned previously, you should wind your spear up into the High Guard while remaining in contact with their spear. While we have illustrated this action with the victor remaining *outside* the opponent's spear here [Fig. 4], the technique works fine if you are *inside* as well. In that case, you must maintain contact with their spear using your armoured leading hand or arm. That you can do this safely with a gauntleted hand is one

Drill 39: Developing *Fühlen* with the Spear

- Practice thrusting at a partner from the High Guard.

- Have them attempt to parry your thrust from the Low Guard.

- Respond by winding your spear or leaving the bind, depending on how hard they parry you. If their point is in presence, wind; if out of presence, pull or change through.

- Your partner should vary the side (inside or outside) of your spear on which they parry you.

- Repeat the above steps, this time by thrusting from the Low Guard.

Fig. 4 Winding at the spear, inside (a) and outside (b).

of the many advantages to fighting in harness! If you do wind inside of their spear, you must be sure, however, to drive your hand sufficiently upward to keep their spear point angled too high for them to hit your head.

As with so many other techniques, this is accomplished with nothing more than a guard transition. Just as with the longsword, winding up into the High Guard, that is, into *Ochs*, allows you to bring superior leverage to bear against your opponent so that their thrust does not hit, but yours does. You must let the sense of *Fühlen*, and your observation of their point's orientation, guide your actions. While in contact with their spear you must decide if you should wind your spear or pull it out of the bind, as in the previous technique.

Voiding an Attack

Simply "not being there" is always a good way to avoid an enemy's attack. If you must react in the *Nach*, Master Peter von Danzig recommends that you *spring to one side out from the spear*[79] when your opponent seizes the initiative and thrusts first. This may be done by combining a cross step with a compass step, so that your point remains directed against your opponent for a thrust of your own. Spring across the line with your left foot and then compass step forward with the right foot, taking you further still off the original line of engagement.

Take care to begin turning your shoulders and hips *before* your foot moves. A spear thrust is very quick and you must

Fig. 5 Rob thrusts, so Christian steps across the line with this left foot to avoid the attack (a-b) and thrusts to Rob's aventail (the mail defense at the neck), compass stepping with the right foot to realign his body (c).

---

[79] Peter von Danzig, *Fechtbuch*, folio 108v.

immediately deny them the target they are seeking with their point. [Fig. 5] This technique underscores the importance of keeping the body's weight on the balls of the feet. You will not be able to pivot properly on the left foot if your weight is placed incorrectly.

Chasing with the Spear

From our study of the longsword, we've learned that *Nachreisen* ("Chasing") is a method for confounding your opponent's timing and management of distance. This concept applies to the spear as well. If your opponent draws back from a bind against your spear, follow their motion and thrust to them as they do so. [Fig. 6] Master Ringeck says: *If you thrust and he parries you and he wants to depart from the spear, then follow after him with the point.*[80] There is a good chance you will disrupt their balance as you do this, as your thrust will be pushing them hard in a direction they were already retreating in. If this happens, rush them and apply one of the Three Wrestlings in the chapter on *Ringen* to bear them to the ground.

Fig. 6 As Rob pulls back to charge a thrust, Christian follows his movement with a thrust to a gap in the armour (a-b).

[80] Sigmund Ringeck, *Fechtbuch*, folio 92r.

Parrying with the Left Hand

You can release your left hand from your spear in order to grab or parry your opponent's spear to the side. This is useful when your opponent has the advantage of weapon length on you. This also works if you have only your sword, having lost your spear. If you try to parry a longer weapon with a shorter one, you will not be able to reach them with a thrust of your own as you do so. Using the left hand allows you to create safety for yourself so that you can bridge the gap. Your opponent might gain the advantage of reach by:

- Fighting with a longer spear than yours.

- Retaining their spear, while you have lost yours and resorted to your sword.

- Fighting with their spear held with their hands far back on the shaft so that the weapon is extended.

If your opponent thrusts upward to your face, parry the thrust aside with your left hand or forearm raised high. [Fig. 7] If they thrust low, parry with your left hand or forearm downward and outward. [Fig. 8] Note that these defenses involve moving your left hand into high and low positions corresponding to *Ochs* and *Pflug*, respectively. As you parry with the left hand, couch your spear under your right armpit and thrust to your opponent. Make sure you power the parrying action with a twist of your hips and shoulders. As always, the whole body is involved in the action, not just the hands.

Fig. 7 Christian sets aside Rob's high thrust with his left hand while thrusting his couched spear.

Fig. 8 Christian sets aside Rob's low thrust with his left hand while thrusting his couched spear.

Drill 40: Fencing with the Spear

- Assume the Low Guard, with your spear held so that its reach is shortened. Have your partner assume the Low Guard, but with their spear more extended.

- Have your partner thrust to your face. Parry upward and outward with your left hand and thrust with your spear couched.

- Have your partner thrust low to the body. Parry downward and outward with your left hand and thrust with your spear couched.

- Both partners resume the Low Guard, their spears extended normally.

- Your partner thrusts to you. Void the thrust by stepping across the line with your left foot, regaining your target by then compassing forward with the right foot.

- Resume the Low Guard. Have your partner assume the High Guard.

- You and your partner come to an inside bind.

- Your partner pulls back their spear to charge another thrust. Follow them as they pull back with a thrust of your own.

Chapter 29:
Fencing with the Half-Sword

When one sees that from the scabbard
both swords are being drawn,
then shall one strengthen.
The protection now truly remember.
— Johannes Liechtenauer

In Chapter 27, I explained how the sword's edge is of little use against a fully armoured knight. To give serious offense to an armoured combatant, the point must be brought against the gaps in their harness, just as in the spear techniques from the previous chapter. To maximize the effect of the sword's point and provide the precision targeting needed to seek out the gaps in the armour, the longsword is held at what some manuscripts call the *Halbschwert* ("Half-Sword"). This name derives from the fact that the left hand holds the middle, or *half*way point, of the blade, while the right hand remains holding the grip. This essentially turns the longsword into a short, nimble, and powerful spear. Other names for wielding the sword in this manner are *Kurzen Schwert* ("Shortened Sword", from the sword's shortened reach in this position) and *Gewappent Hand* ("Armed Hand").

Four guards are described by most Liechtenauer tradition manuscripts for fighting with the half-sword. [Fig. 1] Two of the guards, *usually* numbered as the first and second half-sword guards,[81] correspond to the longsword guards *Ochs* and *Pflug*, just like the first two spear guards. As with the spear, we will call these the *High* and *Low* guards. These are guards for thrusting from above and from below and are positions in which the swords will cross each other and bind.

The third guard is held with the sword across the leading left knee, and is analogous to the longsword guard *Alber*, in its function of provoking attack, and to *Schranckhut*, in its position. This guard is used for parrying high attacks, which involves lifting the weapon up from its position over the knee to a half-sword version of the *Kron* from the longsword teachings.[82]

---

[81] One set of commentaries, ascribed sometimes to Master Martin Huntfeltz and sometimes to Master Lew the Jew, reverse the order of the second and third guards for the half-sword. Master Paulus Kal, on the other hand, completely renumbers them from low to high, with his 1st guard being the lowest one across the knee, and the *Ochs*-like guard labeled the 4th.

[82] As mentioned earlier, *Kron* is depicted in some 16th century works as being a half-sword position, even for unarmoured combat.

The fourth and last guard is the same as the spear guard where the weapon is couched under the right armpit. With the shorter half-sword, the pommel is placed under or at the armpit to stabilize the weapon for a powerful thrust once the point has found a chink in the opponent's armour.

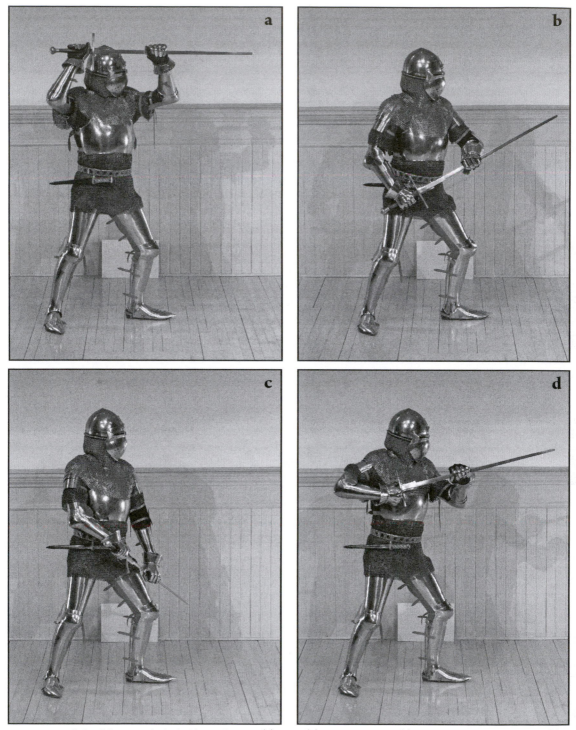

Fig. 1 Guards for fighting with the half-sword: High (a), Low (b), Over-The-Knee (c), and Couched in the armpit (d).

Thus far, the fight with the half-sword would appear to be the same as that with the spear. However, the shorter length of the sword, and its design, which includes a pommel and hilt, give it greater versatility than the spear, in exchange for its diminished range. By grabbing the blade with both hands, the sword can be swung like a poleaxe so that the pommel or hilt strikes the opponent with considerable concussive force. The pommel can also be used to hook an opponent around their neck or elsewhere as an aid in levering them to the ground once the combat moves into grappling range. This is a greater likelihood given the closer-quarters fighting here compared to when the longsword is wielded with both hands on the grip.

We will explore the techniques of the half-sword from the point of view of which guard they begin in, just as the period manuscripts do, and conclude with the strokes with the pommel. As you work through these techniques, bear in mind that everything performed with the spear in the previous chapter can also be done, at closer range, with the half-sword.

Thrusting with the Half-Sword

You can thrust from above to your opponent from the High Guard [Fig. 2] or from below from the Low Guard [Fig. 3], that is, from *Ochs* or *Pflug*. If you cannot reach your opponent with the thrust immediately, you must take gathering steps forward into range. Just as with the spear, if your opponent strongly parries your sword aside, you should pull out of the bind and seek a different opening to attack with the point. Once you have set your point into a gap in their armour, you should move into the fourth guard, Couched, by tucking the pommel in at your right armpit to strengthen the thrust, regardless of whether it originated from above or below.

Drill 41: Developing *Fühlen* with the Half-Sword

1. Assume the High Guard. Have your partner parry your thrusts from the Low Guard.

1. Thrust to your partner's face, neck, or armpit, with your partner parrying inside too weakly to prevent the thrust. Couch your hilt to strengthen the thrust once it hits.

2. Thrust to your partner's face, neck, or armpit, with your partner now parrying *outside* too weakly to prevent the thrust. Couch your hilt to strengthen the thrust once it hits.

3. Thrust toward your partner's face, neck, or armpit, with your partner parrying inside strongly enough to prevent the thrust. Pull from the bind to thrust outside their sword, and then couch the hilt.

4. Thrust toward your partner's face, neck, or armpit, with your partner now parrying outside strongly enough to prevent the thrust. Pull from the bind to thrust inside their sword, and then couch the hilt.

5. Repeat the above steps, but start by thrusting from the Low Guard.

Fig. 2 Christian thrusts from the High Guard, but Rob sets the thrust aside to his left (a-b), so Christian pulls his sword out of the bind to thrust on the other side of Rob's sword (c). He then couches his sword to press the point into the mail (d).

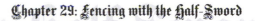

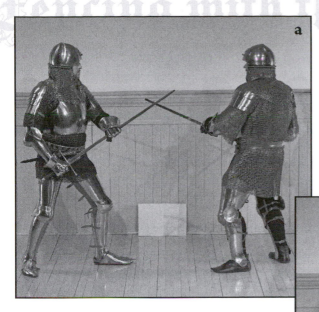

Fig. 3 Here, the same actions shown above are performed from the Low Guard. Christian thrusts up from the Low Guard, but is parried (a-b), pulls through to the other side of the bind to thrust again (c), and couches the sword to press the advantage (d).

Wrestling at the Half-Sword

When fighting from the half-sword grip, you sword can be used as a hooking lever to assist in throwing an opponent down to the ground.

If you thrust, from either above or below, *inside* your opponent's guard and your thrust is parried, you should pull (*Zucken*) out from the bind and thrust *outside* their guard to seek a place to set your point in between the plates of their armour. If, however, they parry again, pushing your sword point to your left side, this makes them vulnerable to a very easily accomplished takedown.

This is one of the few places where passing footwork is used in the armoured combat techniques. Once you've been parried to the left, pass forward with your right foot so that it goes behind their left leg. As you make this step, hook your pommel around the right side of their neck and with a clockwise twist of your shoulders and hips throw them backward over your right knee. Be sure that your weight is more focused on your right foot than on your left. [Fig. 4] Here, forward pressure is brought against their leg and backward pressure is brought against their upper body.

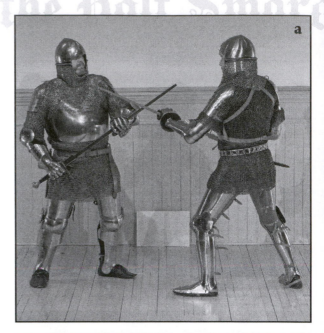

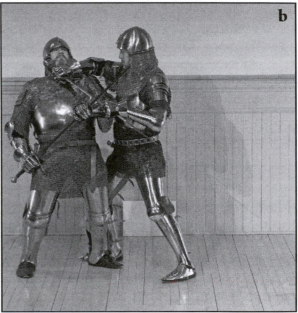

Fig. 4 Rob parries Christian's attack to his outside (a), so Christian passes with his right foot behind Rob's left foot to hook his collar by the pommel and throw him over backward (b).

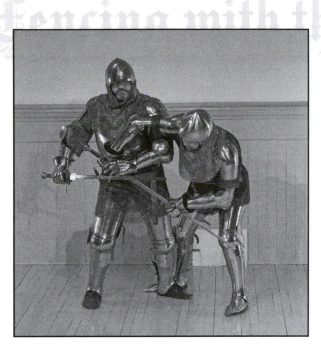

Fig. 5 Rob counters the collar throw of the previous technique by grabbing Christian's sword with his left hand, turning his body to his right, pulling his opponent forward over the hip and onto his face.

Anytime someone goes to throw you backward, you can counter by turning the tables and throwing them forward. So, if someone goes to hook your neck with their pommel in the above manner, let go of your own blade with your left hand and secure their right forearm, hilt, or wrist against your body. Now, thanks to your opponent's action, you already have your left leg in front of their right leg, so a clockwise turn of your shoulder and hips will bring them down. [Fig. 5] A compass step backward with the right foot would add even more power to the throw forward that ensues.

Drill 42: Wrestling at the Half-Sword

1. You and your partner assume the Low Guard.

1. Thrust to your partner. Have the partner parry inside the thrust.

2. Pull from the bind to thrust outside their sword. Have your partner parry outside.

3. Drive your pommel forward around their neck, stepping with your right foot behind their left.

4. Turn your body to your right to throw them backward.

5. Repeat steps 1 – 5, but, as you step, have your partner seize your right arm, wrist, or hilt with their left hand to throw you forward.

6. Repeat all steps, reversing roles.

Thrusting Through with the Point

Durchstechen[83] ("Thrusting Through") is a technique for defending against an upward thrust from the Low Guard with a downward thrust from the High Guard. In some respects, this is akin to the *Meisterhaue* techniques of the unarmoured longsword fencing, for it is a strong thrust into a thrust, much as the Five Strokes are blows which counter other strokes. This technique must be performed simultaneously with their thrust, using the principle of *Indes*.

If you see your opponent is preparing to thrust from below, and you are standing in the first guard, thrust downward as they thrust so that your left wrist blocks their left wrist, with your point reaching over their wrist. As soon as you make contact with them, wind your sword into the Low Guard by pressing down with your pommel, all the while maintaining pressure against them. Once you do this, your point will now be oriented upward, so jab it into the nearest armour gap that presents itself, be it the inside of the elbow, armpit, or flank. [Fig. 6]

To counter this technique, as soon as you feel them thrust against you, wind your sword up into the High Guard. This simple guard transition will at once prevent them from setting their point into your armour and bring your own point into position against their face or neck. [Fig. 7]

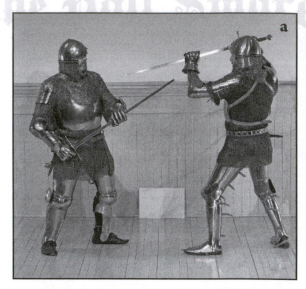

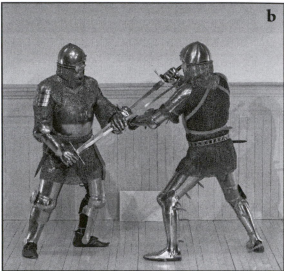

Fig. 6 Rob thrusts upward to Christian from the Low Guard, who jams the thrust with one of his own from the High Guard (a-b). He then winds his sword into the Low Guard to suppress Rob's weapon and deliver a thrust of his own (c).

---

[83] In some manuscripts, including Ringeck, this is called *Durchsetzen*, or "setting through."

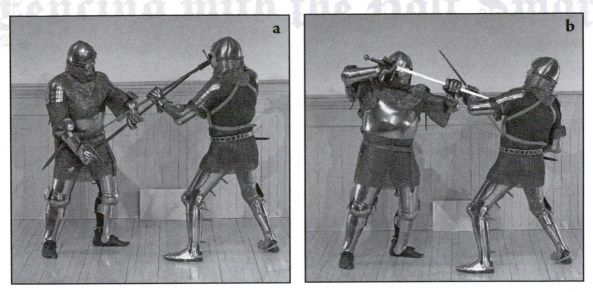

Fig. 7 Rob counters the previous technique by winding up into the High Guard in response to Christian's attempt to jam the thrust from below, delivering a thrust of his own (a-b).

Thrusting Against the Palm

This technique addresses the opposite situation of the previous technique. Here a downward thrust from the High Guard is countered by an upward thrust from the Low Guard. If you see your opponent begin to thrust to you from above, then thrust upward immediately into the exposed palm of their left hand, which is holding the blade of their sword. [Fig. 8]

At first glance, this might sound like a risky technique, as the palm would seem a small target to hit at speed. In practice, however, it actually is not that hard to do and the technique has two safe fallbacks. Should you miss the palm, you can still bind against their sword, from which many other follow-on techniques can be done. If, however, you miss on the right side of their hand, you can drive your point under and against their blade. A sharp pivot of your body to your right will either break their left hand free of their sword or take them off balance. [Fig. 9]

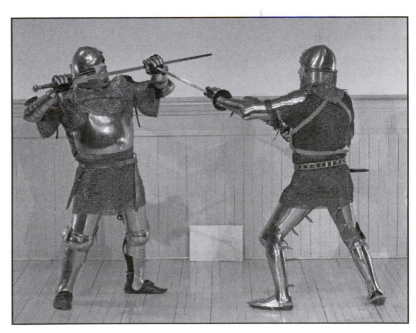

Fig. 8 Christian preempts Rob's high thrust with a thrust to the palm.

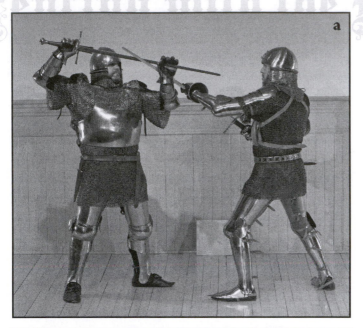

Fig. 9 Missing Rob's palm, Christian thrusts over his hand and under his sword (a) and then uses his sword to lever him backward (b).

Drill 43: Thrusting Through Above and Below

1. Assume the High Guard. Have your partner assume the Low Guard.

1. Your partner thrusts up from below. Thrust down over their left hand.

2. Wind into the Low Guard, pressing them down. Seek an opening with your point.

3. Repeat steps 1 – 2, but as you make contact, have your partner wind into the High Guard to thrust.

4. Assume the low guard. Have your partner assume the High Guard.

5. Thrust to your partner's left palm. Press them backward with your point.

6. Both partners resume their guards.

7. Thrust over your partner's left hand and under their blade.

8. Turn your body to your right breaking your partner's left hand free from the blade or throwing them.

9. Repeat all steps with the roles reversed.

Grabbing the Opponent's Point

If you bind half-sword to half-sword on the inside, you can let go of your blade with your left hand and quickly grab your opponent's point to wrench it aside. As you do this, thrust against your opponent with your right hand holding the grip. You can do this if you've thrust down from the High Guard (perhaps trying to execute a *Durchstechen*), in which case you should let your point fall to their groin for the single-handed thrust. [Fig. 10] You can also grab their point if you have thrust up from the Low Guard, in which case your single-handed thrust should continue up to the face. [Fig. 11] This second version could follow a failed attempt to thrust into the opponent's palm as they thrust down from the High Guard to you.

The technique can be countered by simply winding your sword upward from the Low Guard into the High Guard, which breaks their hold on your point, freeing you once more to thrust to them. [Fig. 12] It is important to practice this transition from the Low to High Guards (that is, from *Pflug* to *Ochs*), as it counters the *Durchstechen* technique that we saw earlier, counters this point grab, and will be used in the next technique as well.

Fig. 10 The combatants form a bind on the inside, with Rob in the Low Guard and Christian in the High Guard (a). Christian grabs Rob's point with his left hand, delivering a thrust to the groin with his right (b).

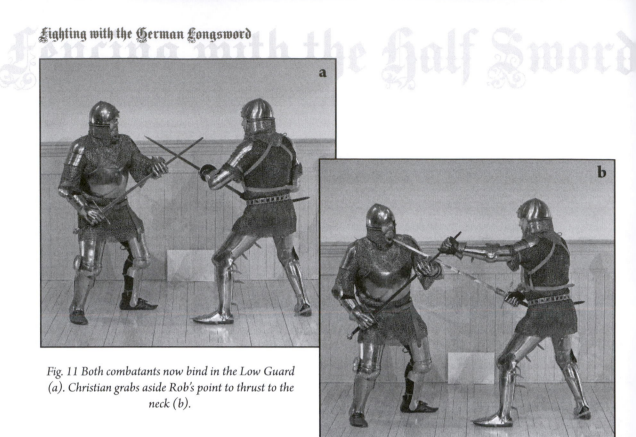

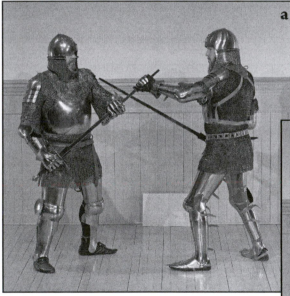

Fig. 11 Both combatants now bind in the Low Guard
(a). Christian grabs aside Rob's point to thrust to the
neck (b).

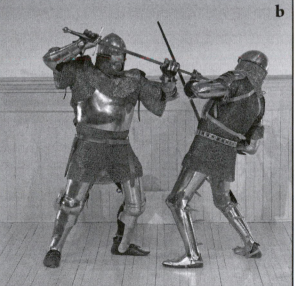

Fig. 12 Rob counters Christian's seizure of his point (a)
by winding into, and thrusting from, the High Guard,
breaking Christian's grip (b).

Fencing with the Half Sword

Drill 44: Blade Grabs

1. You and a partner each assume the Low Guard.

1. Come to a bind on the inside.

2. Grab their point with your inverted left hand and thrust to their face or neck.

3. Assume the High Guard. Your partner resumes the Low Guard.

4. Come to a bind on the inside.

5. Grab their point with your inverted left hand and thrust low to the groin.

6. Repeat all steps, but in case have your partner wind into the High Guard to counter your grab of their point.

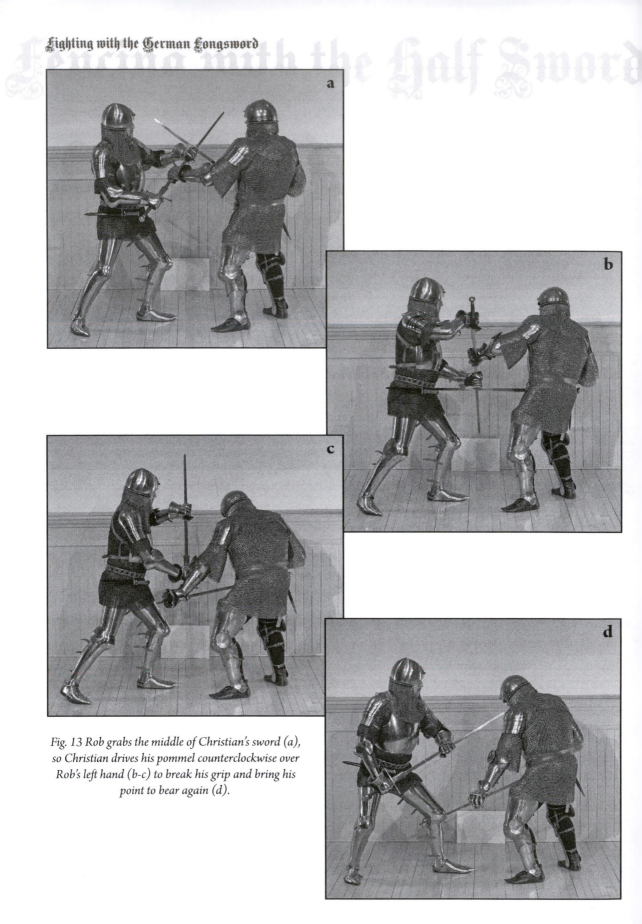

Fig. 13 Rob grabs the middle of Christian's sword (a), so Christian drives his pommel counterclockwise over Rob's left hand (b-c) to break his grip and bring his point to bear again (d).

Countering a Grab Between the Hands

It is generally not a good idea to simply reach for the opponent's blade between their hands, as this merely creates a fulcrum for your opponent to work with and is likely to go badly for you. If someone does this to you, you can move your pommel in an arc, either counterclockwise over their left arm or clockwise under their left arm, to break their grip. Continuing in either direction will bring your point back in line against them in short order. [Fig. 13] Another option is to pass forward with your right foot and smash your opponent in the face with your pommel. [Fig. 14] The last option also naturally sets up the pommel hook takedown described above.

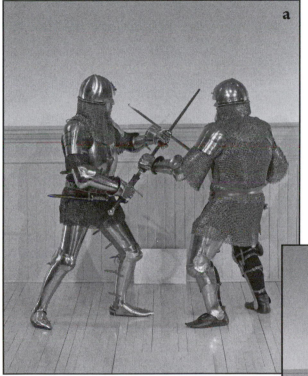

Fig. 14 Rob again grabs the middle of Christian's sword (a), so Christian steps in to smash him in the head with the pommel (b).

Fig. 15 From an inside bind, Christian clamps the swords together with his inverted left hand (a-b). He throws his pommel down and then over Rob's right hand or sword (c) with a pass of the right foot, and then pulls back with a reverse pass of the right foot to disarm Rob (d-e), bringing both points to bear.

Disarming the Opponent

It may happen that both you and your opponent thrust upward from the low guard at the same time and bind inside each other's guards. If this happens, you have a momentary opportunity to disarm them. To do this, open your left hand and grip around the intersection of the two sword blades, clamping them together. Now, move your pommel in a clockwise arc over your opponent's right wrist with a forward passing step of your right leg; the movement of your arms should almost mimic the rowing of a boat's oar. Once you've hooked your pommel over their right wrist, pull your pommel back toward you, continuing the rowing motion, while continuing to hold the blades together with your left hand. This final motion should be accompanied by a backward pass of the right foot. This will relieve them of their sword. [Fig. 15]

Note that the above is essentially the same technique, incidentally, as the second *Schwert Nehmen* technique in the chapter on *Durchlaufen* earlier in this book. The only difference is how we got into the initial bind and in fact this version is easier to perform, as at the half-sword your left hand is already near the point where the blades bind.

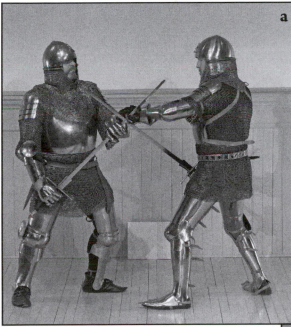

Once again, the transition between the Low and High Guards can counter a technique. If your opponent clasps their blade together with yours, move up immediately into the High Guard, which will break their hold and bring your point against their face. [Fig. 16]

Fig. 16 Rob counters the disarm by winding and thrusting into the High Guard as soon as Christian clamps the blades together (a-b).

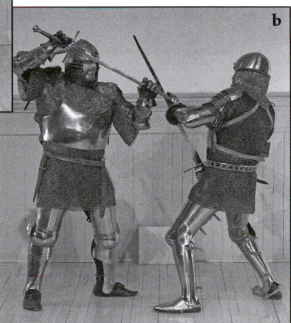

You should find it even easier to perform the sword taking from the outside bind. Should you cross (either initially or after pulling through to the other side) on the outside of their sword, and they parry you strongly, drive your pommel back to the inside and over their right hand. Push your blade against their wrist and pull back your pommel. This push-pull action will relieve them of their sword. [Fig. 17]

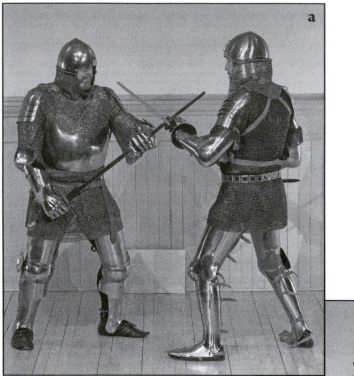

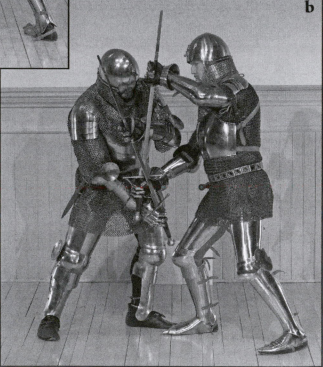

Fig. 17 From an outside bind (a), Christian drives his pommel inside and over Rob's right wrist while pressing his left wrist with the blade (b); a pass forward with the right foot facilitates this. A pass backward would complete the action, prying Rob's sword loose from his grip.

Drill 45: Disarming at the Half-Sword

1. You and a partner each assume the Low Guard.

2. Come to a bind on the inside. Use your left hand to clamp both blades together.

3. With a rowing motion, drive your pommel clockwise over your partner's right wrist, while passing straight forward with your right foot.

4. Pass back with the right foot to finish the disarming action.

5. Repeat steps 1 – 2, but have your partner wind into the high guard, breaking your grasp of the blades and thrusting to you.

6. Both partners resume their guards.

7. Come to a bind on the outside. Drive your pommel inside between your partner's hands to hook the right wrist.

8. Press their left wrist while pulling with the pommel to disarm them.

9. Repeat all steps with the roles reversed.

A Thrust from the Over-The-Knee Guard

Master Paulus Kal's c. 1470 manuscript illustrates a stab to the foot, executed from the third guard, where your sword is held low across the left knee. If your opponent rears back in the High Guard to prepare a high thrust against you, then stab down to the place where the bottom of their *greave* (the defense for the lower leg) meets the top of their *sabaton* (the armour for the foot) – this gap should open up as they chamber a high thrust. You may need to "choke up" on the blade with your left hand to gain sufficient extension with your sword in attacking so low a target. [Fig. 18]

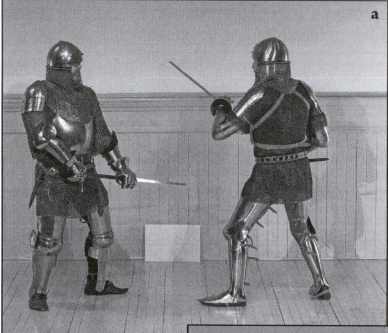

Fig. 18 From the third guard, Over -The-Knee (a), Rob thrusts down into the gap between Christian's greave (lower leg armour) and sa-baton (foot armour) – an opening created by Christian's pulling back to charge a high thrust (b).

Parrying from the Over-The-Knee Guard

The third guard, Over-The-Knee, mimics the functionality of the unarmoured longsword guard *Alber*; it is a guard of provocation from which you can *counter his techniques by parrying*.[84] Much as you can lift your sword up from *Alber* into the *Kron* to answer a high attack, you can

rise up from the Over-The-Knee Guard to a higher position to intercept an attack. If your opponent thrusts to you from the High Guard, lift your sword up to receive the thrust between your hands. Push their point aside to your right and thrust to the face while in the bind. [Fig. 19] This technique can be employed with the half-sword against the spear as well, should you find yourself bereft of yours while your opponent retains theirs, or when *both* opponents are armed with a short spear.

Fig. 19 From the Over-The-Knee Guard, Christian lifts up to parry Rob's high thrust (a-b) and then sets the latter's sword aside to direct his own high thrust (c).

---

[84] Peter von Danzig *Fechtbuch*, folio 66v.

If you encounter strong resistance in the bind and cannot accomplish the thrust to the face, move your pommel in a small counterclockwise arc over their left hand and pull the pommel back hard toward your right side to break their hand free of their sword. This action also has the added benefit of bringing your point once more against the face. [Fig. 20] Maintain contact with their sword at all times to obviate any threat from their point.

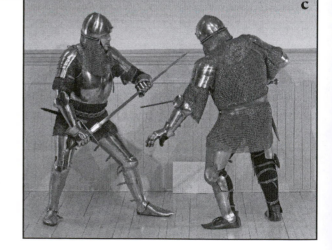

Fig. 20 Christian again parries the high thrust, lifting up from the knee (a), but this time rows his pommel over Rob's left wrist (b) to break his grip on his blade (c).

Drill 46: Using the Third Guard – Over-The-Knee

1. Have your partner thrust to you from the High Guard. Parry the thrust by lifting up your sword from the Over-The-Knee Guard.

1. Have your partner offer weak resistance to your parry. Thrust to their face.

2. Repeat the attack and parry. Now have your partner strongly resist your parry. Maintaining contact with their sword, drive your pommel counterclockwise over their left arm. Pull to break their hand free.

Defending Against a Set Point

The fourth, or couched, guard is used to drive home a thrust into a gap in the armour. If your opponent thrusts into your armpit and moves into the fourth guard to strengthen the thrust, then you must counter them before they can bring all their strength to bear. This can be done by thrusting into their left palm with your point, [Fig. 21] or, using a particularly grim technique, into the back of their gauntlet's cuff. [Fig. 22] You can also move their left hand, and thereby their point, away from you by moving your point over their left wrist and pushing down and away from you. [Fig. 23]

Fig. 21 Countering a set point with a thrust into the palm (a-b).

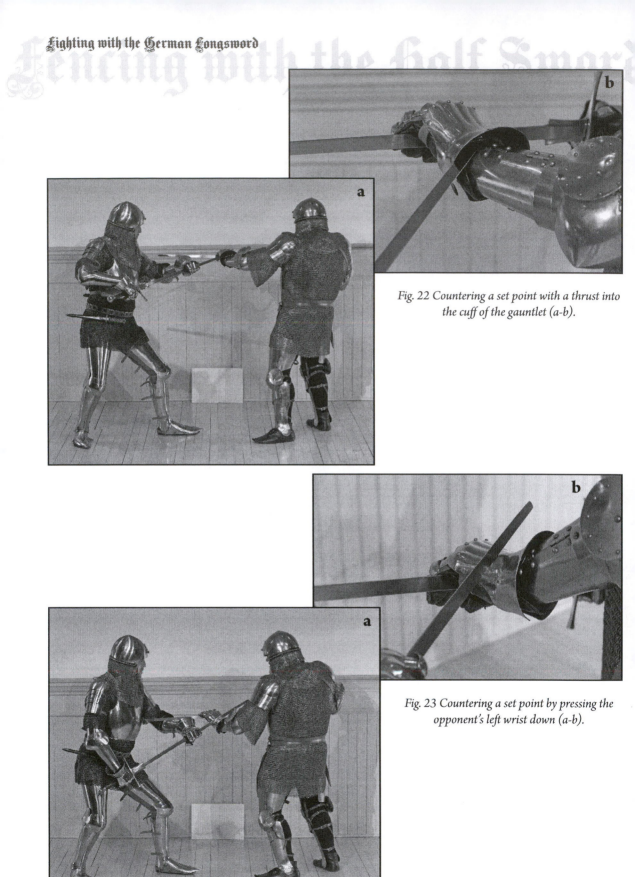

Fig. 22 Countering a set point with a thrust into the cuff of the gauntlet (a-b).

Fig. 23 Countering a set point by pressing the opponent's left wrist down (a-b).

It may happen that each of you has set your point into the other in the Couched Guard. You should then remove their point from you, but in such a way that you can continue to press them with your point. If you have each set into each other's left armpit, compass step back slightly with your left foot so that you come away from their point but remain with your point in their armpit. [Fig. 24] Another, similar, method is to create space by increasing your sword's reach; this is done by moving your pommel to the middle of your chest so that it pushes your opponent away from you while your point stays on them. [Fig. 25]

Fig. 24 Both combatants have set their points (a), so Christian brings his left foot back to free himself while continuing to press Rob (b).

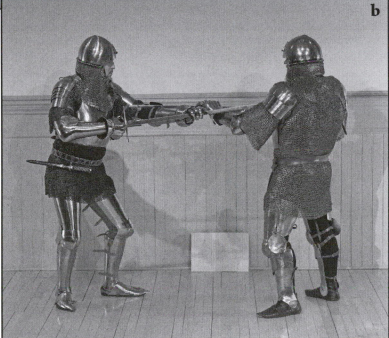

Fig. 25 Both combatants have set their points, so Christian extends his reach by bracing his pommel on his chest (a-b).

Drill 47: Countering a Set Point

Note: *The techniques involving the palm and cuff of the gauntlet must be performed carefully to avoid injury.*

1. Assume the Low Guard. Have your partner set their point into the gap in your armour at the left armpit. The partner should couch their hilt.

1. Thrust into the palm of their left hand, pushing it away and to your left.

2. Repeat step 1.

3. Thrust up and into the gauntlet cuff, pushing it away and to your left.

4. Repeat step 1.

5. Thrust over their wrist, pushing down and away to your left.

6. Repeat step 1.

7. Thrust into your partner's left armpit and step back with your left foot to free yourself.

Strokes with the Pommel

A blow with the pommel or hilt is known in some manuscripts as the *Donnerschlag* ("Thunder Stroke"), or the *Mortschlag* ("Murder Stroke"). Master Liechtenauer's verse calls it the *Schlachenden Ort* ("Battering Point"), from the idea that the pommel counts as a second "point" against the armoured opponent. Liechtenauer advocates the use of these poleaxe-like strokes against the forward extremities, but some commentaries also say to hit the head with them to create a stunning and disorienting effect even through the helmet. A pommel stroke may be struck from either the High Guard [Fig. 26] or the Low Guard. [Fig. 27] In each case, you should feint a thrust before letting go of your right hand from the grip to bring it to help the left in holding the blade. If you don't create a threat with the point first, you will tip your hand too early and your opponent may be able to sidestep or easily set aside the more cumbersome stroke.

Fig. 26 A pommel stroke delivered from the High Guard (a-b).

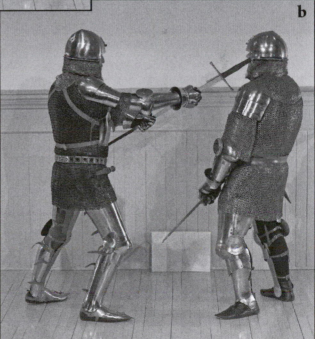

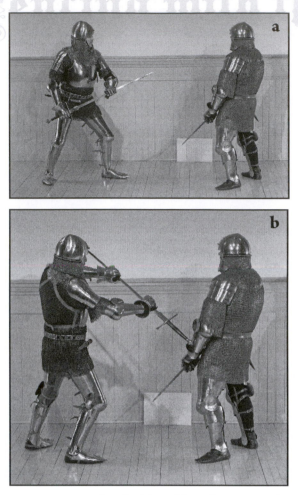

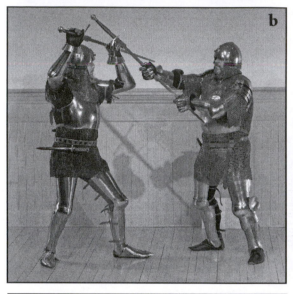

Fig. 27 A pommel stroke delivered from the Low Guard (a-b).

Fig. 28 Lifting up from the knee, Christian catches Rob's pommel stroke near the point (a-b). He then steps across the line with his left foot, freeing his sword and delivering a thrust (c).

Pommel strokes are best parried from the third guard, Over-The-Knee. If your opponent strikes a pommel blow above to you, lift up your sword from your knee into the higher position that resembles the position *Kron*. If it is a particularly powerful-looking strike, try to let it deflect off of the tip of your sword so that the blow slides off toward the ground to your left. As this happens, continue moving your sword up into the High Guard to thrust to their face. [Fig. 28]

If their stroke seems more tentative, though, parry it between your hands on your blade, then move your pommel counter-clockwise over their blade and yank their sword by their hilt with your pommel away from them and to your right side. [Fig. 29] As you do this, your point will come in line, setting up a thrust against them.

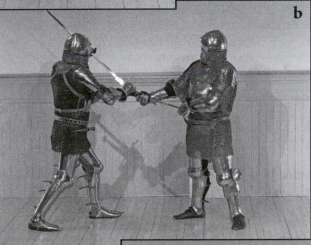

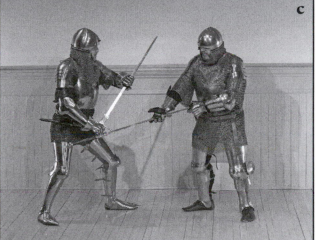

Fig. 29 Christian parries a high pommel stroke between his hands (a) and then rows his pommel counterclockwise to hook Rob's cross (b) to disarm him and come back on guard again (c).

If your opponent strikes to your knee or hip with the pommel, you should still catch the stroke between your hands, but this time by presenting your sword outward, rather than lifting it up into *Kron*. This time, move your pommel clockwise under and then over their sword and then pull to your right side to disarm them. [Fig. 30] Once again, this action will ultimately bring your point into position against them so that you can also thrust.

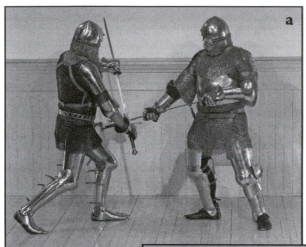

Fig. 30 Christian parries a low pommel stroke between his hands (a) and then rows his pommel clockwise to hook Rob's cross (b), and disarm him (c).

Should your opponent try to sweep you off your feet with a pommel stroke down to your ankle, you can let go of your hilt with your right hand and cast your pommel down and to your left toward the ground to strike away the blow. [Fig. 31] From here, you can drop your sword and step in to wrestle using one of the *Drei Ringen*, the Three Wrestlings, introduced earlier in this book.

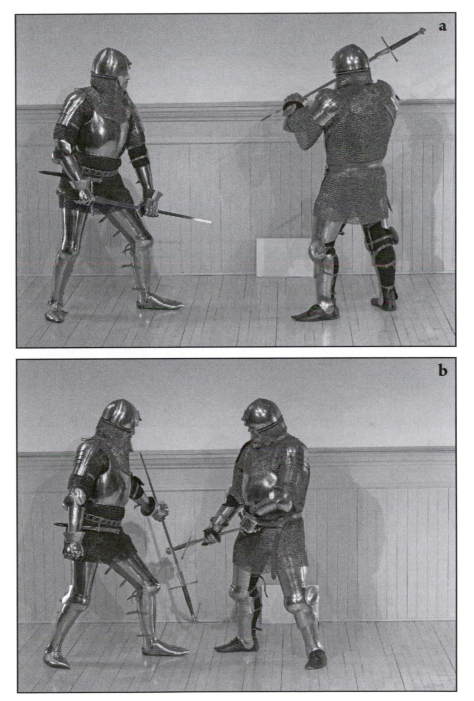

Fig. 31 Rob strikes to Christian's ankle with the pommel, so Christian strikes the attack aside with one hand (a-b). From here, Christian may close to wrestle.

Drill 48: Blows with the Pommel

1. Assume the third guard, Over-The-Knee.

1. Have your partner strike with the pommel to your head. Deflect the blow with your point and thrust to them.

2. Have your partner strike with the pommel to your head. Catch it between your hands to disarm them.

3. Have your partner strike with the pommel to your knee. Disarm them.

4. Have your partner strike with the pommel to your ankle. Strike the blow aside and close on them to wrestle.

Chapter 30:
Conclusion

Be a good grappler in wrestling;
lance, spear, sword and messer
handle manfully,
and foil them in your opponent's hands
— Johannes Liechtenauer

So ends this study of the techniques for armoured combat, and in turn, of the longsword. In this book, I have endeavored to provide a basic primer for the German art of longsword fighting. However, this book has but touched the tip of the iceberg. Detailed study of the manuscripts cited in this volume will yield up a cornucopia of techniques for the longsword. Yet, each of them when studied will reveal the same adherence to the basic principles we have studied and practiced here.

Moving beyond the fight with the longsword, and our study of the spear and half-sword, there are also the techniques for fighting with the poleaxe, the sword and buckler, the dagger, the messer, the dueling shield and sundry wrestling methods. Throughout these other disciplines of the *Kunst des Fechtens* one will find the same concepts of timing, distance, footwork, initiative, and tactile sensitivity that inform the techniques we have learned in this book. As for the specifics of their use, these are subjects fit for other books…

I hope that I have piqued your curiosity in Master Liechtenauer's art and that you will continue to pursue its practice and perhaps even its research. It is my hope and wish that you continue to study, train, and bout with this knightly art in safety and in the spirit of Chivalry.

✦✦✦✦✦✦

Table of Drills

Glossary

Abnehmen [ˈapneːmən] – ("Taking Off") A sudden departure from a bind whereby one's sword is freed to strike to the other side. Similar in meaning to *Zucken*.

Abschneiden [ˈapʃnaidən] – ("Cutting Off") Slicing cuts, delivered from above or below. One of the *Drei Wunder* (Three Wounders).

Absetzen [ˈapzetsən] – ("Setting aside") To deflect a thrust or stroke at the same time as thrusting. The word can also denote a type of parry wherein the opponent's blade slides off of one's own.

Alber [ˈalbər] – ("Fool") One of the four primary guards in Liechtenauer's long sword fighting system. In it the sword is held with the hilt low and the blade angled 45 degrees with the point to the ground. It is a guard that invites an opponent's attack.

After – See *Nach*.

Am Schwert [am ˈʃveːrt] – ("At the Sword") Techniques performed while remaining in a bind with an opponent's sword.

Ansetzen [ˈanzetsən] – ("Setting Upon") To attack with the point.

Aussere Mynn [ˈausər ˈmain] – ("Outer Intention") A type of *Nachreisen* ("Traveling After") that is done by keeping your blade on the outside of the opponent's blade.

Aventail – A drape of mail armour attached to the bottom of a helmet, providing protection for the neck, throat and collar.

Bascinet – The most common knightly helmet of the 14th century.

Before – See *Vor*.

Binden [ˈbindən] – ("Binding") The act of making contact between two swords or other weapons.

Bloße [ˈbloːs] – ("Opening") An opening or target area. In unarmoured combat (*Bloßfechten*), there are four openings: two (left and right) above the belt and two below it.

Bloßfechten [ˈbloːsfɛçtən] – ("Exposed Fighting") unarmoured combat.

Bruch [ˈbrux] – ("Break") A counter-technique, something that breaks an attack.

Buckler – A small, usually round, shield used for foot combat.

Buffalo – See *Büffel*.

Büffel [ˈbyfəl] – ("Buffalo") Period slang term for a cloddish fighter who relies only on strength.

Crown – See *Kron*.

Displacement – See *Versetzen*.

Donnerschlag [ˈdönərʃlaːk] – ("Thunder Stroke") See *Schlachenden Ort*.

Drei Ringen [ˈdrai ˈriŋən] – ("Three Wrestlings") Three basic throwing or takedown techniques found in the Ringeck *Fechtbuch*.

Drei Wunder [ˈdrai ˈvundər] – ("Three Wounders") The three ways of injuring an opponent with a long sword: thrusting, slicing, or striking. All three may be performed from each of the eight windings (*Acht Winden*). See *Winden*.

Duplieren [duˈpliːrən] – ("Doubling") An attack made from a bind wherein one winds the sword behind the opponent's blade to strike or slice them in the face.

Durchlaufen [durçlaufən] – ("Running Through") Wrestling technique performed in longsword fighting in which one "runs through" the enemy's attack to grapple with them.

Durchstechen [durçʃtɛçən] – ("Thrusting Through") Technique performed in half-sword fighting where one thrusts down between the opponent's sword and their body.

Durchwechseln [durçʃvɛksəl] – ("Changing Through") Techniques for escaping from a bind by sliding one's point out from under an opponent's blade to thrust to another opening.

Fechtbuch, pl. *Fechtbücher* – ("Fight Book") Books, in manuscript or printed form, on the art of fencing, especially those produced in medieval or Renaissance Germany.

Fehler [ˈfeːlər] – ("Feint") A deception with the sword that causes an opponent to commit to the defense of one opening while one's intent is to actually attack another opening.

Fühlen [ˈfyːlən] – ("Feeling") The skill of sensing the degree of pressure exerted by one's opponent in a bind. One should determine how to react to an opponent by sensing whether they are "hard" or "soft" at the sword.

Gambeson – A thickly padded coat that sometimes served as a foundation for other armour components, sometimes covered elements of armour and at other times was used as a defense on its own.

Gathering Footwork – A step forward with the rear foot, followed by an equal step forward with the front foot; or, a step backward with the forward foot followed by a step backward with the rear foot.

Gauntlets – Plate armour defenses for the hands.

Halbschwert [halpʃveːrt] – (Half-Sword) Method of wielding a longsword where the right hand holds the grip of the sword while the left grasps the mid-point of the blade. In this method, the sword can be wielded as a short thrusting spear or, with the pommel forward, as an implement with which to hook your opponent and throw them down. Also appears in Ringeck's manuscript as *Kurzen Schwert*, or "shortened sword."

Half-Sword – See *Halbschwert*.

Hard – See *Hart*.

Harnischfechten ['harniʃfɛçtən] – ("Harness fighting") Armoured combat, usually implying foot combat in harness.

Hart [Hart] – ("Hard") Condition in a bind where one is pressing strongly against an opponent's blade.

Hau [Hau] – ("Stroke") A stroke or hewing blow with a sword.

Haubergeon – A shorter version of the earlier nauberk, or tunic of mail. Haubergeons usually came down to the middle of the thigh and could have long or short sleeves.

Hende Drucken [hant drukən] – ("Pressing of the Hands") Slicing technique where one slices under an opponent's hands as they attack from above and then winds the sword's edge so as to slice down onto their hands, thereby pushing the opponent aside.

Hengen – See *Zwei Hengen*.

Hut [hu:t] – See *Leger*.

Indes [in'dɛs] – ("During", "Instantly", or "Meanwhile") Term describing the act of responding almost simultaneously to an opponent's actions, whether using one of the "Five Strokes" to counter a stroke or reacting in a bind based on the degree of blade pressure being exerted by the opponent. This quick reaction allows one to go from a defensive response (*Nach*) into an offensive one (*Vor*).

Krieg [kri:k] – ("War") The second phase of a fighting encounter, when the combatants have moved to close combat range. The techniques used in this close combat are limited to those associated with winding (*Winden*) and wrestling at the sword (*Ringen Am Schwert*).

Kron ['kro:n] – ("Crown") A defensive position wherein one raises the longsword, point upward, to intercept a downward blow on the hilt. Once the attack has been caught, one can rush in to grapple with the opponent.

Krumphau [*Krumphau*] – ("Crooked Stroke") One of Liechtenauer's Five Strokes, directed diagonally downward from one's right side to the opponent's right side, such that the hands are crossed, or from the left side with the hands uncrossing as the stroke is executed. It is usually directed against an opponent's hands or the flat of their sword. The name derives from the crooked trajectory of the blow (krump means twisted) as the sword travels across one's person. The *Krumphau* counters *Ochs*, as it closes off that guard's line of attack.

Kurzen Schneide ['kyrtsən 'ʃnaidə] – ("Short Edge") The back edge of a long sword. When a sword is held out with the point facing an opponent, this edge is the one that is facing up.

Langenort ['laŋənort] – ("Longpoint") A secondary guard described by Ringeck. It is much like *Pflug* ("Plow") except that the hands are extended forward so as to menace an opponent's face at longer range.

Langen Schneide ['laŋən 'ʃnaidə] – ("Long Edge") The true edge of a longsword. When a sword is held out with the point facing an opponent, this edge is the one that is facing down.

Langen Schwert ['laŋən 'ʃve:rt] – ("Longsword") A late medieval hand-and-a-half sword, usually with a sharply tapering point that is suited to thrusting attacks. The longsword is the weapon that Liechtenauer's teachings focus most on.

Long Edge – See *Langen Schneide*.

Long Sword – See *Langen Schwert*.

Leger ['le:gər] – A guard or fighting stance. Liechtenauer's system specifies the use of four guards (see also *Vier Leger*), but other masters, including Sigmund Ringeck, later added other positions to the system.

Liechtenauer, Johannes ['li:çtənauər, jo'hanəs] – German fight master who flourished in the 14th Century. After studying with other masters throughout Europe, Liechtenauer synthesized his own system of fighting which he ensconced in cryptic verse (*Merkeverse*). These teachings were included in the works of many subsequent masters and informed German swordsmanship for more than 200 years.

Mail – Armour composed of interwoven rings of iron or steel, forming a flexible defense nearly impervious to cuts.

Meisterhaue ['maistərhau] – ("Master Strokes") Name for the five secret strokes of Johannes Liechtenauer's system of long sword fighting. The word does not appear in the earlier manuscripts, however. These sword strokes are designed to defend against an opponent's attack while counterattacking them. See *Krumphau*, *Scheitelhau*, *Schielhau*, *Zornhau*, and *Zwerchhau*.

Merkeverse ['mɛrkfɛrs] – ("Teaching Verse") The cryptic verses of Master Johannes Liechtenauer, which were written to obscure their meaning to the uninitiated and serve as a series of mnemonics to those schooled in his fighting system.

Messer ['mɛsər] – A short, falchion-like single-handed sword. The word, which means "knife", may also be another name for a dagger.

Mittelhau ['mitəlhau] – (Middle Stroke) Any horizontal blow, usually directed to an opponent's mid-section.

Mortschlag ['mortʃla:k] – (Murder Stroke) See *Schlachenden Ort*.

Mortstöße ['mortʃto:s] – (Murder Strikes) Blows with hand used to stun an opponent as a prelude to grappling with them.

Mutieren [mu'ti:rən] – ("Transmuting" or "Mutating") A longsword technique, employed from a bind, whereby one winds the sword so that one's point comes down on the opposite side of the opponent's blade to thrust to a lower opening.

Nach [na:x] – ("After") The defensive principle in Liechtenauer's system. When one is forced to respond to an adversary's attack, one is fighting in the After. As it is imperative that one regain the initiative, one employs techniques from the After to get back to fighting in the Before, that is, on the offensive.

Nachreisen ['na:xraizən] – ("Traveling After" or "Chasing") Methods for out-timing your adversary's attack so that you can return to fighting offensively. One can strike right after a missed stroke by your opponent, or right before they strike, for instance.

Nebenhut ['ne:bən hu:t] – ("Near Guard" or "Side Guard") Secondary guard position where one holds the sword at either side of the body with the point trailing slightly backward. The name derives from the sword being near the leg. Similar to the "Tail Guard" of other medieval systems.

Oberhau ['o:bərhau] – ("Stroke from Above") A stroke directed downward from above, either diagonally or vertically.

Oberschnitt ['o:bərʃnit] – ("Slice from Above") A slicing cut that pushes downward from the guard *Pflug* on either side.

Oblique Pass – A passing step where one foot moves forward or backward, past the other, but with an outward component of the movement that takes the fighter off the line of engagement from an attack or potential line of attack.

Ochs [öks] – ("Ox") One of Liechtenauer's four primary guards. The sword is held with the hands crossed high at the right side of the head, with the point directed down towards the opponent's face and the left leg leading. There is also left side version of this guard where the sword is held with the hands uncrossed, with the right leg leading.

Parry – See *Versetzen*.

Pass, Passing Step – Any step that brings one foot past the other, either forward or backward, straight or oblique, so that the trailing leg becomes the leading leg.

Pfobenzagel ['pfobəntsa:gəl] – ("Peacock's Tail") A method similar to the Wheel (*Redel*, see below).

Pflug ['pflu:k] – ("Plow") One of Liechtenauer's four primary guards. The sword is held with the hands crossed at the right side, the hilt at the right hip, with the point directed up towards the opponent's face and the left leg leading. There is also a left-side version of this guard, where the sword is held with the hands uncrossed, with the right leg leading.

Redel ['re:dəl] – ("Wheel") A technique where the point is rotated around the opponent's sword, like the motion of a wheel, until an opening to attack with the point is found.

Ringeck, Sigmund ['riŋək, 'zigmund] – A German fight master of the early to mid-15th Century who interpreted the cryptic writings of Master Johannes Liechtenauer. Ringeck was fight master to Albrecht, Count Palatine of the Rhine and Duke of Bavaria.

Ringen Am Schwert ['riŋən am 'ʃve:rt] – ("Wrestling at the Sword") Techniques for grappling in a bind in longsword combat. These are grouped under *Durchlaufen*, one of Liechtenauer's primary techniques.

RoßfechtenRedel ['rösfeçtən] – ("Horse Combat") Liechtenauer's mounted combat in armour.

Scheitelhau ['ʃaitəlhau] – ("Scalp Stroke") One of Liechtenauer's Five Strokes, a vertical stroke from above with the long edge aimed at the opponent's head or upper chest. It counters *Alber* by means of superior range. The name derives from the primary target of this stroke, the scalp.

Schielhau ['ʃi:lhau] – ("Squinting Stroke") One of Liechtenauer's Five Strokes, a vertical stroke from above with the short edge aimed at the opponent's right shoulder or head. It counters *Pflug* by closing of its line of attack. The name derives from the position of the person striking; one turns such that one is "squinting" at the opponent with only one eye.

Schlachenden Ort ['ʃlaxəndən 'ört] – ("Battering Point") Strikes with the pommel, delivered against an armoured opponent with both hands on the blade. Also called *Mortschlag* and *Donnerschlag*.

Schnitt [ʃnit] – ("Cut") Slicing cut made with either edge of the long sword. One of the Three Wounders (*Drei Wunder*). There are four basic cuts: two directed from above, using a position corresponding to the guard *Pflug*, and two directed from below, from a position like the guard *Ochs*.

Schranckhut ['ʃraŋhu:t] – ("Barrier Guard") A secondary guard that figures in Ringeck's commentaries, but not in Liechtenauer's verse. To stand in the guard you either lead with your right leg with your sword hanging diagonally down almost to the ground on your left side, or lead with your left leg with your sword hanging diagonally down on your right side.

Schwech ['ʃeçv] – ("Weak") The part of a long sword blade extending from the middle of the blade to the point. You can not bind strongly on this part of the sword.

Schwert Nehmen ['ʃve:rt 'ne:mən] – (Sword Taking) Binding and grappling techniques designed to disarm the opponent swordsman.

Setting Aside – See *Absetzen*.

Short Edge – See *Kurzen Schneide*.

Sprechfenster ['ʃprɛ:çfenstər] – ("Speaking Window") One of the techniques of *Zwei Hengen* (Two Hangers). After binding with an opponent's sword, you remain in the bind with your arms extended in the guard *Langenort*. From this position you wait and sense their actions through changes in blade pressure (*Fühlen*). Thus, your adversary's intent is "spoken" through the "window" created by the bind.

Starcke ['ʃtark] – ("Strong") The part of a longsword blade that extends from the crossguard to the middle of the blade. One can bind with strength on this part of the blade.

Strong – See *Starcke*.

Stück [ʃtyk] – ("Piece") A technique or series of techniques strung together.

Überlaufen ['y:bərlaufən] – ("Overrunning") Techniques whereby one outreaches an opponent's low stroke or thrust with a high stroke or thrust. One of Liechtenauer's primary techniques, it also includes methods for reaching over and pulling down an opponent's blade as they attack high.

Unterhalten ['untərhaltən] – ("Holding Down") Wrestling techniques used for holding an opponent once they have been thrown to the ground.

Unterhau ['untərhau] – ("Stroke from Below") A stroke directed upward from below, either diagonally or vertically.

Unterschnitt ['untərʃnit] – ("Slice from Below") A slicing cut that pushes upward from the guard *Ochs* on either side.

Vambrace – A plate armour defense for the forearm. Sometimes this term refers to the entire arm defense.

Verkehrer [fɛr'ke:rər] – ("Inverter" or "Reverser") A technique performed while in a bind by inverting the position of the hilt so that the right thumb is situated beneath the sword. This brings the hilt high while the point menaces the opponent's face.

Versetzen ['fɛrzetsən] – ("Parrying") To parry or block. Liechtenauer's teachings advise against using purely defensive displacements, as they allow one's opponent to maintain the initiative. A proper parry in Liechtenauer's system must contain an offensive component.

Vom Tag ['fŏm ta:k] – ("From the Roof" or "From the Day") One of Liechtenauer's four primary guards, designed primarily as a starting position for strong strokes. One stands leading with the left leg, with the sword held on either the right shoulder or over the head. The guard can also be held at the left shoulder with the right leg leading.

Vom Schwert ['fŏm ʃve:rt] – ("From the Sword") Term describing actions that involve removing one's sword from a bind.

Vor ['fo:r] – ("Before") The offensive principle in Liechtenauer's system. As the control of initiative in the fight is all-important, one should seek to strike before an opponent does, so that the opponent is forced to remain on the defensive. Many of Liechtenauer's teachings describe methods for regaining the initiative if it has been lost momentarily.

Weak – See *Schwech*.

Weich [vaiç] – ("Soft") Condition in a bind where one is exerting little pressure against an opponent's blade.

Winden ['vindən] – ("Winding") A hallmark of Liechtenauer's fighting system; these are techniques where the sword or spear winds or turns about its long axis while binding an opponent's weapon. Winding is used to regain leverage in the bind and to seek out targets by changing the angle of attack without exposing a weakness in one's defense. There are eight basic windings, four performed while binding in the guard *Ochs* and four while binding in the guard *Pflug*. *Duplieren* and *Mutieren* are also types of winding.

Zettel ['tsetəl] – (Epitome) Liechtenauer's verse treatise.

Zornhau ['tsŏrnhau] – ("Wrath Stroke") One of Liechtenauer's Five Strokes, a diagonal stroke from above. It is so named because it is a powerful stroke that an enraged man would instinctively employ.

Zucken ['tsukən] – ("Pulling") The act of jerking one's weapon out of a bind to attack another opening.

Zufechten [tsu:'fɛçtən] – ("Approach" or "Onset") The first phase of combat, where one closes with the opponent.

Zulauffend Ringen [tsu:'laufənd 'riŋən] – ("Wrestling in the Approach") Grappling techniques applied while approaching an opponent.

Zwerchhau ['tsverçhau] – ("Thwart Stroke") One of Liechtenauer's Five Strokes, struck horizontally to the left side of the opponent's head using the short edge. If struck to an opponent's right side, the long edge is used. The *Zwerchhau* counters the guard *Vom Tag*, as it closes off the line of attack of strokes from above. Also rendered as Twerhau.

Zwei Hengen [tsvai heŋən] – (Two Hangers) Positions in which the swords bind. One is where one's sword is held in the bind so that the pommel hangs down, with the point menacing the opponent's face. This corresponds with the guard *Pflug*. The other is where the point hangs down from above to threaten the face, which corresponds with the guard *Ochs*.

Pronunciation Key:

[a:] – father
[ai] – wife, high
[e:] – say
[ɛ] – bet
[ə] – about, common
[i:] – meet
[u:] – boot
[ŏ] – long
[o:] – hole
[y] – pronounced like [i], but with the lips rounded
[y:] – ruse
[j] – year
[ç] – loch, but pronounced in the front of the mouth
[x] – loch, but pronounced in the throat
[ŋ] – sing
[ʃ] – she

Bibliography

Primary Sources

Anonymous, *Fechtbuch* (c. 1430), Ms. KK 5013, Kunsthistorisches Museum, Vienna, Austria.

Anonymous, *Fechtbuch* (15th c.), Cod. Guelf. 78.2 Aug. 20, Herzog August Bibliothek, Wolfenbüttel, Germany.

Anonymous, *Fechtbuch* (15th c.), Cod. Vindob. B 11093, Österreichische Nationalbibliothek, Vienna, Austria.

Anonymous, *Fechtbuch* (c. 1500), Cod. 862, Fürstl. Fürstenbergische Hofbibliothek, Donaueschingen, Germany.

Anonymous, *Fechtbuch* (after 1500), Libr. Pict. A83, Staatsbibliothek Preußischer Kulturbesitz, Berlin, Germany.

Anonymous, *Gladiatoria* (1st half of 15th c.), MS. germ. quart. 16, Jagelonische Bibliothek, Krakau, Poland.

Anonymous, *Goliath* (1st quarter of 16th c.), MS. germ. quart. 2020, Jagelonische Bibliothek, Krakau, Poland.

Anonymous, *Hausbuch* (1389), Codex Hs. 3227a, German National Museum, Nuremburg.

Czynner, Hans, *Fechtbuch* (1538), Ms. 963, Universitätsbibliothek, Graz, Austria.

von Danzig, Peter, *Fechtbuch* (1452), Codex 44 A 8, Library of the National Academy, Rome, Italy.

von Eyb, Ludwig, *Kriegsbuch* (c. 1500), Ms. B 26, Universitätsbibliothek Erlangen, Germany.

Falkner, Peter, *Fechtbuch* (end of 15th c.), Ms. KK 5012, Kunsthistorisches Museum, Vienna, Austria.

Kal, Paulus, *Fechtbuch* (c. 1470), CGM 1507, Bayerische Staatsbibliothek, Munich, Germany.

Kal, Paulus, *Fechtbuch* (late 15th c. copy), Cod. S554, Zentralbibliothek, Solothurn, Switzerland.

Kal, Paulus, *Fechtbuch* (late 15th c. copy), Ms. KK 5126, Kunsthistorisches Museum, Vienna, Austria.

Lecküchner, Johannes (1478), *Fechtbuch*, Cod. Pal. Germ. 430, Universitätsbibliothek Heidelberg, Germany.

_____, (1482), *Fechtbuch*, Cgm. 582, Bayerische Staatsbibliothek, Munich, Germany.

(Jud) Lew, *Fechtbuch* (c. 1450), Cod.I.6.4°.3, Universitätsbibliothek Augsburg, Germany.

Liberi da Premariacco, Fiore dei, *Fior Battaglia* (1409), MS Ludwig XV.13, Getty Museum, Los Angeles, USA.

Mair, Paulus Hector, *Fechtbuch* (1542), Mscr. Dresd. C93 / 94, Sächsische Landesbibliothek, Dresden, Germany.

_____, *Fechtbuch* (1542), Cod. Vindob. 10825 / 26, Österreichische Nationalbibliothek, Vienna, Austria.

Meyer, Joachim, *Grundtliche beschreibung der freyen ritterlichen und adelichen Kunst des Fechtens* (*A Thorough Description of the Free, Knightly and Noble Art of Fencing*). Strasbourg, 1570.

Ringeck, Sigmund, *Fechtbuch* (c.1440), Ms. Dresd. C 487, Sächsische Landesbibliothek, Dresden, Germany.

von Speyer, Hans, *Fechtbuch* (1491), M I 29, Universitätsbibliothek Salzburg, Germany.

Sutor, Jakob, Neu Künstliches *Fechtbuch* (1612), Frankfurt am Main, Germany.

Talhoffer, Hans, *Fechtbuch* (1443), Ms. Chart. A558, Forschungsbibliothek Gotha, Germany.

_____, *Fechtbuch* (1450?), HS XIX, 17-3, Gräfl. Schloss Königseggwald, Germany.

_____, *Fechtbuch* (1459), Thott 290 2°, Königliche Bibliothek, Copenhagen, Denmark.

_____, *Fechtbuch* (1467), Cod. icon. 394a, Bayerische Staatsbibliothek, Munich, Germany.

Wilhalm, Jörg, *Fechtbuch* (1522/23), CGM 3711, Bayerische Staatsbibliothek, Munich, Germany.

_____, *Fechtbuch* (1556), CGM 3712, Bayerische Staatsbibliothek, Munich, Germany.

Secondary Sources

Amberger, J. Christoph, *The Secret History of the Sword.* Baltimore, Maryland, Hammerterz Verlag, 1996.

Anglo, Sydney, *The Martial Arts of Renaissance Europe.* London and New Haven, Yale, 2000.

Arano, Luisa Cogliati, *The Medieval Health Handbook: Tacuinum Sanitatis.* New York, George Braziller, 1976.

Arnold, Benjamin, *German Knighthood 1050-1300.* Oxford University Press, 1985.

_____, *Princes and Territories in Medieval Germany*, Cambridge University Press, 1991.

Blair, Claude, *European Armour.* London, B. T. Batsford Ltd., 1958.

Edge, David and John Miles Paddock, *Arms and Armour of the Medieval Knight.* New York, Crescent Books, 1988.

Finley, Jessica, *Medieval Wrestling: Modern Practice of a Fifteenth Century Art.* Wheaton, Illinois, Freelance Academy Press, 2014.

Forgeng, Jeffrey L., *The Medieval Art of Swordsmanship: A Facsimile & Translation of Europe's Oldest Personal Combat Treatise*, Royal Armouries MS. I.33. Union City, California, and Leeds, UK, Chivalry Bookshelf/ Royal Armouries, 2003.

Galas, S. Matthew, "Kindred spirits: The art of the sword in Germany and Japan," Journal of Asian Martial Arts, VI (1997), pp. 20 - 46

Hils, Hans-Peter, *Master Johann Liechtenauer's kunst des langen schwerts*. Frankfurt am Main, 1985.

Liberi da Premariacco, Fiore dei, Flos duellatorum in arnis, sine arnis, equester, pedester, Francesco Novati, ed., Bergamo, 1902.

Lindholm, David, and Peter Svärd, *Sigmund Ringeck's Knightly Art of the Longsword*. Boulder, Colorado, Paladin Press, 2003.

Oakeshott, R. Ewart, *The Archeology of Weapons*. Woodbridge, UK, Boydell, 1960.

_____, *The Sword in the Age of Chivalry*. London, UK, Arms & Armour Press, 1964.

_____, *European Weapons and Armour*. N. Hollywood, California, Beinfeld Publishing, 1980.

Porzio, Luca and Gregory Mele, *Arte Gladiatoria Dimicandi: 15th Century Swordsmanship of Master Filippo Vadi*. Union City, California, Chivalry Bookshelf, 2002.

Talhoffer, Hans, *Medieval Combat: A Fifteenth-Century Illustrated Manual of Swordfighting and Close-Quarter Combat*. Edited by Mark Rector, London, Greenhill Books, 2000.

Tobler, Christian Henry, *Captain of the Guild: Master Peter Falkner's Art of Knightly Defense*. Wheaton, Illinois, Freelance Academy Press, 2011.

_____, *Fighting with the German Longsword* (1st Edition). Union City, California, Chivalry Bookshelf, 2004.

_____, *In Saint George's Name*. Wheaton, Illinois, Freelance Academy Press, 2010.

_____, *In Service of the Duke: The 15th Century Fighting Treatise of Paulus Kal*. Highland Village, Texas, Chivalry Bookshelf, 2006.

_____, *Secrets of German Medieval Swordsmanship: Sigmund Ringeck's Commentaries on Johannes Liechtenauer's Verse*. Union City, California, Chivalry Bookshelf, 2001.

Wagner, Paul and Stephen Hand, *Medieval Sword and Shield: The Combat System of Royal Armouries MS I.33*. Union City, California, Chivalry Bookshelf, 2003.

Waldburg Wolfegg, Christoph Graf zu, *Venus and Mars: The World of the Medieval Housebook*. Munich and New York, Prestel, 1998.

Waldman, John, *Hafted Weapons in Medieval and Renaissance Europe*. Leiden, Netherlands and Boston, USA, Brill, 2005.

Welle, Rainer, "...und wisse das alle hobischeit kompt von deme *Ringen*": Der Ringkampf als adelige Kunst im 15. und 16. Jahrhundert. Eine Sozialhistorische Und Bewegungsbiographische Interpretation Aufgrund Der Handschriftlichen Und Gedruckten Ringlehren Des Spatmittelalters, 1993.

Wierschin, Martin, *Meister Johann Liechtenauers Kunst des Fechtens*. Munich, Muenchener Text und Untersuchungen zur deutschen Literatur des Mittelalters, 1965.

Zabinski, Grzegorz with Bartlomiej Walczak, *Codex Wallerstein: A Medieval Fighting Book on the Longsword, Falchion, Dagger, and Wrestling*. Boulder, Colorado, Paladin Press, 2002.

Ziegler, Vickie L., *Trial by Fire and Battle in Medieval German Literature*. Woodbridge, UK, Camden House, 2004.